The arts of mankind

EDITED BY

ANDRÉ MALRAUX AND GEORGES SALLES

SCIENTIFIC CONSULTANT

ANDRÉ PARROT

MEMBER OF THE *INSTITUT DE FRANCE*

Early Christian art

André Grabar

EARLY
CHRISTIAN ART

*From the Rise of Christianity
to the Death of Theodosius*

Translated by
Stuart Gilbert and James Emmons

ODYSSEY PRESS · NEW YORK

49 550

Library of Congress Catalog Card Number: 68-10414

Printed in France

Published 1968 by arrangement with Editions Gallimard.
All rights reserved. No part of the contents of this book may
be reproduced without the written consent of publishers,
Odyssey Press, New York,
Trade Division of Western Publishing Company, Inc.

Contents

To my wife

Foreword

When in the early sixteenth century the Romans watched the rise of the majestic new church of St Peter's that Bramante was building in the Vatican, it was described as 'the Pantheon placed upon the vaults of the Basilica of Maxentius.' For the most admired remains of ancient architecture then to be seen in Rome were the domed rotunda of the Pantheon and the great barrel vault of the Basilica of Maxentius in the Forum. These two equally impressive structures belonged to different periods: the former to the first century A.D., when classical art reigned supreme, the other to the fourth century, that is to say to the Late Empire and, in part, to the reign of Constantine, the great promoter of Christian art.

Moreover Bramante's church replaced an earlier Christian foundation, the old St Peter's, built by Constantine on the site of the apostle's tomb. So that Bramante's church of St Peter provides us with a familiar landmark from which we may view in the correct perspective the works of art dealt with in this volume and so better understand the place they occupy in the history of ideas and their material realizations.

These works belong to Antiquity and on this account were admired and imitated when in later times, during the Middle Ages and afterwards, men were looking to the past for guidance in the renewal of art and culture. What then was known of ancient art consisted mainly of works of this late period; they were the most accessible, and that is why they were more often imitated than the others. The architecture, sculpture and painting of later Antiquity naturally survived in greater numbers than those of the previous age, and the Christian character of many of these works facilitated the borrowings from them made by medieval artists. Classical and Late Antique art was drawn on in the Middle Ages just as it was by Bramante when he took inspiration both from the Pantheon and from the imperial basilica in the Forum. And to these two monuments must be added the third one mentioned above, which was also a symbol of its time: the Constantinian basilica of the Vatican which Bramante replaced when he built the new St Peter's. In the sixteenth century it was this new architecture based on Roman models of various types and periods that superseded the Early Christian basilica.

1

Until then—although those Roman models had not been unnoticed or ignored—it was the tradition of the Early Christian basilica and of all the arts fostered by Christianity from the third century on that had prevailed; indeed the art of the Middle Ages was a derivative of Early Christian art.

Not, be it noted, a mere continuation of it. But in many respects the art that is ours today may be traced back to that Christian tradition whose earliest manifestations can be seen in the works we bring together and discuss in the following pages. This fact, needless to say, adds considerably to the interest of our subject and reinforces our conviction that the study of these first ventures of the Early Christians into the field of art—whether in the humble paintings of the catacombs or in the majestic churches of the Constantinian epoch—cannot but be rewarding. These works are the source from which sprang not only St Sophia of Constantinople and Chartres Cathedral but also the art of Michelangelo and Rembrandt.

It will be seen that Christian art begins some three centuries after the founding of Christianity itself. Christian art existed *de facto* before it existed *de jure* and it was born, not as a new artistic language groping for expression, but as an offshoot of the art tradition prevailing at the time when the Christian faith began to spread; thereafter it steadily enlarged its programme. Hence the originality of this early phase in the development of Christian art; it makes its appearance as part of a much larger whole, that of antique art in its decline. There is nothing elementary or primitive in its earliest forms. These are in fact cast in the same mould as contemporary pagan works serving similar purposes; the originality of the Christian sensibility emerges only gradually.

In studying the many reproductions of works and monuments comprised in this volume readers cannot fail to be convinced of a fact that was far from being perceived in former times: the fact that Early Christian art did not replace ancient art but formed an offshoot of it: one that was destined to thrive luxuriantly in years to come, when the other branches withered. But it was only much later that this fact became apparent.

Ancient Christian art passed through two phases, the one we study here being the preliminary one. It came to an end towards the close of the fourth century, with the rise to power in Rome of the Theodosian dynasty. The second phase is represented by the works produced in the fifth and sixth centuries, the first golden age of Christian art.

1. General Characteristics

Geographical and Chronological Survey

While fully aware that all divisions of history into periods must to some extent be arbitrary, we propose to cover in this volume the works of art produced within the frontiers of the Roman Empire from its adoption of the Christian faith until about A.D. 395, in other words the works produced in the first two centuries of Christian art.

The salient feature of this period is the rise of Christianity, no less evident in the realm of art than in all other domains. The spectacular success of the new religion in that field is all the more remarkable since art became affected by the growth of Christianity almost as tardily as the Roman State itself, and much later than literature and philosophy. Like Jewish art whose flowering was so short-lived (and probably following after it), Christian art arose, it seems, or was enabled to express itself in relative freedom, thanks to the policy of religious tolerance practised by the Severan emperors and their successors in the late second century and the first half of the third.

The triumph of Christianity came in the fourth century with the conversion of Constantine the Great. But before we begin our study of the art of this period it may be well to examine some of the less striking but significant Christian works which led up to it. No precise date can be assigned to these early manifestations, but with them begins, to all intents and purposes, the history of that Christian art which was destined to inspire the artists of all the lands of Europe and the Near East for nearly two thousand years to come.

So far as art is concerned Antiquity may be said to end with the Arab invasions of the first third of the seventh century. But it comprised two fairly distinct periods: the first, with which we deal in the present volume, lasted, broadly speaking, until the end of the fourth century; the second extends from Theodosius I to Justinian and Heraclius. The dividing line between them cannot be sharply drawn; it may be dated either to the beginning of the reign of Theodosius I (379) or to the momentous political event which took place in 395: the separation of the Eastern and the Western Roman empires.

It was not to any political event of this order that the new art owed its wide success, but rather to the bold and active policy of the Theodosian dynasty in religious matters.

It was they who, from the close of the fourth century on, elevated Christianity to the rank of a State religion and closed down the last pagan temples. In this volume we shall describe Christian art as it was practised before these drastic innovations; first, in the age of the persecutions when, under the pagan Roman government, the artistic activities of Christians were necessarily clandestine; next, under Constantine and his immediate successors, that is to say during the decades following the imperial edicts of religious toleration by which the Christians benefited. From this time date the tentative beginnings of Christian art on the grand scale. But this trend was checked by several emperors converted to Arianism or advocates of a return to paganism, with the result that large-scale Christian art did not get into its stride until after this intermediate period, which can be dated, roughly, to the middle of the fourth century and covers a considerable part of its last half. For the patronage of the whole-heartedly Christian and Catholic emperors, notably Theodosius and his sons, did not take effect immediately. It is at this point that the present volume ends, its subject being exclusively pre-Constantinian and Constantinian Christian art—i.e. what is known as Early Christian art—considered under its two most characteristic forms, one private and the other supervised by the Roman State. The large-scale art, on the other hand, which began under the Theodosian dynasty and continued uninterruptedly until the Arab invasions of the seventh century, can best be studied as a whole in another volume of this series; following on Early Christian art, it is the art practised by and under the Christian Roman Empire.

The Christian works anterior to the Peace of the Church (313) constituted a foreign element in the body of Roman works produced in the second and third centuries, and in them we find a sort of preamble to the Christian art of Antiquity. They can be envisaged either in the context of the pagan arts of the declining Roman Empire or in their relation to the later, full-fledged Christian works. We prefer to take the latter course, since Christian art after Constantine owed several of its distinctive traits to reminiscences of this Early Christian art. Thus it seems rewarding to survey this earlier art before dealing with that of the period when Christianity had become the State religion. Moreover—differing in this from the usual practice—we shall group together all Christian works of art prior to the seventh century in a single category: the art of 'Christian Antiquity.'

Only by approaching it from this angle can the importance of this period in the general history of art, of its discoveries and inventions and of the part it played in shaping medieval art, be fully appreciated. True, this creative effort, limited to the field of art, may have done less to guide and foster the growth of Christendom than did the activities of the theologians, poets, liturgists and founders of monasticism during the same period. None the less a comparison with these other activities is certainly permissible and in some respects the art of this period played a similar role by laying the foundations of a tradition that lasted into the Middle Ages and even later.

It was to the Roman State that Christian art owed its vast expansion in the fourth century, for its beginnings go back to the edicts of religious toleration and the great churches founded by the emperors. Here, too, a tradition was established that was to last over a long period and it is not too much to say that if the date of the conversion of the Empire and the birth of large-scale Christian art had been different, the latter would have transmitted through the centuries a very different aesthetic.

1. *Rome. Aerial View.*

2. *Constantinople. Aerial View.*

It is generally assumed that the decline of the classical tradition in art was connected with the political and social upheavals of the third century, which affected both the economic structure of the Empire and its religion. There is much to be said for this view, and it would seem that the classical aesthetic shared in the partial collapse of so many other Roman institutions during this age of transition.

But we must not overlook the fact that Christian works of the third century (frescoes in the catacombs and in the baptistery of Dura-Europos, and sarcophagus reliefs) were little affected by the decadence of contemporary Roman art and followed the canons of the classical tradition. This may well have been due to the humble nature of these works; they came from the workshops of unenterprising craftsmen who thought it safer to conform to traditional models.

A few years after the Peace of the Church came an event of exceptional importance. After being for centuries the political capital of the Mediterranean world and the seminal centre of all the artistic activities of the Empire, Rome, on the initiative of Constantine, ceded these roles to Constantinople on the Bosphorus (in 330).

Over a long period artists and craftsmen from Rome and other cities of the Empire flocked to the new capital, where monuments and buildings befitting its new political status were being erected. During the fourth century Byzantium took, but did not give—a process that was to be completely reversed in the fifth century.

In confirmation of this we have only to consider the edifices built by Constantine in his capital. We know of them only by written descriptions, reminiscences in ancient records. All the same they must not be overlooked, any more than the Constantinopolitan foundations in Jerusalem. All these were prototypal works which set the style of religious architecture in many parts of Christendom for centuries to come. The influence of the Constantinian churches in both cities—in the political capital and in the religious capital (it was said of Constantine that he founded a 'New Jerusalem')—can be clearly seen in many later edifices.

The Christian art of Antiquity not only spanned many centuries but extended over a vast area. In this volume we shall deal with works from all the provinces of the Roman Empire, which at the beginning of the period we are concerned with reached from the Euphrates to the Atlantic, from the British Isles and the Crimea to Nubia and the Sahara. In the third and fourth centuries a similar art was current throughout this area and there were many imitations, exact or remote, of the monuments of Rome. From the third century on the Christians utilized this art, adapting it to their religion. (The Jews, it would seem, had already done the same thing.) Though we have only scanty information regarding the forms these imitations took in the third century, before the reign of Constantine, traces of them have been found in Syria, Egypt, Greece, Italy, Gaul and Spain.

In the fourth century Christian art gained ground throughout the length and breadth of the converted Empire, and nothing could indicate more clearly than this widespread triumph the bond between Christian art in its early period and the imperial government. Like the Christian religion, Christian art owed its vast expansion to the Pax Romana, and the rapidity of its spread over an enormous area to the excellence of the system of communications made available to artists and craftsmen by the central power. Thanks to the Romans, travelling had become simpler and safer; this facilitated pilgrimages,

3. *Jerusalem. General View*

notably to Palestine, and these in turn helped to make certain works of Christian art more widely known. For centuries to come the arts of Christendom were to benefit by the favourable conditions created by the Roman Empire in their early phase and the impetus given by the adoption of Christianity as the State religion.

The Empire not only ensured a vast field of action for works of Christian usage and inspiration but also imposed on them a certain unity of style and subject matter. Of the provinces enriched by a long spell of peace some kept to the themes current in the great cities, interpreting them however in a somewhat rustic manner, often racy of the soil, while others revived indigenous art traditions that had existed before the Roman conquest. Encouraged by Rome, provincial art had thus developed more or less pronounced local idioms, and when the earliest Christian art made its appearance in the provinces in the favourable climate of the Pax Romana, it followed the lead of its predecessors and neighbours, and in turn developed regional characteristics. In other words, the Empire lay at the origin not only of the overall unity of Christian art in the Mediterranean area and the outlying provinces from Mesopotamia to Spain and Great Britain, but also of the diversity of forms grafted on to this basic unity.

8

4. *Rome. Trajan's Column, detail: Dacian Peasants before the Emperor.*

The Social Background

What were the social conditions under which Early Christian art developed, and what is known about the artists and their patrons?

With few exceptions (some of which are famous), such as the creations sponsored by Constantine and Justinian, and those of the great architects employed by the latter, whose names are known, the records are silent as to the individuals taking part in the artistic activities of this period, even when their names are mentioned. We are therefore forced to consider rather the *categories* of men, artists and patrons who were responsible for the works of art. Information of this kind is easier to come by and in a sense more valuable; for though we may learn little from an isolated reference to an individual, information bearing on a social group, a class or category of men and on all that was most typical in their activities and aims, has every chance of being more rewarding.

There is ample evidence as to the general nature of the social background of the Christian art of Antiquity, meaning by that the Christian communities commissioning it. At first these small groups of believers were recruited chiefly in the great cities of the Mediterranean world, above all in the poorer districts of these cities. The Jewish element —strongly Hellenized—predominated; but though Levantines were in a majority, the native Christians of each province of the Empire were also well represented.

5. Medal of Septimius Severus. Cabinet des Médailles, Bibliothèque Nationale, Paris.

In Rome these communities included men and women (chiefly the latter) belonging to the privileged and wealthy class, and evidently this was also the case in the East. In the small town of Dura-Europos on the Euphrates there was in the early third century a 'Christian House' with a baptistery adorned with frescoes; this points to the existence of a well-to-do Christian community having a good social status. But neither here nor elsewhere are there any inscriptions stating whether the edifice or the paintings were due to the munificence of an individual donor or to a joint enterprise on the part of the local believers. Perhaps we may assume that the same custom prevailed among the Christians as among the contemporary Jewish communities (who, however, sometimes recorded the names of their wealthy benefactors, for example in certain mosaic pavements at Aquileia). If so, the Christian funerary monuments—frescoes, sarcophagi, engraved slabs, mosaics—were presumably commissioned by the heads of more or less well-to-do local families.

A visitor to the catacombs of Rome cannot fail to be struck by the rarity of cubicula decorated with paintings, despite the great number of cemeteries in general use. Only prosperous families could afford the cost of a frescoed tomb. In a third-century pagan hypogeum recently brought to light in northern Bulgaria, several slaves are represented, showing that the owners of the tomb had a certain number of servants in their household. Under St Peter's, tombs of slaves have been found in the mausolea of wealthy men,

10

6.   *Rome.   Column of Marcus Aurelius, detail: Execution of Barbarian Prisoners.*

7.   *Sabratha, Theatre.   'Pulpitum,' Central Niche, detail: Septimius Severus sacrificing to the African Gods.*

8. *Medal of Diocletian. Cabinet des Médailles, Bibliothèque Nationale, Paris.*

their masters. In another hypogeum (fourth century) which was recently uncovered in Rome under the Via Latina, the paintings in adjoining vaults reflect different beliefs, pagan and Christian. This seems to have been a private family tomb, which continued to serve as such, though the members of the family belonged to different confessions. It is evident, in fact, that despite changes of religion the successive owners of family hypogea kept to a similar artistic programme—a fact of considerable interest since it shows that Jews and Christians alike had no qualms about conforming to the Roman tradition of funerary paintings.

The custom of building private burial vaults, which had begun before the Peace of the Church, lasted two or three centuries with little change, except that in the later ones inscriptions sometimes record the intentions, hitherto unspecified, of the person or persons commissioning the frescoes. It was not until about the sixth or seventh century, according to the locality, that this type of decoration, due to private initiative, died out. But meanwhile Constantine had inaugurated the era of imperial control of the arts of Christendom, an era that marked the beginning of large-scale Christian art and was to last as long as the Empire.

The Christian emperors felt it incumbent on them to build churches, to decorate and furnish them and to supply them with costly liturgical vessels, exactly as their pre-decessors had done for the temples of the gods. The custom had developed above all

12

9. *Salonica. Arch of Galerius, detail: Triumph of the Emperors.*

in the half-century preceding the Peace of the Church, when Aurelian and Diocletian were active patrons of the arts. Naturally enough these emperors favoured particularly the places where the gods whose special protection they invoked were worshipped, and Constantine conformed to this practice when Christianity became the State religion.

Constantine was the first emperor to patronize Christian art on a large scale. The great buildings commissioned by him in Rome, Antioch, Palestine and elsewhere, marked a wholly new departure in the evolution of Christian art. Henceforth it always had an official status, being in great part financed and supervised by the government in power, and it displayed the usual characteristics of arts associated with an 'establishment': a taste for luxury, the use of expensive materials often brought from distant lands, rapid execution, aesthetic eclecticism and a cult of the grandiose. Often, too, we find reflections of the palace art of the new capital. A letter from Constantine to the Bishop of Jerusalem sets forth his programme for the church he wishes to have built on Golgotha: the large sums of money to be spent on it, the materials he will provide, the means of transport he will put at the bishop's disposal. Certain distinctive features, such as a ceiling in an exceptionally costly wood, are suggested in the letter, but the general layout and execution are left to the decision of the local authorities and architects.

In Constantine's lifetime and shortly after his death several members of his family built luxuriously appointed churches of the same type as those erected under the emperor's personal control. Then came a cessation of activity, due perhaps to the persistent conflicts between the Arian emperor and the magnates of the orthodox Church, but from 379 on Theodosius I revived the practice of imperial patronage and spent large sums building churches and adorning them on a lavish scale, particularly in Rome.

13

10. *Rome. Arch of Constantine, detail: The Emperor distributing Largesse.*

His sons, his grandson Theodosius II and nearly all the fifth- and sixth-century emperors kept to this practice, which now became traditional, even compulsory, in Rome, Milan and Ravenna, as well as in Constantinople.

Though it was the capitals that chiefly benefited by the imperial largesse, some provincial towns shared in it: among them Jerusalem (where Constantine thought of founding a Christian metropolis), Ephesus, Alexandria and various cities in Cilicia, Syria and Samaria.

The rulers of the Germanic kingdoms established in the outlying provinces of the empire followed the example of the emperors. Once converted, they made a point of performing their Christian duties by erecting churches, martyria and monasteries. Moreover at quite an early date—before the fifth century—high officials within the Empire proper began to follow the emperor's example. In the capitals, the larger cities and the rural areas where the first monastic establishments were founded, in Gaul and Italy, Syria and Egypt, senators, patricians, consuls and 'counts' *(comites)* built churches, sometimes of considerable size; an example, almost intact, is the fifth-century church at Sohag in Egypt.

But the most active church-builders outside the eastern capital were the high dignitaries of the Church, the bishops of Rome and of the many provinces of the Empire. For in the order of precedence instituted by Constantine and his successors the bishops ranked beside the highest state officials and already in the fourth century enjoyed the many privileges accruing to this status.

14

11. *Medal of Constantine and his Ideal Model Alexander the Great. Cabinet des Médailles, Bibliothèque Nationale, Paris.*

Thus the bishops, who in the West belonged to senatorial families, regarded the building of churches as one of their normal functions in sixth-century Gaul (St Gregory of Tours is an outstanding example). In size and ornamentation the edifices built by them vied with those of the emperors. Examples are the cathedral of Bishop Theodore at Aquileia and the first church of Santa Maria Maggiore in Rome.

In addition to places of worship, the cathedral precincts included secular buildings, centered around the episcopal palace, the bishop's private residence. We get an idea of the ground plans, if nothing more, from the remains of the Lateran palaces and those at Salona in Dalmatia, Side in Pamphylia, Gerasa and Bosra in Palestine, Jemila in North Africa. Sometimes the cost of these buildings was defrayed by the bishop himself, if he came of a wealthy family. St Paulinus, Bishop of Nola, a native of Gaul, spent a fortune on gorgeously decorated edifices in honour of St Felix, a martyr revered in his diocese. From the days of Constantine the bishops in all parts of the Empire had ample funds at their disposal, provided both by the government and by the donations of private individuals.

That the lower clergy, too, gave commissions on occasion for Christian works of art is evidenced by many inscriptions on mosaics, chiefly in Syria but also at Aquileia, in Greece and in North Africa. The works they commissioned were naturally on a smaller scale, but the mere fact of their existence may surprise students of medieval art, in which works due to the enterprise of the minor clergy are rare and vouched for only in its latest period.

15

12. *Consular Diptych of Stilicho: Stilicho, Serena and Eucherius.   Cathedral Treasury, Monza.*

16

13. *Rome.   Sarcophagus, detail: Portraits of Wife and Husband.   Museum, Basilica of San Sebastiano, Rome.*

Socially, this was something new in the Empire. True, there had always been pagan temples endowed by worshippers with works of art: statues, temple furniture, precious jewellery. Some of their most generous patrons were the emperors. But in the provinces such richly endowed temples were few and none had at its disposal funds in any way comparable to those which the emperors, Constantine to begin with, expended on the Christian churches. Moreover the general conception of the provincial foundations, their artistic 'programme,' was not as closely bound up with the imperial religious policy and other forms of governmental action.

Historians have always spoken admiringly of the rapidity with which, beginning in the reign of Constantine, the Church built up a network of religious institutions throughout the length and breadth of the Empire by bending to its service the administrative system, the bureaucratic regime and the material resources of the Roman State. Some recent studies have dealt with the results of this policy in a domain which, while

14. *Rome. Roman Calendar of 354 (after a drawing by Peiresc). Rome.*

it does not fall within the province of art history in the strict sense, touches on that of the works of art produced during this period; I have in mind the elaborate vestments prescribed for bishops and certain portions of the church service which reflect the usages of the imperial liturgy. Similarly, the residences of bishops and the churches, the mural and movable paintings associated with the cult and also the statuary (so far as it was tolerated by the Church) evidence the high status assigned to the institutions, dignitaries and personnel of the Church in the social order of the Empire.

The freedom of choice allowed the private patron as regards the works of art commissioned by him was considerable, but it varied greatly from one period to another. *A priori* an art favoured by all-powerful monarchs and by the high ecclesiastics of a

18

15. *The Emperor Valentinian I (?), detail. Barletta.*

16-17. *Rome. Medal of the Emperor Valens. Kunsthistorisches Museum, Vienna.*

Church which they actively supported was bound to reflect the ideas and tastes of these rulers and dignitaries. Their conception of the glory and grandeur of God and the splendour of his epiphanies, of his relations with man, of the saints, his servants, and of the church, the House of God, were necessarily embodied in the manifold creations of the architects, mosaicists, painters and goldsmiths who were employed by local dignitaries and remunerated by the State, the Church establishment and its prelates.

Under these conditions patrons of the arts could control to a large extent the activities of artists and craftsmen, and, as we shall see at a later page, the surviving monuments have features that evidently corresponded to the taste of the rulers and prince-bishops: churches resembling the halls of palaces, gorgeous mosaics, cycles of triumphal images. The Christians of earlier times had cultivated a very different type of art, without any trace of the spectacular effects that came in with the reign of Constantine. For in those early days there were no Christian emperors, no high-ranking Church dignitaries to give commissions to artists and artisans, and the bishops, far from being assimilated to the great office-holders of the pagan State, were men of humble extraction, leading simple lives, so that the only funds available for building were those provided by their congregations, which consisted mostly of men as impecunious as themselves.

As was to be expected, the characteristics of this earliest Christian art, as stabilized at the time of the Peace of the Church, persisted long after Constantine, but only in the domain for which this archaic art had been originally intended. In other domains—those opened to Christian artists after the triumph of Christianity under Constantine—the artists' tastes and forms reflect the new social and economic order that developed after the Peace of the Church. The art that thus came into being was destined, in its turn, to outlast the social conditions that had given rise to it. However, this was to become apparent only later, since those conditions remained much the same throughout the period we are dealing with and up to the Arab invasions.

20

18. *Statuette of an Empress. Cabinet des Médailles, Bibliothèque Nationale, Paris.*

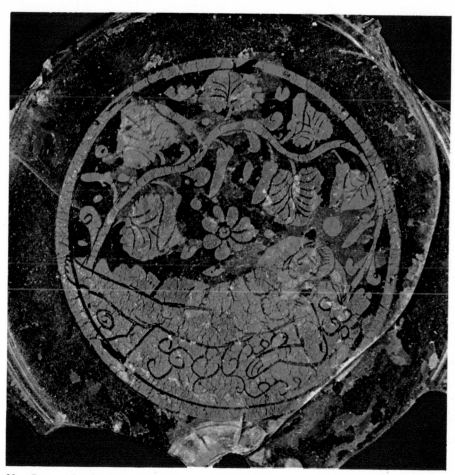

20. *Rome. Jonah. Museo Cristiano, Vatican City.*

Programmes

The scarcity of extant monuments (only a minute fraction have survived) precludes a detailed analysis of the artistic programmes of this period and we must confine ourselves to mentioning the salient characteristics of such few works as are available. These, however, provide sufficient data for a more or less accurate appraisal.

By the 'programme' of an art is meant the totality of themes, political, religious or topical, which it utilizes. These are determined by the factors of time and place, by social conditions and the function of the works of art; the programme necessarily varies with any changes affecting one or another of these factors.

The Christian art of Antiquity did not always keep to the same programme. Here again a spectacular and far-reaching change was brought about by Constantine's championship of the Christian faith. Before the Peace of the Church, Christian art seems to have been limited in its applications and reserved mainly to burial places. In Rome and Naples, in Provence and almost everywhere in the Mediterranean area Christian tombs were adorned with frescoes and, more rarely, mosaics; with sculpture (on sarcophagi) and engraved tombstones. The church architecture of this early age is represented

23

19. *Aquileia, Cathedral of Bishop Theodore. Jonah.*

21. *Provence. Sarcophagus, detail. Church of Saint-Sauveur, Brignoles.*

by a very small number of surviving edifices and they have no artistic interest. It would seem that until the reign of Constantine Christian places of worship usually consisted simply of rooms included in ordinary dwelling-houses and the Christian art of the period played no part in them.

That, however, there were exceptions to this rule is proved by the early third-century baptistery at Dura-Europos on the Euphrates. Quite possibly the baptisteries were given iconographic decorations earlier than the churches properly so called—this for a

24

22. *Rome, Catacomb of SS. Pietro e Marcellino. The Raising of Lazarus.*

reason we shall deal with later. In any case the content of the imagery at Dura differs so little from that of the Christian tombs in Rome and elsewhere that there can be no question of an enlargement of the programme. It is, rather, an adaptation of the same art (normally reserved to sepulchral decorations) to another function, that of adorning a baptistery.

Though the Dura baptistery is the only example we have for the pre-Constantinian period, it may safely be assumed that what was done in a humble provincial town like

25

23.   *Rome, Catacomb called Coemeterium Majus.   Adam and Eve.*

Dura was also done in larger, more prosperous cities.   Perhaps the extension of iconographic paintings to the walls of Christian places of worship was suggested by the contemporary practice of the Jews, who were now beginning to adorn the walls of their synagogues with religious paintings.   Both sects were free to do so, thanks to the toleration in religious matters practised by the Severan emperors and their immediate successors. Indeed these emperors seem to have actively encouraged the building in Galilee of monumental synagogues adorned with symbolic imagery.

Without going further, at this stage, into the ideology behind the Christian art that figured in the tombs, we may point out that this art kept strictly to its sepulchral function and never aspired to any systematic exposition of Christian doctrine.   It is doubtful whether the clergy ever took any steps to control or standardize this Early Christian sepulchral art.   There are no allusions to it in any contemporary writings of the Fathers (a famous passage in the works of St Clement of Alexandria speaks only of Christian symbols engraved on seal-rings) and in a general way the early theologians showed no interest in iconography.   The Christian use of funerary images must have begun, in prac-

26

24. *Rome, Catacomb of the Via Latina. Adam and Eve.*

25. *Sfax.* *Funerary Mosaic: Orant. Tunis.*

tice, as an imitation of similar customs already current in the pagan world (the Jews may have been the first to fall in line), and the Doctors of the Church neither sanctioned nor encouraged it *expressis verbis.*

All the same there are two points suggesting an intervention by the Church: first, the judicious choice of subjects, presupposing a fairly thorough knowledge of Christian doctrine; secondly, the close connection between Christian picture cycles and imagery in Italy, Gaul, Africa, Egypt and even Syria. Evidently the artists decorating Christian tombs were more closely supervised than the available texts might lead us to suppose; they must have been supplied with models or verbal descriptions of the prescribed imagery, in much the same way as rules, oral or written, were transmitted in other fields, in order to ensure the uniformity of Christian observances throughout the Empire.

Constantine's edicts opened up new fields of activity to Christian art; first and foremost, that of large-scale architecture. This included from the start several types of edifice all of which had precedents in an earlier age and whose general conception owed nothing to Christian influence. Churches were modelled on the Roman assembly halls,

26.   *Rome.   Sarcophagus, detail: Orant.   Museo Torlonia, Rome.*

27. *Aquileia, Cathedral of Bishop Theodore.   The Good Shepherd.*

and the mausolea of Roman cities served as prototypes for the monumental tombs of prominent Christians, which soon became the scene of commemorative ceremonies. Some baptisteries conformed to the same architectural tradition, while others were inspired by the large public fountains and the great Roman *thermae* equipped with *calidaria* and swimming-pools.   Before the Christians, other religious sects had adapted certain types of Roman public buildings to the uses of communal worship, for example the Mithraists and, in particular, the Jews.   The architects of the Constantinian period may have been guided by this precedent.

Besides these officially sponsored places of worship, imitated again and again in later times, there existed, after the reign of Constantine, many other churches which but for the conversion of the Empire would never have come into being and which had

29.   *Rome.   The Raising of Lazarus.   Museo Cristiano, Vatican City.*

developed, stage by stage, out of the pre-Constantinian *domus ecclesiae* or 'church houses' (in Syria).   However, though enlarged, improved and more artistic, Christian architecture of this type did not make any notable progress after the Peace of the Church, and it soon died out.

As regards secular architecture, the adoption of the Christian faith by the emperors and the Roman State had effects that were mainly negative: temples and theatres (but not hippodromes) ceased to be built, and public baths, which hitherto had been the largest, most conspicuous buildings in every Roman city, were erected only at rare intervals. On the other hand, the construction of municipal buildings continued steadily between the fourth and sixth centuries.   The newly founded cities, beginning with Constantinople (in 330) and several provincial capitals built in the reign of Justinian, were provided with all the necessary public buildings, laid out in accordance with the urban planning adopted in the age of the Hellenistic kingdoms.   In the first half of the fifth century Constantinople

28.   *Rome, Catacomb of San Callisto, Crypt of Lucina.   The Good Shepherd.*

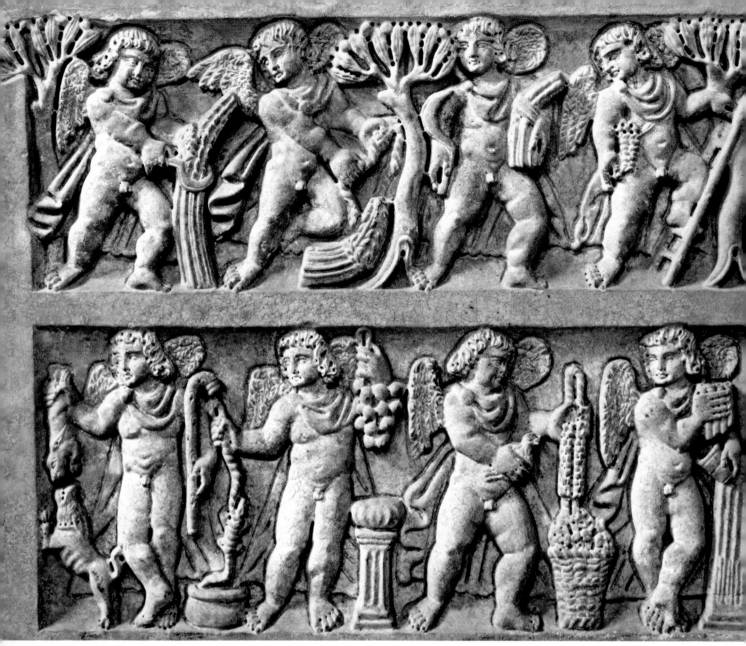

30. *Rome, Catacomb of Pretestato. Sarcophagus with Vintaging Scenes. Museo Laterano, Rome.*

was girdled with new defensive walls which were not only a masterpiece (new for the period) of military engineering but a work of art in their own right.

However, apart from the improvements made by the engineers employed by Theodosius II on the walls of Constantinople, there were few innovations in the domain of secular architecture and its brief flowering under Justinian was soon followed by a marked decline.

While less spectacular, perhaps, than in the case of architecture, the consequences of the new religious orientation made themselves felt no less in Christian iconography. As things stand, the surviving monuments enable us to judge of the resulting changes only from the end of the fifth century on. It is possible that before this the Constantinian basilicas had been adorned with paintings containing images of a new kind; but no trace of them remains, apart from a few fragments and drawings of lost mosaics. However,

32

judging by these fragments, the religious imagery of the imperial mausolea (Santa Costanza in Rome, and perhaps Centcelles near Tarragona) contained nothing new.

Just when a new iconography made its first appearance is an open question, but there is ample evidence of its existence in the Theodosian period: church mosaics, tomb frescoes, sarcophagus reliefs, and ivory carvings. Usually this imagery served a doctrinal or didactic purpose. Out of the mass of available themes the Christian iconographers selected a relatively small number, preferably those for which there had been precedents in the earlier iconography, for example themes that had served to exalt the reigning monarch. This is why Christian imagery gave so large a place to celebrations of the majesty of the omnipotent Redeemer, to scenes glorifying the victory of Christ and his saints, to ceremonies of coronation and investiture, to representations of Christ the King giving their mandates to his disciples. We are often told that this triumphal iconography was directly influenced by imperial art, but the point might be better made

31. *Rome, Tomb of the Aurelii. Jonah thrown overboard from a Boat with a Square Sail.*

32. *Dura-Europos, Synagogue.* *The Triumph of Mordecai.* *Damascus Museum.*

in another way. When the Christian iconography took form the emperors had just
been converted and the imperial art exalting them had reached its peak. Christian art
took over the formulas used to extol the glory of the monarch and adapted them to
Christian uses. Not only certain basic themes, such as that of the emperor 'in majesty,'
but also the specific places where they figured in the church, were suggested by practices
obtaining in pagan temples, and perhaps also in the imperial law-courts.

At the same time another iconographic programme, wider in range if less spectacular, was being disseminated in the illustrated books made under the auspices of the

34

33. *Rome.* *Sarcophagus, detail: Christ seated above a Personification of the Cosmos.* *Museo Laterano, Rome.*

34. *Rome, Underground Basilica of Porta Maggiore. Mythological Scene.*

Church. These cycles of narrative scenes, interpreting in pictorial terms the text of the Scriptures, were created for books, but there and elsewhere they were often used not merely to illustrate the Bible story but also with an homiletic purpose, and this in fact became the explicit and most generalized function of Early Christian imagery.

This was a new application of religious iconography; there was no precedent for it in the imagery of Greco-Roman paganism. In the latter descriptive scenes from mythology and history had been currently employed but were rarely intended to convey religious truths. It was only in the later period of Antiquity, and chiefly in the mystery religions, that recourse was had to this procedure; for example in the underground basilica of Porta Maggiore in Rome and the recently discovered tomb under the Via Latina, where the Labours of Hercules are obviously meant to symbolize man's struggle for salvation from his lower self.

Already in the Dura synagogue (c. 200) frescoes illustrating Old Testament themes had been used to instruct the Jewish community in certain tenets of their faith. The

36

35. *Rome, Catacomb of the Via Latina. Hercules in the Garden of the Hesperides.*

36. *Rome, Catacomb of the Via Latina.   Jacob and his Sons arriving in Egypt.*

appearance of similar scenes in Christian art, leading to a considerable enrichment of the iconographic programme, took place no later than the middle of the fourth century. We have an early example in the frescoes just referred to in the Via Latina tomb, where Old and New Testament scenes are grouped together with the evident intention of demonstrating a specific religious doctrine.   At the same time this picture cycle belongs to the iconographic tradition of the emperors' triumphal arches which likewise included 'salvational' themes.   It was in Early Christian art, however, that a practice arose which became widely current in the Middle Ages: that of depicting incidents recorded in the Bible in such a manner as to indicate their bearing on the Christian verities and more especially the typological significance attaching to them.

Secular painting and sculpture continued to flourish after the Peace of the Church, but few works of this kind have survived.   As in the case of architecture, we know of a certain number of specific works that were ordered by the emperor; none of these has survived, but parallels can be found in the mural decorations of temples dedicated to the cult of the emperors, the illustrated calendars and ivory carvings made for the Roman aristocracy, and the statues of provincial dignitaries of the Empire.   Nothing in the programme of this secular art, whether governmental or aristocratic, shows any great change from that of the previous centuries; at most, there was a new emphasis on those official aspects of secular art which remained unaffected by the decline and eclipse

37. *Rome, Catacomb of the Via Latina. Cain and Abel bringing Offerings.*

of paganism. We have in mind the imperial and governmental figurations (of which there were not so many in previous centuries), whose relative frequency appears to correspond to a genuine revival of the art of the Roman monarchy after its conversion to Christianity.

This interdependence between monarchical iconography and Christian iconography can be traced back through the Theodosian period to the time of Constantine or even earlier, pending the developments it was to undergo later. This is a fact of considerable importance, and one that gives us a better insight into the nature of Early Christian art.

As noted at a previous page, the art examined in this book is generically a branch of antique art; Christian art did not supplant its predecessor but grew out of it. It is a mistake to believe that antique art was *in extremis* when it gave birth to Christian art.

For three or four centuries the new aesthetic developed within the context of classical Antiquity and its emergence does not mean that we are already in the Middle Ages.

True, medieval art was, later, to take over some of its methods and forms, but this aesthetic (as we shall see) still pertained to Antiquity, for the term 'antique art' need not be restricted to the classical Greco-Roman aesthetic. There were some arts of Late Antiquity—just as there were some very early 'antique' arts (for example Mycenaean and Etruscan)—which lay wholly outside the pale of 'classical' Greek and Roman art.

During the last centuries of Antiquity the social order for which artists catered, though less stable and less wealthy than in the past, maintained the standard of gracious living which had been assured it for several generations by the Pax Romana, seconded by the rise of the Hellenistic kingdoms. A steady flow of commissions led practitioners of all the arts to adapt themselves to the very diverse requirements of the vast cosmopolitan world the Empire had now become, and to keep in constant touch with the various traditions which persisted simultaneously in the Greek, Roman, Gaulish, Iberian and Levantine art centres.

The emperors, the Senate, the aristocracy, high officials and municipal and religious organizations continued to build enormous edifices, lavishly decorated and equipped with all possible architectural amenities. So arranged as to cater for every form of public and private activity, these buildings were provided with spacious halls, storerooms, baths, fountains, inner courts and gardens. Not only were new edifices erected but old ones were completely renovated, when this seemed called for. Care was taken to situate the various rooms, large and small, at convenient distances from each other so as to facilitate easy communication between them, with special regard to the purposes they served. There were numbers of doors placed at suitable spots, outside corridors sheltered from sun and rain, and inner atria with free access to light and air. When more rooms were needed, an upper storey or a vaulted basement was added, and staircases installed to serve them. According to the function of the building or group of buildings, special care was taken to achieve an overall effect of grandeur and to ensure the comfort and convenience of the interior appointments.

Owing to their empirical practice of seeking the solution best adapted to the circumstances, Early Christian architects gave their work a remarkable variety of forms. None the less, since certain structural arrangements inevitably recurred in buildings serving the same purpose, specific architectural types began to emerge. But they were not yet standardized and a good deal of latitude was permitted in their execution. Also, the practice of joining together independent buildings led to a variety of solutions, whether the architectural complex had been planned in advance or was the end-product of subsequent enlargements.

The figural arts of Late Antiquity are less well represented than its architecture. But the surviving works and fragments brought to light by excavation point to a taste for imagery that, so far as we can judge, had not existed to the same extent in classical Antiquity. Current throughout the Empire in workshops staffed by craftsmen familiar with a wide variety of techniques, this imagery ranged over many different styles with a versatility enabling it to be adapted to programmes and monuments of all descriptions. As in the case of architecture, alongside original works of very different kinds, certain forms tend to recur, and types gradually emerge, though so far there is no question of stereotyped formulas.

In grafting itself on to the architecture and iconography of Late Antiquity, Early Christian art took over the traditions of the various workshops it patronized. This is why in its first phase it lacked the unity of inspiration and execution it might have had if its course had been shaped by the ecclesiastical authorities. On the whole the eclecticism of Late Antique art rules out any effective differentiation on a geographical basis between the first types of Christian architecture and imagery; we cannot endorse the views of those who would draw distinctions, often arbitrary, between the works originating in the large Greek or Latin cities (Antioch, Alexandria, Jerusalem, Rome, Milan), basing these distinctions on theological or aesthetic considerations. Thus, apart from a few isolated cases where the local idiom is unmistakable, we see no need to discuss the question of the place of origin of given types or forms of edifices and images, so long as we are dealing with the art of Late Antiquity.

This period cannot be prolonged beyond the fourth century. By then the changes taking place in political and economic life and in religious beliefs and practices were leading to a new orientation of art which, meanwhile, had come wholly under the control of the Christian authorities, ecclesiastical and civil.

Forms and Aesthetic

The subject of this volume is *art*, not the culture of the age as revealed by its works of art. However rewarding inquiries of the latter kind may be, they have no place, or only a minor place, in a series entitled 'The Arts of Mankind,' whose proper study is aesthetic facts *per se*, not their corollaries. This does not mean that we shall examine these facts in isolation from their historical context, their places of origin, their natural frame of reference. But we shall never lose sight of what it is that confers on certain buildings, paintings and sculptures of the period concerned, the dignity of 'works of art.' In dealing with the existing monuments attention will be given to the materials of which they are made, the techniques employed, and in describing their forms we shall try to define the aesthetic both of individual works and of groups of homogeneous works. And, for a proper understanding of each specific case, it is helpful to determine the place which the group to which it belongs occupies in the over-all evolution of the art forms of the period.

As already pointed out, we shall deal with the art produced in workshops located in all parts of the far-flung Roman Empire as it existed between the third and seventh centuries, and above all with works of Christian inspiration. To begin with, all that was truly new about this art was its inspiration; the techniques and forms, the choice of the material and scale of the works according to their function, were in the main traditional. Thus, young though it was, this art had nothing 'primitive' about it, none of those traits which so often distinguish the initial phase of an art movement, traits that catch and gratify the eye because of their naive charm—also, perhaps, because of our tendency to compare the life of an art form with that of a living being that is born, grows up, reaches its prime, then falls into a decline. Early Christian art provides neither

38. *Dura-Europos, Synagogue. Head of a Prophet, detail. Damascus Museum.*

of these gratifications; it was born old (except for the novelty of its themes) and saddled with the burden of an age-old Mediterranean tradition. It came to be rejuvenated, but only later, when Western civilization had declined to such a point that certain races which hitherto had had no effective influence on it began to take an active, vitalizing share in creative art. But this was only long afterwards, in the Middle Ages, and only in Western Europe. In the countries around the Eastern Mediterranean the same phenomenon occurred, but outside the pale of Christendom, in the lands which came under Arab sway in the seventh century, and whose artistic activities were now controlled by the invaders. Elsewhere, after resisting the onslaughts of Germanic, Slavic and other barbarians, the Eastern Empire succeeded in maintaining all the traditions inherited from

Antiquity on a level that precluded any imposition by the newcomers of drastic changes in a culture as specific and as highly developed as the one associated with Christian art—except in faraway Russia, from the fifteenth century on. So it was that in the Middle Ages Byzantine art remained as little naive or 'primitive' as was Mediterranean art as a whole during the period covered by this volume.

The art that flourished in Rome and its dominions, under the emperors, kept to the aesthetic of classical Greek and Hellenistic art. In the early days of the Empire, Greek artists played an active part as sculptors, painters and architects in all the Roman towns and provinces. Often graceful and sensitive, their art conformed to a canon which, by and large, derived from the masterpieces of the great age of Greek art. So familiar was this ideal that even the most mediocre artists could reproduce its characteristic traits instinctively, almost with their eyes shut. It spread to distant lands, beyond the frontiers of the Empire; Indian craftsmen, for example, did their best to imitate it. For a long time there was, in short, no aesthetic *problem*, except, in certain cases, that of adapting classical forms to works of a new order.

Such were the conditions under which in the second and third centuries Christian themes made their first appearance in paintings and reliefs. These works, as said above, conformed to the tastes and technical procedures of contemporary Roman art—or, more exactly, of the types of art already current in the towns or regions where these Christian works were executed.

It seems to me that all we have been told about the 'profound influence' of the Christian faith on these works, *qua* works of art, is wide of the mark. And, since it would be absurd to assert that the faith of the early Christians lacked depth (rather, the contrary is true), we may assume that this view is due to a misinterpretation of the facts. The men who planned and executed the murals—for example those in the Dura baptistery—felt that they were providing exactly what their fellow-believers needed by depicting Christian *themes*. The forms were those of all the paintings and carvings they saw around them. Evidently it never struck them that the expression of Christian ideas might call for a new style and new forms.

Of the works immediately following the edicts of toleration and the conversion of the Empire little can be said. What we know of the Christian edifices founded by Constantine himself, by his associates or by members of his family (e.g. the basilica at Bethlehem and the rotunda of Santa Costanza in Rome) gives no inkling of the beginnings of a specifically Christian aesthetic. The same applies to the Calendar of 354; here we can hardly expect to find any reflection of the new faith, for though the calendar was made for a Christian its illustrations are confined to portraits of emperors, personifications of cities and astrological themes—typically pagan motifs.

However, about the same time (the middle of the fourth century) efforts were made, chiefly in sarcophagus reliefs, to convey something of the aura of divinity emanating from Christ, and even hints of the spiritual grandeur of the apostles, beginning with St Peter and St Paul. But, while conforming closely to the Christian ideology in general and more especially to that of the Christians who had inherited Constantine's conception of the converted Roman monarchy as an earthly counterpart of the heavenly kingdom, these early Christian artists neither reacted against the art tradition of the past nor attempted to adapt it to a figuration of the new, transcendental ideas peculiar to a revealed religion.

True, it was now that artists began to figure forth the godhead of Christ, using the representations of the emperor 'in majesty' as their models. This, however, was nothing new, for depictions of the 'majesty' of Jupiter, Bacchus, Isis and other deities had been current in the art of the imperial epoch, and in fact the adjustments made by the Christian artists were iconographic rather than stylistic.

Even so, the noble gravity imparted to the figures of Christ and the apostles in sarcophagus reliefs of the second half of the fourth century and in contemporary frescoes in the catacombs may justly be regarded as among the first manifestations of a specifically Christian religious sentiment. Probably it was first expressed in the large-scale compositions (mosaics in Constantinian churches). It soon came to characterize all the sacred figures and lasted over many centuries; in the West until the rise of Gothic art, and permanently in Byzantium.

Contemporary architecture exhibits a number of features which appear to be of Christian inspiration. It comes as something of a surprise to find, in every province of the Empire from the end of the fourth century on, so many churches having the same form, that of a three-aisled basilica. The remarkable uniformity over so wide an area—aesthetically the interiors of all these basilicas have a family likeness—may be accounted

39. *Rome (?). Sarcophagus: Christ and the Apostles, detail. Louvre, Paris.*

40. *Rome (?). Sarcophagus, detail: Head of an Apostle. Louvre, Paris.*

42. *Rome. Sarcophagus, detail. San Sebastiano, Rome.*

for by the fact that the early Christians found the basilical hall best suited to the requirements of their liturgy. From the moment when he entered the basilica by the central
door the worshipper's gaze was guided by two parallel rows of columns advancing
towards the altar, the spiritual journey's end and token of the Divine. For the choir and
communion table in front of the apse arrest the dual forward movement of the columns
and by their very immobility suggest the everlasting world of God, outside space and
time. This is borne out by the distribution of the images and by the symbolism of the
sacred edifice itself as explained by the earliest Christian writers: the choir standing
for the intelligible heavens, the nave for the earth (i.e. the material world), the pictures
in the choir representing the consummation of the act of Salvation, those in the nave
the stages leading up to it.

Certain forms and procedures, alien to classical art, seem uniquely Christian in
spirit. Everywhere, for example, the figures are portrayed with wide-open eyes, Christ
and the Virgin to begin with. Here, presumably, since the eyes are 'mirrors of the soul,'
the Christian artist's object was to reveal the innermost being of these holy personages.

47

43. *Rome, Catacomb of Commodilla. The Donatrix Turtura, detail.*

44. *Rome, Santa Maria Maggiore. View of the Interior.*

Accordingly the mundane aspects of the scenes are disregarded, their settings contain a bare minimum of furniture and architecture. The figures themselves, apart from the faces with their big, staring eyes, lack plasticity and their attitudes and gestures are quite unlike those of real life. They have no weight, no real contact with the ground, but seem to hover lightly just above it. The space surrounding the figures and objects is sketchily indicated, everything is flattened, schematized. Clearly, for the artists who made these images, material reality counted for nothing, and one can only suppose that this habit of shutting their eyes to the physical world was a consequence of their whole-hearted adoption of the new faith, in which the spiritual world was man's sole concern. Though unconfirmed by any Christian writings of this period (texts dealing with such matters are rare), it

45. *Dura-Europos. Cult Relief: The Syrian God Aphlad and a Priest Sacrificing, detail.*

seems safe to assume that there was a connection between the decline of literal imitations of the physical world and the rise of Christianity.

What exactly was this connection? Put quite simply, it may have been no more than the fact that, indifferent to the beauties of the visible world and its 'vain appearances,' the early Christians contented themselves with the most summary depictions of things seen and discountenanced any sort of naturalism. They may have held that artists, seeking as they did to glimpse the world invisible, did best not to linger on the material side of things. This attitude is comprehensible in view of the affinities between the Christian ideology and the art forms which developed at the close of Antiquity; and it is noteworthy that the more or less abstract forms which had then come into favour

46. Palmyra. Relief: Procession of Women. Palmyra Museum.

persisted in the arts of the early Middle Ages and at Byzantium—arts distinguished by their intense spirituality.

None the less, recent discoveries and a closer study of Late Roman monuments have proved, first, that the decline of the classical aesthetic and the art of rendering with objective fidelity the outward aspects of the visible world did not begin in the Christian artists' workshops; and, secondly, that the last phase of antique art (when it strongly diverged from classical tradition) originated independently of Christianity and before the emergence of Christian art.

Well before the founding of the Christian Empire there had come into favour an art that was in no sense progressive, but dependent on models of an earlier age, which the artist copied to the best of his ability. These models, or their prototypes, were Greek and, being still accessible to later generations, they enabled artists and patrons of the arts to keep in contact with a body of classical works spanning several centuries. Every man of means in Italy prided himself on owning works of this type. Roman temples were crowded with them, and still more had survived in Greece. Some were masterpieces in their own right and thanks to them the classical aesthetic was transmitted from one generation to another. This led to an idealization of the creations of a more or less distant past and, since no account was taken of the interval of time that had elapsed, discouraged artists from striking out in new directions. Much the same thing

51

47. *Heads of Two Tetrarchs, detail. Piazza San Marco, Venice.*

happened in the Middle Ages, when artists habitually drew inspiration from Antiquity and made a practice of reproducing ancient prototypes.

Needless to say, neither in the Middle Ages nor in Antiquity did this reluctance to break away from ancient models reduce art to a state of pure stagnation. New elements inevitably crept into the traditional handling and modified it. But this was followed by a revived enthusiasm for the antique, a *renovatio*, in the course of which ancient models were once again assiduously imitated. In some cases this renewal was limited in scope, in others it covered a wider field. Whenever it was patronized by the Emperor, it affected the whole Empire. Archaizing movements of this type had been promoted by Augustus, Hadrian and Gallienus, and similar 'renaissances' seem to have taken place in the reigns of the Christian emperors Constantine and Theodosius.

During the middle and second half of the fourth century there was a spate of conscious, often remarkably adroit imitations of classical works, commissioned by the aristocracy of the capital, who still kept to the pagan faith.

From now on the practice of imitating more or less ancient works came into favour, and it was to retain its popularity all through the Middle Ages. This idealization of Antiquity led to a revival of art forms of widely differing periods and these frequent, though never generalized, reversions to the past tended to link together, through the ages, the productions of artists in all parts of Europe.

There were several reasons why the artists imitating classical models did not copy them literally. A study of the more marked deviations from classical taste and the traditions of Greek art throws light on the rationale of the alterations of classical forms

52

and the innovations made, many of which lasted into the Middle Ages. Before manifesting itself in Rome, the decline of the classical aesthetic can be seen in provincial works, such as the statues produced in Egypt, Gaul and England, the reliefs in the temple of Baal at Palmyra, the sculptures of Dura-Europos and those of Aphrodisias in Asia Minor (dating to the third century). In other words, provincial artists, while following the example set by the great Mediterranean cities, transformed their imitations of classical models into works couched in an original style; and this was due both to a different

49. *Edessa. Funerary Mosaic of Moqimu (copy).*

48. *Palmyra, Tomb of the Three Brothers. Funerary Portrait.*

cultural climate and to differences in their training. In the third century there was a steady flow of provincials into Rome and the newcomers played an ever-increasing role in the public and private life of the city, with the result that works of art produced in the capital, even in the most highly esteemed workshops, came to reflect the local idioms of the provincial arts.

Thus in the reliefs on the Arch of Constantine in Rome (314), an eminently official work commissioned by the Senate and presented to the Emperor to commemorate his victory at the Milvian Bridge, we find a tendency towards a rugged primitivism, characteristic of the provincial workshops and resembling that of the reliefs on the Arch of Galerius at Salonica, erected some years earlier.

The reliefs on the Arch of Constantine and the porphyry statues of tetrarchs (St Mark's, Venice, and the Vatican Library) show how great was the influence exerted by the provinces on even the most official art of Rome. This need not surprise us when we remember that the Empire included not only peoples of many different races and cultural backgrounds, but also social and ethnic groups which had formerly had distinctive aesthetic traditions of their own. This applies chiefly to the eastern provinces where, in the climate of the Pax Romana, the regional arts of earlier days had flowered anew. Here provincialism was marked by national characteristics or, rather, by a reflection of the traditional aesthetic and techniques peculiar to each region.

In Egypt, Syria and parts of Asia Minor these traditions, in all that differentiated them from the classical norm, were a legacy of the Mesopotamian arts of an earlier age, transmitted by the Iranians. It was by way of her eastern provinces that Rome became acquainted with the arts of Asia, in the form of objects produced by native craftsmen who, after assimilating the highly advanced art of nearby Persia (Parthian, then Sassanian), adapted it to the taste of the Roman customers for whom they catered.

Common to the provincial arts and the arts of the East were certain characteristics which became widespread in Late Antiquity and were later to be distinctive of the art of the Middle Ages. These characteristics were schematic design; a simplification of forms (often reduced to geometric figures); concentration on a few expressive traits that are maintained and emphasized (while others are attenuated or suppressed in the interests of clarity); a disregard of space and of the relations between objects which would indicate their size; indifference to plastic values, to weight and lighting (leading to the absence of any fixed source of light and therefore of cast shadows); a preference for purely surface effects as against those suggesting the third dimension.

It will be noted that these characteristics are the same as those of the Christian works of Late Antiquity discussed at an earlier page, and it is evident that we here have antecedents of their style. Several factors contributed to these changes and enabled the provincial and Oriental arts to stamp their imprint on works produced in the chief cities of the Empire—Rome to begin with. One of the main factors was of a demographic order. As a result of the long-lasting Pax Romana the number of provincials residing in Rome and the other large cities had greatly increased in the age preceding the Christianization of the Empire. If proof be needed, we have only to recall the racial origins of the emperors and high officials of this period; also the dissemination of Oriental religions in all parts of the Empire, most notably in Rome.

50. *Rome. Sarcophagus, detail: Plotinus (?) surrounded by Female Figures and Disciples. Museo Laterano, Rome.*

As was to be expected, the chief patrons of the arts were members of the wealthy and privileged class in the capital, and artists were naturally guided by their tastes. It was in workshops financed by these patrons that the masterpieces, destined to serve as prototypes, were produced. Thanks to the long spell of peace and prosperity a large body of art lovers had grown up who gave regular employment to artists and encouraged them to make copies of the works that they preferred.

But, in the process of imitating a model, simplifying it with an eye to reproduction and adapting it to different materials and dimensions, the art of the original was always modified to some extent. Equivalents or substitutes were created and thus a new style developed in which planes were simplified, drawing was schematized, perspective reduced or eliminated altogether, details of costumes were emphasized and modelling was summarily indicated.

55

In other words the development of the techniques of reproduction, due to the rising demand for works of art in an age of prosperity, led to certain stylistic changes which merged with those already introduced by the provincial and Oriental arts. Nor must we forget that the aim of imperial official art was to remind every spectator, Roman or foreign, of the power and beneficence of the monarchy. This propagandist art, which more than any other depended on the techniques of reproduction and was produced on a larger scale, contributed to the creation of a simple, conservative style, the stability of whose procedures made it easier to grasp the significance of the accepted imagery.

This art, which prepared the way for the one that was soon to be diffused by the State-sponsored Church, was an art intended for the masses and readily comprehensible by them. Flourishing more than ever after the conversion of imperial Rome to Christianity, this art left its mark on the works which were now being reproduced in large numbers throughout the Empire. They had to appeal to the masses, and it was this necessity that determined the style of these works—the most widely diffused because promoted by the all-powerful emperors.

It is harder to say to what extent the tastes of individual members of the cultured élite contributed to the decline of the classical aesthetic tradition and the triumph of the new art. Few of the Doctors of the Church give any helpful information on the subject in their writings, nor have they anything to say about the psychological, doctrinal or metaphysical content and purport of the images.

We learn more from the pagan writers of Late Antiquity. I have in mind the Neo-Platonists, above all Plotinus, who shows a deeper understanding of art and refers more frequently to it than any of his disciples. In the *Enneads* he justifies a way of seeing nature that disregards the appearances of things, their dimensions, colours, transient aspects, with the result that they become diaphanous, devoid of weight and substance. Contemplating nature in this manner does not necessarily mean viewing it from outside; indeed the point of vision is often located in the object, so that it can be viewed from within, almost as though the beholder formed part of it.

The organ of this way of seeing was what Plotinus called the 'inner eye,' a term which became widely current among the Christians of the Middle Ages, and which, as used by Plotinus, pioneer of introspective mysticism, had a metaphysical significance. Thus in other passages of the *Enneads* Plotinus envisages the possibility of contemplating the irrational nucleus immanent in all material entities. This contemplation, he held, enabled a total, direct apprehension of the essences of objects, instead of the analytic, discursive apprehension of normal life. He even speaks of the 'dematerialization' of reality by means of procedures approximating to some of those most commonly used in the art of Late Antiquity and the Middle Ages: the abolishment of space, foreshortening, perspective, the horizon line; of the opacity of solid bodies and 'the light of common day.' Only when material things become transparent *inter se* and accessible to the mind's eye are we able to discern those spiritual values which constitute the only *true* reality and are therefore the sole objects worthy of our interest and the artist's contemplation.

At the close of Antiquity and in the early Middle Ages Plotinus was widely read, not only by the last of the pagans (above all the Neo-Platonists, his disciples) but also by Christian writers, who often quoted, approvingly, passages from the *Enneads*. So there are grounds for believing that the teachings of Plotinus had an influence on the art of this period. Whether or not he personally contributed to the introduction or diffusion of the new aesthetic in the Empire, he must have seen its earliest manifestations and grasped what it was aiming at. Neither then nor later do we find any shrewder, more searching analyses of the art of the age than those of Plotinus—provided we admit that this art had a spiritual function. In any case he makes it clear that the Christians and adherents of the other revealed and mystical religions which flourished at the end of Antiquity did not merely endorse the spiritual message of the art of their time, but may well have inaugurated this art or (at the very least) that they approved of it, shaped its course and ensured its survival over a long period.

Thus, thanks chiefly to Plotinus, we can see why it was that the most enlightened spirits of the age encouraged an abandonment of the traditional classical aesthetic, incapable of expressing the irrational substratum of current religious thought, and tried to replace this art with another, employing different forms and methods. As we have seen, many of these changes were suggested to the vanguard artists of the day by the more or less uncouth provincial schools, by the techniques used for mass production, and by works of art imported into the Empire from the Near East.

2. Christian Painting and Sculpture before the Peace of the Church

As the title of this chapter implies, Christian art before the Peace of the Church (313) is known to us only in two forms, to the exclusion of all others. The present state of our knowledge is necessarily fragmentary and one-sided. The widespread destruction of Christian places of worship, particularly during the last persecutions under the Tetrarchs, may well have swept away not only whole groups of early buildings but also many small artefacts of Christian inspiration, in glass or metal, which must certainly have been in existence by this time. However, though the yield has been sadly meagre, recent excavations in Syria, Rome and Dalmatia have brought to light some vestiges of third-century Christian places of worship.

We shall, then, begin with these remains of very ancient monuments and describe some of the most interesting. But though they have much historical and documentary importance, they hardly belong, so far as architecture is concerned, to the domain of art. Thus when we speak of third-century Christian art, all we really have to go on are the two forms of art named in the heading of this chapter: painting and sculpture.

Early Places of Worship

The ruins of a very early Christian church came to light in 1931-32 at Dura-Europos, a Roman frontier town on the Euphrates, when the site was excavated by a Franco-American expedition led by Michael Rostovtzeff. There is no question that this edifice predates the Peace of the Church, for its remains were found in a protective embankment made by the townsfolk of Dura a little before 256 to reinforce the defences of the town against a possible attack by the Persians (which actually took place). Like other buildings in the immediate vicinity of the fortifications, the Christian church was sacrificed for purposes of defence. It would seem that the burying of the church was regarded as a temporary measure. But as the improvised earthworks proved ineffective and the Persians

59

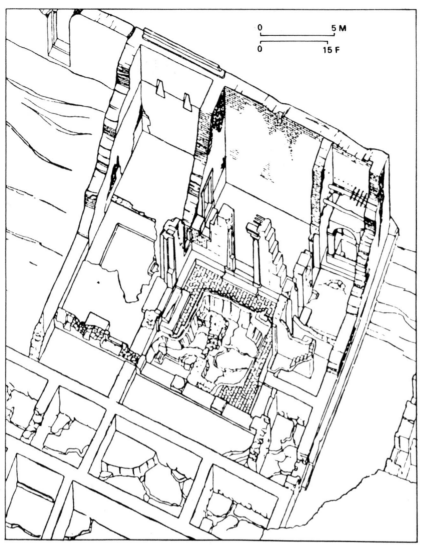

52. *Dura-Europos. Isometric View of the* 'Christian House.'

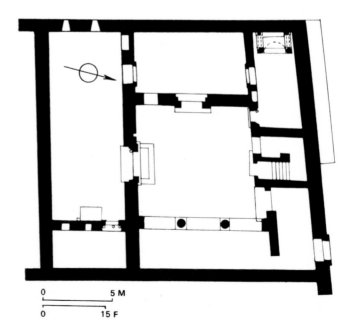

53. *Dura-Europos. Plan of the* 'Christian House.'

60

captured the town, the buried buildings had to wait seventeen centuries before being restored to the light of day by the Franco-American expedition. To the very fact that the earth-works failed to check the invaders we owe the preservation of this unique specimen of third-century Christian architecture, elsewhere obliterated by the ravages of men and time.

The structure of the Dura church has nothing in common with that of the basilica which became the standard Christian place of worship in the fourth century. Indeed it cannot properly be called a church; it was only a house owned by Christians, some rooms in which were set apart for services. The Christian House at Dura resembled other houses in the town and those in other Roman cities of the East. It included a roughly square courtyard (with sides about 25 feet long) on to which opened, on the ground floor and the one above, rooms of various sizes and serving different purposes. It would appear that the upper floor served as the owner's private residence and contained bedrooms and living rooms, while the five rooms on the ground floor (or one or two of them) were utilized for Christian worship. Our uncertainty on this point may seem surprising, but it merely stresses the curious fact that, with the exception of one on the ground floor, none of the rooms has any distinguishing feature showing what it was used for. Neither the layout nor what remains of the decoration enables us to decide which was the meeting-room of the Christian community and where the services took place—with the exception of one long narrow room on the right of the entrance. That this served as a baptistery is proved by the wall paintings and a ritual object discovered in the course of the excavations.

We have here, then, a place of Christian worship dating to the first half of the third century, which strangely enough has nothing distinctively Christian except for the deco-ration and a stone-built font in the room used for baptism. All the rest answers to the purposes of ordinary domestic architecture and only the exceptional size of one of the ground-floor rooms leads us to surmise that this room was the one used for collective worship.

These ruins at Dura are not only of sentimental interest; they have also an historical significance, despite the very few specifically Christian characteristics found in them. For they not only show that at the time when the Christian House was built the members of each congregation had special places used exclusively for communal worship, but also that the rooms reserved for these gatherings had no distinctive architectural features or even any special type of decoration. The one exception to the rule, so far as the absence of decoration and liturgical appurtenances is concerned, is the room used for baptism (the paintings in the Dura baptistery will be discussed later).

As for the curious 'neutrality' of the architecture of the Christian House at Dura, we find the same phenomenon in Christian edifices of the same period in Rome. This 'neutrality' becomes all the more remarkable when we compare, in this same town of Dura, the Christian House with the nearby, approximately contemporary synagogue.

The Jewish community of Dura must have been larger than the Christian. Their place of worship was similarly located in a private house but this formed part of a much larger group of non-religious buildings; moreover the room reserved for services, as it existed in the third century, presupposes a deliberate architectural planning not found in the Chris-tian House. For though around it there were several dwelling-houses having the same layout as the Christian House (an inner courtyard with rooms of various kinds abutting

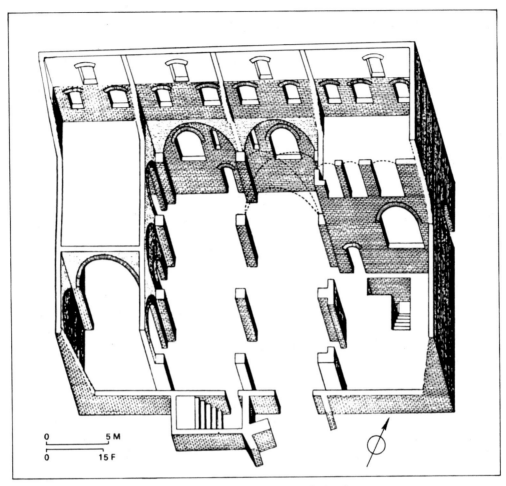

54. *Rome, San Martino ai Monti. Isometric View of the Original Church.*

on it), the house in which the synagogue was located had this peculiarity: part of the building was separated from the rest by a blind wall. The house of the synagogue comprises a courtyard with three porticoes behind which is a large room whose width exceeds its depth. Two doors lead into it, a large central door by which the men entered, while the smaller side-door was probably reserved for the women. In the back wall of the synagogue, facing the central entrance, was a ciborium, a recess in which stood the cupboard containing the Torah (a roll of the Mosaic books of the Old Testament). Against the wall was a bench, running all round the room and providing seating accommodation for the congregation.

All this goes to show that the Jewish community held its services in a room which had been built specially for this purpose and incorporated in a small architectural complex, while a few steps away the Christians contented themselves (except in the case of the baptistery) with making a few, hardly noticeable alterations in an ordinary private house. Without dwelling for the moment on the architectural features of the Dura synagogue (these will be discussed when we come to deal with other ancient synagogues and their architecture as compared with that of the Christian churches of the same period), we would

62

draw attention to one point: the differences between the two places of worship at Dura can be accounted for when we remember that, in the period of the Severi, when these buildings were made, the Jewish religion was officially recognized by the Roman government, but Christianity was not. Thus the Jews were entitled to have their own places of worship, whereas the government officially ignored, and could not legally recognize, the existence of premises specially equipped for Christian worship. This gave the Roman authorities the right, in the sporadic periods of persecution, to confiscate and destroy Christian churches. But the remains discovered at Dura prove that—except in these periods—the Christians ventured to adapt certain premises to the requirements of their rites, but that the alterations they made were so slight that they did not catch the eye of passers-by or even of those who entered the courtyard of the house.

According to Eusebius several pre-Constantinian churches were enlarged and refitted during the reign of Constantine in virtue of the edicts of tolerance. So we may assume that these churches were originally quite small, perhaps as little conspicuous as the room set apart for worship in the Christian House at Dura. But the speed with which the architects of the Constantinian period transformed them, once Christianity became legitimized, suggests that larger and more dignified buildings may well have existed. The fact must be borne in mind that between the Christian House at Dura and the churches of around the year 300, over half a century had elapsed. Despite the dating proposed by the excavators, the remains of the earliest Christian church at Emmaus in Palestine do not seem to predate the Peace of the Church.

To this period may be assigned the oldest churches of Rome, those described as *tituli*, the first parish churches in the capital of the Empire. Excavations made beneath several Roman basilicas of the Middle Ages have brought to light buildings which may have been used for Christian worship before the reign of Constantine.

Cases in point are the old houses buried under the churches of San Clemente and Sant'Anastasia; in each the room where Christian services took place was on the upper floor (there were two storeys), while the ground floor consisted of shops and storerooms. Unfortunately, since the rooms on the upper floor were destroyed when the medieval basilicas were built, we know very little about just those parts of the buildings which would have been most interesting in this context. Still, so far as can be ascertained, the 'churches' of the *tituli* in Rome were, as at Dura, quite undistinctive rooms forming part of large private houses.

The house which in the third century contained the so-called 'Titulus Equitii' (a parish church in Rome) is in a better state of preservation, since the basilica of San Martino ai Monti which replaced it was erected, not above, but alongside the 'Christian House.' It therefore gives us a better idea of the general look of the rooms used for Christian services in third-century Rome. Here, as at Dura, the room was on the ground floor. It was a relatively large one (55½ by 44 feet) and roofed with high groined vaults supported by free-standing pillars and pilasters engaged in the walls. This main room was surrounded by other vaulted rooms, the ones on the upper floor (no longer extant) communicating with those on the ground floor by a monumental staircase. This is the largest surviving Christian edifice of the pre-Constantinian period. But here we come up against a difficulty, due to the absence of any definite proof of an architectural arrangement indicating

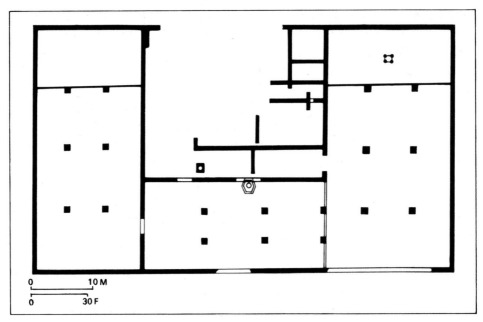

55. *Aquileia. Plan of the Cathedral of Bishop Theodore.*

that this place was actually used for the celebration of Christian services as early as the third century. Indeed the same difficulty arises in respect of all the buildings of this type, unless exceptionally, as at Dura, church furniture or third-century Christian wall paintings have been discovered in them. These doubts arise from the very nature of these edifices, since pre-Constantinian Christian churches were devoid of any distinctively Christian features.

Another monument is sometimes cited as an example of Christian architecture in third-century Rome. This is the 'Titulus Byzantii' beneath the church of SS. Giovanni e Paolo. But an archaeological examination of what remains of the walls, vaults and paintings throws doubt on its Christian character. Some fine substructures have been found beneath the basilica of Pammachius (c. 450), and a famous *confessio*, but there is nothing in the architectural arrangement, and no wall painting, to make it certain that this was a Christian church in use before the Peace of the Church.

A final, indirect piece of evidence regarding the churches of this very early period is provided by the ruins of some Christian edifices of the early Constantinian epoch whose design may reflect that of churches built before the Peace of the Church. One is the cathedral of Aquileia founded about 314 by Bishop Theodore; another, the church of Marusinac at Salona on the Dalmatian coast, in its original form (cf. plan, page 183). In both cases the structure has nothing of the basilical plan and there is no trace as yet of the type of Christian place of worship which came into favour in the fourth century throughout the Mediterranean area.

Only the foundations of the Aquileia cathedral have survived and the architecture they reveal is so simple in design that it is easy to form a reliable idea of the general aspect of the original building. There were two large rectangular halls side by side, but some hundred feet apart, each being in effect an independent unit. The northern hall is about

64

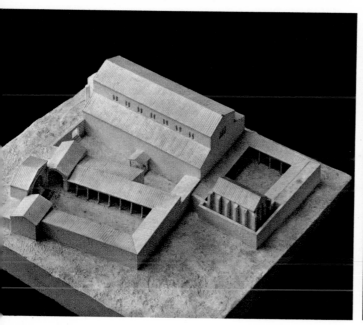 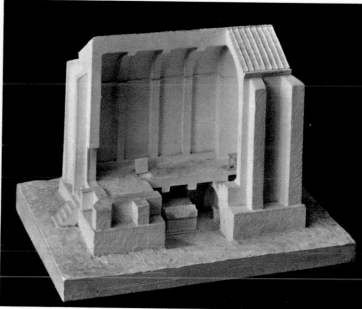

56. *Salona. Basilica and Martyrium of St Anastasius (reconstruction)*. 57. *Salona. Martyrium of St Anastasius (reconstruction)*.

123 feet long by 56½ wide; the southern, about 121 by 65½ feet. These two halls, like the smaller rooms connecting them, formed part of an architectural complex with a façade common to both overlooking a street in Aquileia. While we can only guess at the precise liturgical function of each of the two halls (on the basis of certain references, unfortunately not very clear, to a practice obtaining in the early Middle Ages of using similar paired but separate buildings as cathedral churches), some of their architectural characteristics call for mention here. For one thing these halls have a very simple layout, without any specific adjunct such as an apse. Within the rectangle formed by the walls of the room were six square pillars, and these pillars and the surrounding walls were clearly too flimsy to support vaults. Evidently, then, these halls had wooden roofs, but there is no knowing what shape they were given. It would have been interesting, in particular, to ascertain whether the roof above the chevet of the southern hall was disposed transversely as was the famous floor mosaic (illustrating the story of Jonah) below it. For it seems very probable that the roof was given the same layout as the mosaic pavement, in which an evident distinction is made between the nine panels in the nave, on the one hand, and, on the other, the single panel in the chevet.

This arrangement tends to show that the order of the ritual had an influence on the structure of the southern hall at Aquileia, and also foreshadows the later basilicas with a transept (a transverse hall in the chevet). But at Aquileia this influence is only hinted at, by the layout of the mosaic pavement and perhaps that of the roof as well, whereas a little later the basilicas with transepts translated the same programme into architectural terms. The foundations of Bishop Theodore at Aquileia have much to tell us about the nature of Christian architecture previous to the adoption of the basilical plan. It shows that when the Christians opted for this plan in the fourth century they did not come to it wholly unprepared.

Painting

Though hardly anything remains of the Christian architecture of the period preceding the edicts of tolerance, many paintings have survived. It is true that the extant works show no great variety, but we have whole sequences of them, proving the existence of well-established practices in this domain. It can be said without hesitation that there existed in the third century a Christian painting which had a well-defined field of application and an iconographic and functional programme which presupposes a tacit acquiescence on the part of the Christian communities or, more probably, the existence of instructions issued by the Church authorities.

The Christian paintings of this early period have a very special interest for the light they throw on the religious value then assigned to images. For it must not be forgotten that they are the earliest figurations of a religion which had originally dispensed with any iconography and, failing to divine the enormous importance religious imagery was later to assume, had begun by ruling it out entirely. It is evident that when, around the year 200, the Christians broke with this rule they had good reasons for doing so and that these, their first images, must have had a specifically Christian purpose.

What, then, was this religious function, which was deemed important enough to warrant the inclusion of an iconography in a religion which aspired to commune with God solely 'in the spirit'? To answer the question without doing injustice to the motives guiding the promoters of this art, we must examine its manifestations, its forms and functions, in the milieu in which it came to birth. The first thing we note is that Christian figure painting began with the cycles of images displayed on the walls of a baptistery, at Dura-Europos (we have already described the location of this room in the 'Christian House'), and on the walls and ceilings of the Roman catacombs, i.e. the subterranean burial chambers of the Roman cemeteries.

In both cases the decorations were clearly made with an eye to their aesthetic effect (this applies particularly to the catacombs). But the choice of subjects—to be discussed later—suggests that there was also a didactic purpose behind them. These paintings represent figures and events whose choice and combinations show that all are intended to convey a similar message. They are images of God's loving-kindness towards those who put their trust in Him; also of the efficacy of the sacraments, paradigms of salvation, and of the path to be followed in order to share in the privilege of the Eucharist. It was thought fit to inculcate these lessons both in the baptistery, where neophytes were initiated into the faith, and also in the tombs, where the Christian, his journey done, entered into the new life beyond the grave. In both cases these images recalled the salvation of others who had kept the faith; in one for the edification of the neophyte, in the other for the consolation of the bereaved. This art in the form of religious images is Christian through and through. But it is noteworthy that it should have made its appearance when it did (long after the birth of Christianity itself) and have been mainly associated with funerary rites, for reasons extrinsic to Christianity.

As we point out elsewhere, the origins of this Christian imagery may probably be connected with the beginnings of Jewish figural art, which go back to the reign of the Severi. It was then that, yielding to the widespread taste for pictures (like that prevail-

58. *Rome, Catacomb of the Giordani. Orant.*

ing nowadays), each religion took to inventing an imagery of its own, the Jews presumably setting the precedent for the Christians. The Jews of Dura had no hesitation about painting pictures in large numbers, even on the walls of their synagogues, following in this the practice of the pagan communities around them. The Christians did not go so far as that, anyhow in their 'church' at Dura, but they evidently approved of having a few pictures on the walls of one of the most sacred rooms of their House, the one used for baptism—perhaps because the sacrament of baptism assimilated this room to the tomb of the 'old Adam,' reborn by the rite of baptism to eternal life. In any case many Christian tombs of the period were also decorated with figural religious paintings, a practice frankly paralleling that of the pagans. Nothing, indeed, could be more banal than the decorations, with mythological subjects, figuring in pagan tombs. The continuity of this tradition is attested by many decorations, among them those in the Porta Maggiore hypogeum and in the pagan cubicula of the Porta Latina catacomb, where mythological characters and incidents serve as paradigms of the dead man's lot in the next world. This method of pictorial demonstration was taken over by the Christians, with the difference that their themes were drawn from the Old Testament stories or prayers for the dead evoking them.

The influence of this tradition—and consequently of the precedents which led the Christians to give their first religious paintings this orientation—is borne out by one of the most striking characteristics of Early Christian art. The great majority of the third-century paintings are treated in a very summary and succinct manner; the artist confines himself to a few splashes of colour on the walls and to a quite small number of figures or objects. The same tendency to extreme abridgement had already appeared in the decorative paintings and stuccoes made in the first century A.D. in Rome. This almost hieroglyphic imagery, suggesting more than it actually represented, had a great vogue in Rome where—a significant point—it was being used in the decoration of pagan tombs at the very time when the Christians took over some of its characteristics in their earliest murals and in the catacomb paintings.

It will be best to begin our survey of the first Christian wall paintings with an account of those in the Dura baptistery, this for two reasons: first, their early date (beginning of the third century), and secondly because they are unique of their kind, since all the other extant murals, whether equally early or later in date, belong to sepulchral art.

The discovery of the Christian wall paintings at Dura came as a great surprise; it had always been taken for granted that the existence of any above-ground Christian place of worship, and *a fortiori* of religious murals, was an impossibility in this early age. But there was no denying the facts; the Dura baptistery and its paintings exist, and they date to the beginning of the third century.

The baptistery was a long rectangular room with a wooden roof. At one end stood a stone-built font shaped like a sarcophagus; above it was a ciborium resting on two columns. The vault of the ciborium is bright blue, spangled with stars, and on the end wall behind the font is a composition prefiguring later apse paintings. On a red ground the Good Shepherd is seen carrying a ewe on his shoulders, preceded by his flock. Adam and Eve, too, are represented, in a curiously narrow Garden of Paradise. Thus the purport of the panel over the baptismal font is evident: it tells of the old Adam who sinned and the new Adam, Christ, who redeems the victims of original sin.

68

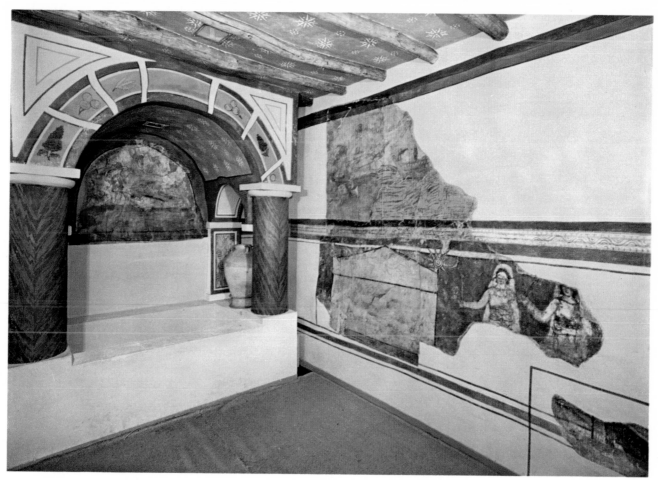

59. *Dura-Europos. 'Christian House,' Baptistery: Overall View. Yale University Art Gallery.*

60. *Dura-Europos. 'Christian House,' Baptistery: The Good Shepherd and his Flock. Yale University Art Gallery.*

61. *Dura-Europos. 'Christian House,' Baptistery: Healing of the Paralytic. Yale University Art Gallery.*

62. *Dura-Europos. 'Christian House,' Baptistery: Christ and St Peter walking on the Water. Yale University Art Gallery.*

Barely half the paintings on the walls remain. Keeping to a decorative scheme of Hellenistic origin, the artist disposed them in two registers, of approximately equal size, one above the other. The upper contained a sequence of scenes with small, rather clumsily drawn figures on a white ground. Undivided by frames, these scenes represented the miracles of Christ; only two of them—the healing of the paralytic man and St Peter walking on the sea—have survived. Other instances of divine succour in time of need, drawn from the Gospels and perhaps also from the Old Testament, probably figured on other parts of the walls, this cycle corresponding to that of the paradigms of deliverance so frequent in contemporary catacombs. Since this was a baptistery, the imagery naturally related rather to the salvation of the neophyte than to that of the Christian after death, as in the underground tombs. The miracles of Christ on the upper part of the wall were treated sketchily.

The handling of the paintings on the lower register, below a stucco cornice, is completely different; they contain large, monumental figures on a uniform red ground. There seem to have been several scenes, though only one can be made out; it represents the three Maries bringing myrrh to the sepulchre of Christ. Carrying tapers, they approach a large sarcophagus of which only one of the short sides is shown, adorned with two stars serving as acroteria. This last detail, as well as the absence of the angels and the lid of the sarcophagus resting against the mouth of the cave, differentiates this image from the usual rendering of the scene. Evidently the Christian artist employed at Dura followed an icono-

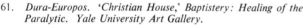

63. *Dura-Europos. 'Christian House,' Baptistery: The Woman of Samaria at the Well. Yale University Art Gallery.* ▶

graphic tradition that soon became obsolete (or nearly so). On the other hand the monumental proportions and solemn style of the imagery have no equivalents in other third-century paintings and anticipate the majestic art of the fourth century. The presence of this image evoking the Resurrection and the place it is given on the wall relate no doubt to the symbolic value of the baptismal rite as signifying the death and resurrection of the Christian, prefigured by Christ's.

On the same register, but in places which did not allow of larger pictures, are traces of two scenes inspired, it seems, by the prayers in the Order of Baptism: the Woman of Samaria at the well and David's victory over Goliath. Some scholars have seen in them references to doctrines peculiar to the Syrian theologians and liturgists. But since these men lived at a later period, this view seems to us untenable. There are better grounds for stressing the resemblances between the Dura paintings and those in the contemporary Roman catacombs. It is only the layout of these decorations and the style of the small scenes at the top of the walls that affiliate the Dura paintings to those of other paintings (but pagan ones) dating to the first centuries of our era in a nearby province, notably those at Kerch in the Crimea.

64. *Dura-Europos, Mithraeum. Mithras Hunting. Yale University Art Gallery.*

However, for a better understanding of the paintings in the Dura baptistery, they should be compared with other wall paintings at Dura: the slightly earlier ones in the Mithraeum and the contemporary (or near-contemporary) murals in the synagogue. The style of both shows a stronger Iranian influence than do the Christian frescoes in the baptistery. In the Mithraeum, as in the synagogue, most of the paintings are on a monumental scale which is paralleled in the baptistery only by the large composition showing the Holy Women at the tomb.

So it is not surprising that Iranian influence should manifest itself in the Christian paintings of Dura chiefly in this particular scene. We need only compare the processions of donors in the Mithraeum, that of the three Maries in the baptistery, and two women in the scenes with Elijah at the synagogue. This style is akin to that of the funerary mosaics at Edessa, several of which are contemporary and give us an idea of the type of art prevalent in the chief city of the region, an art stemming from both the Greco-Levantine and the Parthian tradition.

72

65. *Dura-Europos, Mithraeum. Portrait of Zoroaster (?). Yale University Art Gallery.*

66. *Dura-Europos, Synagogue. Overall View with the Torah Shrine. National Museum, Damascus.*

67. *Dura-Europos, Synagogue. The Crossing of the Red Sea; The Abandoned Temple, detail. National Museum, Damascus.*

68. *Dura-Europos, Synagogue. The Temple of Dagon devastated by the Ark; The Childhood of Moses, detail. National Museum, Damascus.*

69. *Dura-Europos, Synagogue. The Miracle of the Well—Elijah resurrecting the Son of the Widow of Zarephath. National Museum, Damascus.*

70. *Dura-Europos, House of the Scribes. Portrait of Heliodorus. Yale University Art Gallery.* ▶

71. *Dura-Europos, Synagogue. Figure of a Man. National Museum, Damascus.*

77

OMPHALE HERCVLES

CASSIA
MANEEETA
PRISCILLA
FECIT

72. *South Italy.   Votive Relief of Cassia Priscilla.   Museo Nazionale, Naples.*

73. *Rome, Barberini 'Mithraeum.'   Mithras and Scenes of the Cosmogony, detail.*

74. *Rome, Cemetery under St Peter's. Vine-Shoots and Christ as the Sun God.*

The frescoes in the Dura baptistery are the only Christian paintings of the period preceding the Peace of the Church that have so far been discovered in an above-ground edifice. Unless, that is, we are justified in adding to them the mosaics in a small burial chamber in the cemetery beside the Via Cornelia in Rome and occupying what was to be the site of the Constantinian basilica of St Peter in the Vatican. Unfortunately its attribution to the mid-third century is dubious. As at Santa Costanza in the next century, the vault decoration consists of interlacing vine-shoots with, in the centre, the figure of Christ, who has the attributes of Apollo, a quadriga and horses. Seven rays light up the nimbused head of this symbolic image, in obvious allusion to Christ 'light of the world.' The tesserae of the wall mosaics have fallen and only the outlines of the figures can still be seen: the Good Shepherd, the Fisher of Men, and Jonah cast into the sea and swallowed by the whale. The themes of this small iconographic cycle are the same as those on the earliest

80

Christian sarcophagi—with the exception, perhaps, of the solar symbol. This personification of the sun reappears, however, in a fifth-century mosaic in Sant'Aquilino, Milan; it is characteristic of the imagery favoured by the Christian iconographers preceding and contemporary with Constantine.

The small group of mosaics described above are evidence of the practice that had now developed of adorning the walls and vaults of mausolea in open-air cemeteries with illustrations of Christian themes. Thus they help us to 'situate' the paintings in the Roman catacombs which, it is clear, drew inspiration from the wall paintings in built-up mausolea. But while these mausolea have been destroyed (or are known to us only by fragmentary remains uncovered in excavations on the Via Cornelia and the Via Triumphalis, beneath St Peter's and on Isola Sacra at Ostia), the underground galleries of the catacombs and all the paintings in them, pagan and Christian, have survived more or less intact.

It is to the catacombs, almost exclusively, that we owe our knowledge of large-scale Christian painting prior to the Peace of the Church, and they are to be found only in places where the nature of the soil lent itself to this type of subterranean cemetery, as at Rome, Naples and Syracuse. For this early period the Roman catacombs are virtually the only ones to preserve frescoes which derive from the wall paintings in built-up mausolea; and the relationship between them is all the more apparent since a frescoed decoration in the catacombs is always limited to a single burial chamber or to an arcosolium—in other words, to the underground equivalent of an individual above-ground tomb. Thus each mural in these underground galleries has the air of being an isolated work, exactly as it would have been in an above-ground mausoleum. For, contrary to what might be supposed, the Roman catacombs were not given painted decorations as a matter of course. Only a very small number of cubicula or arcosolia were frescoed, those owned by the few well-to-do Christians of the period; and they alone could afford to complete the adornment of their family vaults with handsome carved sarcophagi. These wealthier Christians, however, do not seem to have been quite so ready to spend money on the tombs of the martyrs; their sarcophagi were not decorated with figure carvings and it was only three or four centuries later that the tomb of the sainted Pope Cornelius, then the object of a special cult, was adorned with paintings.

So far, the only known instance of a private underground tomb previous to the age of Constantine is the 'Cappella Greca' in the catacomb of St Priscilla. Though subsequently joined to the catacomb, it was originally an independent tomb. After the Peace of the Church, however, a good many tombs of this type, some pagan, others Christian (or Christian in part), were constructed. This was probably due to the change in the social status of Christian families, with respect to other Roman families, after the triumph of the Church; the number of converts in the well-to-do classes increased after the promulgation of the edicts of toleration. Fortunately, thanks to local conditions, the remains of some Christian paintings have been preserved, in private burial chambers at a shallow depth in an ancient cemetery at Nola, near Caserta (in the vicinity of Naples). These paintings, originally very fine but now in a poor state of preservation, may well date back to the age of the Severi (c. 200), in which case they number among the earliest examples of Christian painting. Their iconographic programme is the same as in the Roman catacomb paintings, but with a greater range of Old Testament subjects.

75. *Rome, Catacomb of Domitilla. Birds beside a Vase.*

Now that the catacomb paintings have come to be studied in the context of similar Roman works, it is clear that even the earliest of them can hardly have been made much before the year 200. The oldest paintings in the catacombs are, then, roughly contemporary with the frescoes in the Dura baptistery. The burial chambers known as the Flavian Hall in the catacomb of Domitilla and a similar decoration in the so-called Crypt of Lucina (beside the catacomb of San Callisto and subsequently joined to it) on the Via Appia furnish the best examples of this, the most archaic type of painting. It consists of frescoes entirely covering the vaults and walls of the burial chambers and having an elegance and lightness typical of the style of decoration prevailing in Rome in the late second and early third century, for example in the pagan mausoleum of the Nasonii (160-180) and the 'House of Diana' at Ostia (195). A creamy white ground is criss-crossed with thin red and green lines, at once enlivening and unifying the painted surfaces. The vaulted ceilings are generally square, with a circular motif inscribed within the square. The same thin lines demarcate the central circle, and this is surrounded by geometric designs.

82

76. *Rome, Catacomb of Domitilla. Ceiling Painting.*

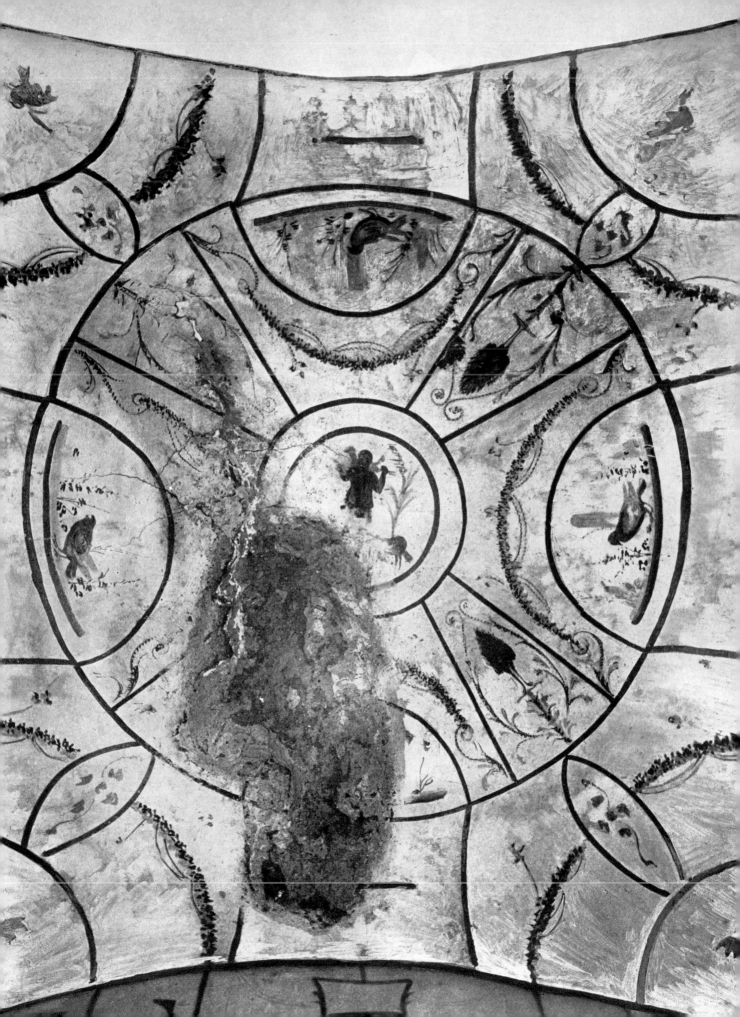

77. *Rome, Catacomb of Pretestato, Crypt of San Gennaro. Air Shaft with* **Paintings**.

78.   *Rome, Catacomb of SS. Pietro e Marcellino.   Jonah thrown into the Sea.*

79. *Rome, Catacomb of Priscilla, Cappella Greca.   Head in a Medallion.*

80. *Rome, Catacomb of Domitilla. Cubiculum of the Good Shepherd.*

81. *Rome, Pagan Mausoleum under San Sebastiano. Birds and Vine-Shoots.*

87

82. *Rome, Catacomb of San Callisto, Crypt of Lucina. Fish and Eucharistic Bread.*

83. *Rome, Catacomb of Domitilla. Orpheus and Animals.*

84. *Rome, Catacomb of Domitilla.   Orpheus-Christ with Animals, detail.*

The artists responsible for the Flavian Hall and the Crypt of Lucina were merely applying to Christian sepulchres the decorative schemes that were in common use in similar contemporary pagan tombs.

There is nothing comparable here to the Pompeian frescoes of two centuries earlier, with their simulated architecture and views in *trompe-l'œil* of distant buildings and landscapes. This illusionist art had gone out of fashion and been replaced by the decorative style described above: abstract, uniform grounds, a regular pattern of fine-spun lines, often of different colours. An art, in short, existing on a single but indeterminate plane, which is unaffected by the presence of an occasional figure or group of figures, small and lightly indicated, located here and there within the very simply designed frames described above.

89

86. *Rome. Sarcophagus, detail: Bath of a New-born Babe. Museo delle Terme, Rome.*

Some elements of this style of decoration had made their appearance as early as the first century A.D. Thus the vaulting of the underground (Pythagorean) basilica at the Porta Maggiore in Rome was already decorated with an elaborate network of tenuous frames—but in stucco, not painted—containing vignettes of tiny, elegant figures usually placed in the centre of the scene, with an empty space around them. Here, too, we find a preference for small, dramatic motifs, agreeable to the eye, however serious the subject, some of them culled from mythology, evoking gods and the Pythagorean mysteries. To heighten the effect of lightness, flying figures, birds in flight and 'levitations' heavenwards were frequently included.

85. *Rome, Villa of Livia. Orchard closed off by a Balustrade. Museo delle Terme, Rome.*

88. *Rome. Underground Basilica of Porta Maggiore. Mythological Scene.*

89. *Rome, Roman Edifice in the Farnesina Gardens. Scene of a Rustic Sacrifice. Museo delle Terme, Rome.*

87. *Rome, Catacomb of the Via Latina. Hercules and the Hydra.*

90. *Rome, Catacomb of Pretestato, Crypt of San Gennaro. Winter.*

91. *Rome, Catacomb of Domitilla. Eros.*

The earliest paintings in the catacombs, those we have mentioned and others as well (for example the pictures in the so-called Chapel of the Sacraments in the San Callisto catacomb), often represent birds flying across an open space, *putti* with outspread wings, and airborne monsters. In the corners of ceilings there are also personifications of the Seasons borrowed from the repertory of the ancient mausolea. Christian subjects do not invariably predominate in the earliest works. These are small-scale paintings subordinated to the pattern of geometric lines which determine the layout of the decorative scheme and immediately catch the eye of the beholder.

Everything indicates that the artists were primarily concerned with the decorative effect of the paintings. Thus we find figures of Orants—ideal evocations of Christian prayer—recurring at selected points on the same ceiling and alternating with 'historical' Christian subjects. This arrangement, too, illustrates the priority given to decorative effect—the very feature of these Christian paintings that was taken over entirely from contemporary non-Christian art.

92. *Rome, Catacomb of Pretestato, Crypt of San Gennaro.   The Harvest, detail.*

93. *Rome, Catacomb of Pretestato, Crypt of San Gennaro.   Winter, detail.*

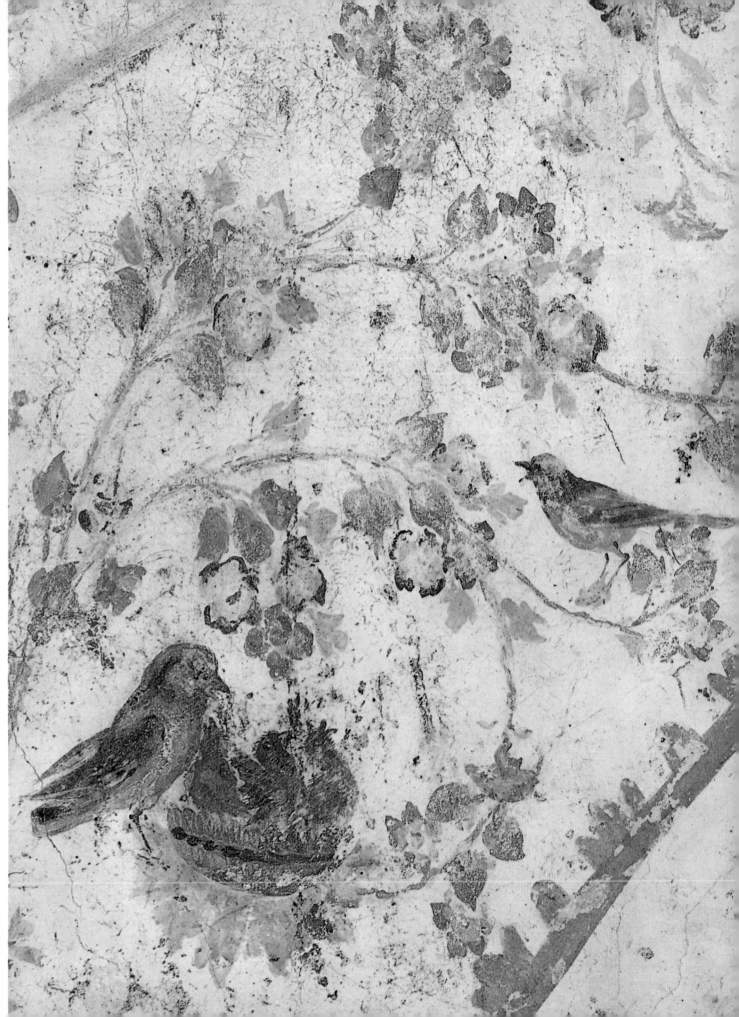

94. *Rome, Catacomb of Priscilla.* *The Good Shepherd; Isaiah (or Balaam pointing to the Star) with the Virgin and Child.*

There are some cases (only a few, however) in which this derivation from the mural decorations of the period is made more apparent by the use of stucco ornaments. The best known are those in the catacomb of Priscilla on the Via Salaria: some stucco fragments setting off certain elements in a scene of a mother suckling her child beside a standing figure. These are thought to represent Isaiah prophesying the birth of the Messiah in the presence of the Virgin and Child.

In the famous chapel of this catacomb, the Cappella Greca, other stuccoes (purely decorative motifs composed of large fronds of acanthus) garnish the intrados of the arches forming the main vault.

No precise dates can be assigned to the paintings in the catacombs; the men who made them were artisans who did not aim at novelty and, deliberately or as a matter of course, imitated ancient models of various periods—not necessarily those nearest to them in time. In the absence of any inscriptions a study of their style and technique, even of their content, does not lead to any definite conclusions. Given the nature of this art, only an inscription or some clue extrinsic to the actual paintings would make it possible to date them with any accuracy. Unfortunately, as things stand, no indications of this kind are available in the case of the pre-Constantinian paintings; we have to make shift with a very approximate chronology. The early third-century frescoes in the Flavian Hall (catacomb of Domitilla) and in the Crypt of Lucina (catacomb of San Callisto) are followed by those in the five burial chambers known as the Chapel of the Sacraments (catacomb of San Callisto), which presumably date to the first half of the third century. To the same period may be assigned the Virgin and Child with Isaiah in the catacomb of Priscilla, and the fresco cycle, very different but no less impressive, in the Cappella Greca of the same catacomb; also, perhaps, the fragmentary scenes supposed to illustrate the Passion in the Catacomb of Pretestato (sc. Praetextatus). One of the works of the late third century calls for special mention: the portrait of a girl or young woman as an Orant which forms part of the decoration of a burial chamber in the Catacomb of Priscilla. She stands in

95. *Rome, Catacomb of Priscilla. Isaiah (or Balaam pointing to the Star) with the Virgin and Child.*

97. *Rome. Sarcophagus, detail: Orant. Palazzo
Sanseverino, Rome.*

98. *Italy. Sarcophagus of Flavius Julius Catervius,
detail: A Philosopher. Cathedral, Tolentino.*

the centre of the tympanum of an arcosolium, between a man and a woman, both seated,
and a few other figures. We shall revert to this famous figure at a later page; meanwhile
we would draw attention to its high artistic quality, comparable with that of the frescoes in
the Cappella Greca. We must not be taken to imply that this peculiar excellence was a
purely Christian contribution to the Roman art of the time; such, indeed, is not our
impression. But since this is a work of art wholly in keeping with contemporary taste
and usage in Rome, it has an interest as pointing to the fact that, well before the triumph
of their faith, certain members of the Christian community could enlist the services of
great artists (who may themselves have been Christians).

    This fresco of a young Orant, known as the 'Donna velata,' is among those which supply
the closest links between the art of the catacombs and that of the Christian sarcophagi
previous to the Peace of the Church. The affinities between the two arts appear most

101

clearly in the case of identical themes, for example the representation of a fisherman (i.e. the Saviour as a 'fisher of men'). The so-called Chapel of the Sacraments offers several examples of themes which also figure on the earliest Christian sarcophagi. On these, too, we often see a shepherd carrying a lost sheep on his shoulders (an ancient motif taken over by the Christians for representations of Christ as the Good Shepherd), accompanied by a dog and his flock, and scenes of shepherds milking ewes in a pastoral setting, a rocky landscape with rustic huts. To a group of sarcophagi with these reliefs corresponds a group of archaic paintings in the catacombs.

When we examine all the Biblical themes used by the catacomb painters and the sculptors of Early Christian sarcophagi, we find that the great majority are drawn from the Old Testament, predominant among them being signal instances of the deliverance of God's faithful servants in an hour of need: Daniel in the lions' den, Jonah cast forth by

99. *Rome. Nereid Sarcophagus, detail: Fisherman. Museo di Pretestato, Rome.*

100. *Rome, Catacomb of San Callisto, Chapel of the Sacraments. Jonah thrown into the Sea.*

the whale, Abraham stayed from sacrificing Isaac, the Three Children in the fiery furnace, Noah saved from the Flood and (among the smaller number of Gospel scenes) the raising of Lazarus and the healing of the paralytic man. On the whole, these scenes are visual counterparts of prayers said in the Office of the Dead, in the form it is known to have had since the early Middle Ages, and also of the invocations in other Christian prayers. The same practice had obtained in the earlier Jewish and Gnostic liturgies; there, too, the suppliant recited a series of the prayers which, when addressed to God by righteous men in time of danger, had been answered.

This correspondence between the iconographic themes and the prayers in current use has been thought sufficiently close to explain the presence of this imagery in the catacombs and on sarcophagi—an explanation that in my opinion is well founded. But these Christian paintings and carvings may have been preceded by similarly inspired Jewish images. Noah saved from the flood and Daniel in the lions' den, both with their arms raised in prayer, were familiar themes in the Jewish iconography of Antiquity. Moreover the Christian prayers did not include all possible instances of deliverance; these paradigms were carefully selected, the number of examples cited varied from one prayer to another, and the same is true of their iconographic equivalents.

103

102. *Rome, Catacomb of Priscilla, Cubiculum of the 'Velatio.'* The Three Children in the Fiery Furnace.

About the year 300 themes connected with deliverance began to figure more frequently than hitherto in the frescoes on ceilings and arcosolia and in sarcophagus reliefs. This tendency gained ground during the fourth century; indeed, to this century date the first concrete examples of the 'salvation cycles' illustrating specific paradigms of deliverance in the prayers of the Office of the Dead. (The prayers themselves, be it noted, cannot be traced back beyond the early Middle Ages.) At first, however, these historical scenes from the Bible were very few in number, and Christian themes made their appearance in art in the form of symbolic figures invested with an hieratic aura: the Good Shepherd (i.e. Christ) and the Orant (i.e. the Christian suppliant). Soon the range of these symbolic images was enlarged by assigning a symbolic value to certain Old Testament themes. Thus Adam and Eve evoked man's first disobedience and Original Sin; the Adoration of the Magi, the foundation of the Church; the baptism of Christ, the sacrament of baptism; the miracle of the loaves and fishes, the sacrament of the Eucharist.

These evocations of the sacraments which prepare the Christian for salvation occur repeatedly and much stress was laid on them. For this type of Early Christian imagery related not only to the lot of the individual after death but also to the salvation of mankind in general. Its repertory was enlarged after Christianity became the State religion, when as a consequence of its official status new themes were introduced.

105

101. *Greece. Relief: Orpheus. Byzantine Museum, Athens.*

103. *Rome, Catacomb of SS. Pietro e Marcellino. The Baptism of Christ.*

104. *Rome, Catacomb called Coemeterium Majus. Orant between Two Shepherds.*

105. *Rome, Catacomb of San Callisto, Chapel of the Sacraments. Eucharistic Meal.*

106. *Rome, Tomb of the Aurelii. The Heavenly Jerusalem (?).*

In this volume we are concerned only with *Christian* works of the third century. But mention must be made of several mausolea decorated with paintings of the third and even the fourth century, in which Christianity is curiously blended with other beliefs, Christian subjects being juxtaposed with others of a non-Christian nature.

The most striking example of this hybrid, para-Christian art, for the middle of the third century, is the underground tomb of the family of the Aurelii on the Viale Manzoni in Rome. In one of the two burial chambers the Good Shepherd figures on each of the four segments of the vault and Christ is represented on a hill-top, at the foot of which a flock of sheep are grazing.

While some other paintings—for example a triumphal entry into a city and an orator haranguing a crowd of people in a courtyard—lend themselves to a Christian interpretation, this seems to be definitely ruled out in the case of certain scenes. The decoration of this tomb is thus a work of some complexity: not painted for a Christian milieu, it none the less includes some Christian themes.

How did this come about? Should we assume that the orthodox Christian iconography ramified into other strata of society? The image of Christ seated in front of a flock (differing from that of the Good Shepherd carrying a lamb) has no known parallel in ancient Christian painting and sculpture. That, however, may be due simply to the fact that so little of either has survived. After all, there are frescoes in the Dura baptistery—

108

107. *Rome, Tomb of the Aurelii. The Sermon on the Mount.*

108. *Rome, Jewish Catacomb, Villa Torlonia.   The City of Jerusalem and Temple Candlesticks.*

wholly Christian these—of which no parallels are to be found in the contemporary art of Christian Rome.

It is quite possible that the prototype of the Shepherd-Christ in the family tomb of the Aurelii existed in a Christian art that had flourished in Rome (or elsewhere) and of which nothing has survived. Or it may be that the artists employed by the Aurelii invented their Christian imagery *ad hoc*, suiting it to the taste of Gnostic patrons—which would also explain the absence of images of this type in normal Early Christian art. Be this as it may, the existence of this very early heterodox imagery, without any equivalent in the orthodox monuments, has an interest and perhaps some importance. It suggests a possibility that the earliest Christian art may have originated in a para-Christian milieu, presumably Judeo-Christian or Gnostic, before being taken up by the Church.

At first sight this problem may seem to have no connection with the history of art. But in actual practice the doctrinal significance attaching to each of these images changed with the religious climate in which they arose and this led to changes in the way they were conceived and represented. Moreover the problem of the religious function of these images has another bearing on the history of art. While the first Christian art grew naturally out of the Roman art of its time, may there not have been a reciprocal influence? May not this new Christian art have influenced other religious arts of the period? That this possibility should be allowed for is evidenced by the facts set forth above.

Though different teams of artists were employed in the catacombs even when the tomb chambers adjoined—as was the case with the Priscilla and Giordani tombs—all alike conformed to the customs of the period. This is why, from the historical viewpoint, most

110

109. *Rome, Tomb of the Aurelii.   An Apostle (?).*

110.   *Rome, Catacomb of Priscilla, Cappella Greca.   Eucharistic Meal: 'Fractio panis.'*

111.   *Rome, Catacomb of SS. Pietro e Marcellino, Hall of the Tricliniarch.   Celestial Banquet.*

112. *Rome, Catacomb of Priscilla, Cubiculum of the 'Velatio.' The Magister.*

of their frescoes, *qua* works of arts, are in the main stream of Roman painting. However, in some of the finer frescoes on Christian themes we can trace the hand of a genuinely original artist. Examples are the paintings in the Cappella Greca and in the cubiculum of the 'Velatio' (with the famous Orant called the 'Donna velata,' to which we drew attention at an earlier page); they are the work of highly gifted painters.

Two at least contributed to the wall paintings in the Cappella Greca. One worked on a red ground like that of the first-century frescoes in Pompeii and Rome. On the red underpainting he superimposed animated scenes, containing figures in strenuous movement depicted with rapid brushstrokes and aptly placed patches of more or less diluted white. Such was his adroitness that he often got his effect with a single stroke, but when the subject called for detailed treatment he individualized faces and gave its full value to every gesture, as in the group of participants in an 'agape.' The scenes on one of the upper zones of the walls—Daniel in the Lions' Den, the Raising of Lazarus, Abraham's Sacrifice—have elaborate architectural settings, reminiscent of the 'sacred landscapes' of the Roman fresco painters of the first centuries of our era.

113

113. *Rome, Catacomb of Priscilla, Cappella Greca.* *Story of Susanna (before the restoration of 1952).*

These landscapes with architectural settings of various kinds link up the Christian paintings in the Cappella Greca with the frescoes adorning interiors of another kind. I have in mind the mural decorations of the third decade of the third century when, it seems, a taste prevailed in Rome for paintings with picturesque motifs, extensive architectural settings, many figures, sometimes crowds of people assembled in front of buildings or in landscapes strewn with flowers. It is in the partly Christian, partly pagan tomb of the Aurelii on the Viale Manzoni, in Rome, mentioned above, that we have the best examples of the architectural aspects of these themes, while on the walls of a Christian dwelling-house called the 'Triclia,' on the Via Appia, we see, side by side or one above the other, groups of persons gathered for a meal. (One panel, now in a very bad state of preservation, seems to represent the miracle of the loaves and fishes.)

114

Both in the tomb of the Aurelii and in the Cappella Greca, these landscape paintings occupy the same position, at the foot of the vault, and this common feature of the two sets of decorations—one partly Christian, the other purely Christian—corresponds to a layout current in Roman decorative painting of the period.

In another burial chamber, just at the entrance of the Cappella Greca, figures painted in dark colours stand out on a white ground. The small paintings on the ceiling, which like those on the upper part of the walls are badly damaged, are peopled with tiny, wispy figures, as in the Adoration of the Magi. Lower on the walls, however, above a stucco plinth simulating slabs of coloured marble (there are other stucco reliefs on the intrados of the arches in the room behind), a broad frieze depicts the story of Susanna, with tall, slim figures moving gracefully in a fluent rhythm. Though the figures were brushed in rapidly, the painter took pains to add plastic values to the silhouettes by presenting them on two planes, one darker than the other.

In the Gospel scenes in one of the chambers of the Catacomb of Pretestato, we find similar effects, but these are perhaps later works. The identification of their themes (the Healing of the Woman with an Issue of Blood, the Woman of Samaria and the Crowning with Thorns) remains conjectural.

114. *Rome, Catacomb of Priscilla, Cappella Greca. Susanna and the Elders (before the restoration of 1952).*

115. *Rome, Catacomb of Priscilla, Cubiculum of the 'Velatio.' Orant called 'Donna velata' between the Magister and the Mother and Child.*

Very different is the art which so enchants us in the cubiculum of the 'Velatio,' particularly the painting of the 'Donna velata' to which it owes its name. Whereas the light and graceful motifs of the ceiling have equivalents elsewhere, this portrait of the dead woman as an Orant is remarkable for its intense colours and fully modelled volumes. The maker of this fine picture must have been a practised easel painter, for this use of bright, full-bodied colours and graduated tones producing a three-dimensional effect, as well as the precise delineation of the face, is seldom found in frescoes. Fourth-century Orants are treated on the same lines, and in their case the influence of the easel portrait is even clearer—for example in the portraits of two young girls as Orants on either side of the arcosolium in the Trasona catacomb.

Chronologically, the series of catacomb paintings previous to the Peace of the Church ends with the large group of frescoes in the cemetery of San Callisto. These figure in a burial chamber facing another chamber where an inscription *in situ* dates it to 308 or 309, in the time of Pope Marcellus I. There is every likelihood that these frescoes date to the same years, just before the edict of toleration. A whole wall is decorated with a 'paradise garden' full of plants and birds, with, in the lowest register, a balustrade and basins from

116. *Rome, Catacomb of Priscilla. Orant called 'Donna velata,' detail.*

which doves are drinking. All these were motifs currently used in Roman garden scenes, such as the fresco in the Villa of Livia at Porta Prima and that on the wall of the staircase facing the *confessio* beneath the church of SS. Giovanni e Paolo in Rome. Five figures, likenesses of the persons buried in the tomb, are depicted in the garden as Orants, with their names inscribed; it is accordingly known as the cubiculum of the 'Cinque Santi' (five saints). They wear sumptuous garments like the later saints of Christian art, but also like the young women in the Trasona catacomb.

Dating to 308-309, the five Orants in the catacomb of San Callisto come after the 'Donna velata' (late third century) and foreshadow the Orants in the Trasona catacomb (fourth century). Thus they mark a date in the history of the Christian funerary portrait and prove that on the eve of the triumph of Christianity the preference for a real likeness of the dead man or woman had made itself felt among the early Christians, who hitherto had not dared to go farther than an idealized image of the deceased, as a depersonalized Orant without any signs of age or sex. From the 'Donna velata' on, by way of the five Orants in the San Callisto catacomb to the Trasona Orants, the abstract formulas of earlier works are superseded by increasingly lifelike portraits.

117

117. *Rome, Catacomb of Priscilla, Cubiculum of the 'Velatio'. Mother and Child.*

118. *Rome, Catacomb of Trasona, Tomb of the Two Orants. Portrait of a Young Woman, detail.*

The lesson of these sepulchral portraits warns us against trying to draw any hard-and-fast dividing line between catacomb painting before and after the Peace of the Church. The rapid development of Christian art after the triumph of the Church naturally brought about changes in the art of the catacombs; in particular a habit of imitating the mosaics and paintings in contemporary churches and mausolea. But in fact this interrelation had long existed and the changes made under Constantine were not so far-reaching as is commonly supposed.

After Constantine the catacombs continued to be the normal burial places and the custom of adorning the tombs of well-to-do Christians with wall paintings lasted until the early fifth century and even later.

Cycles of images from the Old and New Testaments remained in favour and their iconography changed little. The same decorative schemes figured on the ceilings, the only innovations being in the style of the frames: broad bands, sometimes suggesting depth, instead of simple circumscribing lines.

True, fourth-century Roman painting was far from being restricted to these continuations of the art of the previous century. But it is important to stress this continuity, since despite the fact that the turn of the century was also a turning point in history, the changes made in funerary art were slight as compared with those in other art forms; in sepulchral art the triumph of the Church took effect belatedly and even then only to a small extent.

119. *Rome, Catacomb of San Callisto, Cubiculum of the 'Cinque Santi.' Orant, detail.*

120. *Rome, Catacomb called Coemeterium Majus. Orant between Two Shepherds, detail.*

LIVIA NICARVS
LIVIAE PRIMITIVAE
SORORI FECIT
Q V AN XXIIIIM VIII

122. *Rome. Sarcophagus of Livia Primitiva, detail:* **The Good Shepherd.** **Louvre, Paris.**

Sculpture

The sculptors who carved the reliefs on sarcophagi worked under much the same conditions as the catacomb painters. Here, too, when the man commissioning them was wealthy a master-craftsman was called in and the sides of the coffin were adorned with finely executed bas-reliefs. Outstanding works of this kind were often used as models by less competent executants and these copies, as was to be expected, are but pale reflections of the lost originals.

In the absence of inscriptions or other chronological indications, dated or reliably datable sarcophagi (such as that of Livia Primitiva in the Louvre) are no less rare than works of high artistic quality. For these unoriginal sarcophagus reliefs do not lend themselves to any certain classification or dating. These difficulties are easily accounted for when we remember that there is no clue to the number of workshops, in Rome and in Provence, where the sarcophagi were made.

Hence, inevitably, an uncertainty both as regards the idiosyncrasies of specific workshops and as regards the distinctions characterizing works produced at different dates. We have no means of knowing whether any given innovation was made by a single workshop, then imitated by others with an unspecified time-lag, or by several workshops at once. To form any conclusion we would need to know the conditions under which the general adoption of this innovation took place (if it did take place) and the time it took for these changes to materialize.

The problem is further complicated by the fact that we are equally ignorant of the part played by the patron in determining the style and execution of the work. He may

123

123. *Rome. Sarcophagus of Baebia Hertofila. Museo delle Terme, Rome.*

have specified the type of sarcophagus he wanted, and this may not necessarily have been the most recent one. In works of this kind, there must often have been reversions to the past, for funerary art depended more than any other on the acquired taste and sensibility of the patron.

If we have lingered on the problems raised by the Christian sarcophagi and stressed the hopelessness of any attempt to date them with more precision, this is because several archaeologists have failed to take into account the inherent difficulties of the problem, the absence of positive data for fruitful research. The chronologies they put forward are valid only on the most general lines and, when closely analysed, are found to lack any foundation in reality.

It is clear, however, that the sarcophagi utilized by the early Christians were sometimes 'pre-fabricated,' since in several cases, while the reliefs are otherwise entirely completed, we find only a rough outline of the portrait which was to figure in the centre of the front. Evidently the details of the dead man's lineaments were added when the sarcophagus was delivered to his family. This proves beyond all doubt that a standardized type of sarcophagus was generally accepted and remained in current use over a fairly long period.

124

124. *Rome. Sarcophagus, detail: Shepherd and his Flock. Museo delle Terme, Rome.*

125. *Auletta. Pagan Sarcophagus: Ariadne and Vintaging Putti. Museo Nazionale, Naples.*

126. *Rome. Sarcophagus, detail: Orant and Bucolic Scene. Museo Laterano, Rome.*

126

127. *Rome. Sarcophagus, detail: Good Shepherd and Bucolic Scene. Museo Laterano, Rome.*

Like the catacomb paintings, the reliefs on Christian sarcophagi derived from contemporary works of pagan art. The traditional element in these reliefs is still larger, or anyhow more perceptible, since we are in a position to identify their pagan antecedents: these we have not only for the general category of sarcophagi adorned with figure reliefs then in vogue, but also for each of the most important types of Christian sarcophagus in use in the third century. The very variety of their motifs and decorative schemes reflects the pagan sarcophagus reliefs of the period. Thus the pastoral theme of shepherds and their flocks in landscape settings so popular with the third-century Christians had already figured on many pagan sarcophagi. On these again we find the characteristic decorative layout of a great many Christian sarcophagi: a central relief separated by strigils from two reliefs at the ends of the coffin. The Christians kept to this conventional layout, changing only the themes of the reliefs. In other cases, even the pagan themes were retained, for

127

128. *Rome. Sarcophagus, detail: Young Woman listening to a Philosopher. Palazzo Sanseverino, Rome.*

129. *Italy. Sarcophagus of Flavius Julius Catervius. Cathedral, Tolentino.*

130. *Rome. Sarcophagus, detail: Jonah. Santa Maria Antiqua, Rome.*

example the likeness of the deceased in an *imago clipeata* (sometimes replaced by a shell); the group of philosophers whose company the deceased will share in the Other World, since he has been initiated into the true wisdom, i.e. Christian doctrine; a group of musicians evoking the harmony of the celestial spheres, the dead man's new abode; masks of the seasons at the two extremities of the coffin, symbols of the eternity of the after-life; a curtain in front of which is the portrait of the dead man; dolphins and sea monsters reminding us of his voyage to the Other World; or scenes of the hunt, an ancient funerary theme taken over by the Christians as an allusion to Christ, hunter of souls.

129

131. *Rome. Sarcophagus, detail:* **Orant** *listening to a Philosopher. Santa Maria Antiqua, Rome.*

To begin with, the Christian element in sarcophagus reliefs is unobtrusive, limited to the purely allegorical figure of the Orant, along with the Good Shepherd. Before the time of Constantine only a very few subjects, all drawn from the Bible, were added to the repertory of themes. The story of Jonah, unlike the other paradigms of deliverance taken from the Bible, was often represented in two or three successive episodes. The popularity of this subject may be due to its analogies with the theme of the journey oversea to the Hereafter and also with the adventure of the beautiful young shepherd Endymion (assimilated to Jonah) on whom Zeus bestowed eternal life in an unbroken slumber.

132-133. *Sarcophagus, details:* **Story of Jonah.** *Ny Carlsberg Glyptothek, Copenhagen.*

134. *Rome. Sarcophagus, detail: Shepherd carrying a Ewe. Museo dei Conservatori, Rome.*

135. *Rome. Sarcophagus with Old and New Testament Scenes, detail: Daniel. Museo Laterano, Rome.*

The repertory of themes also included those of Daniel in the lions' den, Moses striking water from the rock, the Three Children in the fiery furnace and above all the Raising of Lazarus.

To them were added, towards the close of the third century, the Adoration of the Magi, the Fall of Adam and the Miracle of the Loaves and Fishes, this last with its illustration of a shared repast prefiguring the Eucharist. Similarly, the scene of the Baptism of Christ, which appears on the short side of a sarcophagus (No. 23893 in the Museo delle Terme, Rome), was probably intended to serve not only as a recall of that event but also as an allusion to the sacrament of baptism. Thus while the stories of Jonah, Daniel and Lazarus were reminders that God succours those who trust in Him, the scenes of the Baptism and the Miracle of the Loaves and Fishes evoked the sacraments whereby the dead Christian had entered on the path of salvation.

136. *Rome. Sarcophagus with Old and New Testament Scenes, detail: Adam and Eve. Museo Laterano, Rome.*

137. *Rome. Sarcophagus of Baebia Hertofila, detail of the lid. Museo delle Terme, Rome.*

138. *Fragment of a Sarcophagus: Story of Jonah. Santa Maria in Trastevere, Rome.*

135

139. *Sarcophagus, detail: Baptism. Museo delle Terme, Rome.*

140. *Italy. Sarcophagus, detail: Daniel, Jonah and an Orant. Museum, Velletri.*

141. *Italy. Sarcophagus of Flavius Julius Catervius, detail: Adoration of the Magi. Cathedral, Tolentino.*

142. *Provence. Sarcophagus with both Pagan and Christian Motifs, detail. Church of Saint-Sauveur, Brignoles.*

In Provence, where a number of very ancient Christian sarcophagi have been preserved, the Brignoles (or La Gayole) sarcophagus is remarkable for the beauty of its reliefs. Carved in Greek marble with a wholly Hellenic fluency of execution, this is none the less a Provençal work, probably dating to the first half of the third century. On the damaged front we see, alongside some rather puzzling motifs (e.g. the head of a personification on the left), some beautifully carved figures: a fisherman, a female Orant beside a flock of sheep, a Good Shepherd, and a seated philosopher who seems to be talking to him.

143. *Provence. Sarcophagus with both Pagan and Christian Motifs. Church of Saint-Sauveur, Brignoles.*   139

144. *Rome. Sarcophagus, detail: Seated Philosopher. Museo Laterano, Rome.*

The handsome sarcophagus from the Via Salaria (No. 181, Lateran Museum, Rome) is remarkable for the classical, monumental style of the figure reliefs placed between two protomes of rams (a reminiscence of pagan sarcophagi).

The central place on the front of the sarcophagus is occupied by the Good Shepherd and a female Orant, both of these figures retaining something of their original pagan significance: that of personifications of the philosophic concepts of Philanthropy and Piety. Here, however, they are converted into allegories of Christ and the Christian virtues of the dead woman. It is in a garden, surrounded by the flock (another pagan

145. *Rome. Sarcophagus, detail: Orant and Group of Women. Museo Laterano, Rome.*

theme), that these symbolic figures are placed, and symmetrically disposed at the two extremities of the main composition are two seated figures: a man with a book and a matron with a scroll. Beside each are standing figures, two men on either side of the seated man, a woman just behind the matron. The matron's face is given the most distinctive features; presumably she is the dead woman listening to the words the man is reading out.

The interpretation of this scene, and even its Christian character, remains conjectural but there is no question of its high merits as a work of art.

146. *Rome. Sarcophagus, detail: Orant. Museo delle Terme, Rome.*

Very different is the style of another famous sarcophagus (No. 23893, Museo delle Terme, Rome). Despite the salience of the reliefs, separated by rows of flutings (strigils), the effect produced is pictorial rather than sculpturesque; indeed the central figure of the Orant, with her over-large hands, the birds surrounding her at different levels and the trees on which they are perched remind us of a painted picture. This impression is conveyed even more strongly by the lower reliefs on the ends of the sarcophagus, illustrating the Baptism of Christ and a flock of eleven sheep.

The fronts of some sarcophagi of this period form a single composition, made up of small scenes grouped together side by side in no very strict order. The relief is low and fairly uniform, and landscape elements between the figures enhance the pictorial effect. The best example of this method is Sarcophagus No. 119 in the Lateran Museum, Rome, on which several independent iconographic themes are skilfully interlinked with a view to forming a picturesque whole, agreeable to the eye. While the reliefs on other sarcophagi are arranged with an eye to architectural effects, here the sculptor has aimed at creating the effect of an organized, continuous space.

But everywhere, conforming to the taste of the period, the sculptors who carved these sarcophagi (like their contemporaries, the painters of the catacomb frescoes) tend to subordinate the exact rendering of Biblical themes to aesthetic considerations.

142

147-148. *Rome. Sarcophagus, details: Story of Jonah. Museo Laterano, Rome.*

3. The Art of the Fourth Century

The adoption of Christianity as the State religion of the Roman Empire and the transfer of its capital to the shores of the Bosphorus affected art in many ways. In ancient times art was so closely bound up with religion that the sudden decline and eclipse of paganism, the meteoric rise of Christianity, the imperial patronage accorded it and the power now vested in the Church had far-reaching effects on the course and functions of art.

These momentous events took place in the first thirty years of the fourth century, and art forms must have been affected at once. It was then that the first Christian churches founded by a Roman emperor were built, while in Rome herself the pagan cemeteries were razed to the ground and replaced by shrines and churches erected on the graves of martyrs, notably St Peter's (after 326). From now on the treasuries both of the provinces of the empire (at Jerusalem and elsewhere) and of the imperial household could be drawn on liberally to defray the expenses of the Christian foundations sponsored by the emperor and the bishops.

It is easy to imagine what effect this sudden afflux of wealth had on Christian art, which hitherto—when not compelled by active persecution to keep in hiding—had had no support but what a few private persons of limited means could give it; and we have seen how much the sepulchral arts of third-century Rome achieved despite the meagreness of their resources.

Unfortunately the art historian today is in no position to study the first works of art produced after the triumph of Christianity, to evaluate their innovations or trace their initial development; the number of surviving works is too small. The few remaining ruins and the fragments brought to light by excavation have much to tell the archaeologist about the building techniques employed, the layout of the early places of worship and their decorative schemes. But for the art historian this is inadequate. How can he appraise the artistic qualities of Christian architecture in the reign of Constantine when only one entire building and part of another remain intact? How can he analyse the Christian figure arts of the period when, for the whole of the fourth century, there is

145

150. *Rome. The Arch of Constantine.*

not a single illuminated manuscript of a Christian book and but one group of wall mosaics with, in effect, only two Christian images?

True, some of the fourth-century catacombs undoubtedly reproduce wall paintings from churches and shrines no longer in existence, and their documentary value is great. But the art historian (again, as distinguished from the archaeologist) must bear in mind that these murals are only copies made by mere artisans of lost originals. So that the historian of fourth-century Christian art is severely handicapped; his field of observation is restricted to a very small number of works, so few that he cannot allow himself to generalize.

146

151. *Rome. Arch of Constantine, detail: Distribution of Subsidies.*

It so happens that for the Constantinian period (which witnessed the birth of large-scale Christian art), and indeed for the whole of the fourth century, the surviving pagan monuments are more impressive than the few Christian works that have come down to us. I have in mind the Arch of Constantine and its reliefs, the rotunda of Romulus, and the vaulted Basilica of Maxentius (finished by Constantine), all in Rome; the ceiling painting in the imperial palace at Trier; the illustrations in the Calendar of 354, with its portrait of Constantius I; and the ivory diptychs carved for the great senatorial families of the Nicomachi and the Symmachi.

It would of course be a mistake to conclude that works wholly in the spirit of pre-Christian Roman art predominated in the fourth century. But the works just referred to, and some others (besides the palaces, baths and public buildings of all kinds erected by Constantine in his new capital of Constantinople and also at Nicomedia, Antioch, Arles, Trier, Ostia, and elsewhere—buildings known to us only from texts and a few ruins) prove that an art and architecture with nothing specifically Christian about them continued to flourish, and indeed to form a considerable part of the work commissioned by the emperors converted to Christianity and by the Roman senators who remained hostile to it.

In this field the only significant change was that pagan temples ceased to be built. For the rest, things went on as before and this is why, if the beginnings of Christian architecture are to be seen in the right perspective, they must be placed within the context of the great imperial and senatorial monuments of the fourth century.

The Arch of Constantine, erected by the Senate near the Colosseum to flatter the emperor (then still a pagan) after his victory over Maxentius at the Milvian Bridge in 312, kept to the traditional style of Roman triumphal arches. Symbolizing a victory which was later celebrated as a triumph of Christ and his vicegerent Constantine, the arch is covered with sculptures, pagan through and through, which glorify the 'Unconquered Sun' as the emperor's guide and guardian. The arch was erected in some haste and—anticipating a practice that was soon to become common—adorned in part with reliefs taken from the triumphal monuments of previous emperors (of the second century). But to these were added some new reliefs representing episodes in the public life of Constantine, his battles and his largesse. The style of these reliefs resembles and continues that of works produced under the Tetrarchs (notably the sculpture on the Arch of Galerius at Salonica). They are crowded with robust, ungainly figures; the realism of details strikes a contrast with the schematic treatment of draperies, bodies and the composition of the scenes; and there is a tendency to replace plastic volume by chiaroscuro effects. It seems likely that provincial craftsmen from the north or perhaps the Balkans had a hand in the reliefs on the Arch of Constantine.

152. *Salonica. Arch of Galerius, detail: A Sacrifice.*

153. *Salonica. Arch of Galerius, detail: Scenes of War and Triumph.*

At about the same time, close by, an edifice was completed which had been begun by Constantine's vanquished rival Maxentius: the great basilica which still stands beside the Via Sacra in the Forum. Alongside the circular *heroum* for his son Romulus, Maxentius founded and Constantine completed (modifying its axis) this magnificent basilica whose mighty tunnel-vaulting has been imitated by so many architects from Bramante on. Not until the sixth century do we find another edifice vaulted with an equal boldness and sweep: the domed church of St Sophia in Constantinople. In Italy nearly a thousand years were to pass before any comparable buildings were erected: Santa Maria del Fiore in Florence and St Peter's in Rome (if we disregard the cupolas of St Mark's in Venice as being too little Italic). Until Renaissance architects again attained the technical proficiency of the Romans (attested throughout the Empire by the ruins of so many other buildings of imperial times), the vaulted Basilica of Maxentius in the Forum dominated for centuries all the Christian edifices erected there amid the ruins of ancient temples and houses.

In the two fields of small-scale painting and ivory-carving several fourth-century works have been preserved which also continue the tradition of classical Roman art.

The pictures in a Calendar, illuminated in 354 in Rome for a man of exalted rank, achieve a high level of excellence and, once again, remain quite untouched by Christianity. These paintings revert in the middle of the fourth century to a pagan iconographic tradition, and so successfully as to prove that the prestige of that art had by no means declined several decades after the conversion of the Empire. Yet the man who commissioned the Calendar was a Christian. He retained the customary imagery of the Roman calendars: astronomical figures and evocations of pagan festivals. But he asked for, and got, a new version of them—proof enough that this art was still very much alive in the mid-fourth century. There were other patrons of art in Rome, in the latter half of the century, who were trying to encourage a return to the purest classical style. This tendency can be observed in the work of the ivory carvers employed by members of the Roman aristocracy. The rather lifeless Atticism of their art was probably the expression not only of a conservative taste but also of the hostility to Christianity which prevailed in the great senatorial families on the eve of the reign of Theodosius I. The best examples of this Atticism are the leaf of a diptych in the Musée de Cluny, Paris, and another in the Victoria and Albert Museum, London; one represents a priestess of Ceres, the other a priestess of Bacchus, sacrificing at an altar. Very close to them in style, and probably of approximately the same date, are two other diptychs, one at Liverpool (Asclepius and Hygieia), the other in the Louvre (a priest of the imperial cult presiding at the games).

The vaulted Basilica of Maxentius enables us to form an idea of palace architecture in the fourth century. It was from this time on, beginning probably with the Tetrarchs, that the 'Sacred Palace' came to play the leading role in the field of civil architecture, a role which it continued to play at Byzantium for many centuries to come. Since Diocletian, every phase of official life in the Palace had been regulated by a complicated ceremonial. For its observance a whole series of suitable rooms, halls, porticoes and courtyards was required; and the variety of their functions called for large, well-planned buildings which, while perfectly adapted to the daily needs of palace life,

154. *Rome. Basilica of Maxentius (also called Basilica of Constantine).*

should at the same time impress the public with the might and majesty of the monarch.

As it happens, neither the imperial palaces of Rome nor those of Constantinople have been preserved; nor are the remains even sufficient to trace their ground-plan. The sole surviving palace is that of Diocletian at Spalato (Split) in Dalmatia, dating to the first years of the fourth century. But it is not a very typical example, for it is a fortified palace combining the features of a military camp and an imperial residence. So for our present purposes we may disregard the plan of the palace and note above all its aulic aspect: the great colonnade enclosing the forecourt in front of the vestibule of the palace, whose porticoed façade carries a pediment in the manner of a pagan temple. This grandiose entrance was probably similar to the entrances of the great palaces in the capitals, about the time of the promulgation of the edicts of toleration (313). Libanius' description of the palace of Antioch shows that its frontage resembled that of Spalato.

151

155. *Spalato. Palace of Diocletian: Main Entrance preceded by an Arcaded Portico.*

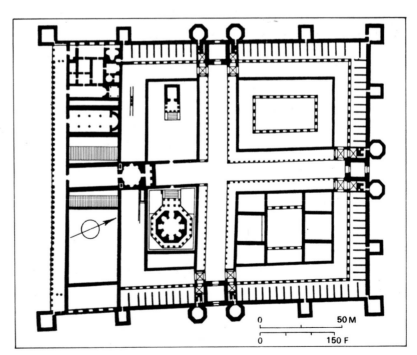

156. *Spalato. Plan of Diocletian's Palace.*

157. *Rome. Diptych of the Nicomachi and Symmachi. Musée de Cluny, Paris; Victoria and Albert Museum, London.*

Like the palace of another Tetrarch, Galerius, at Salonica, Diocletian's palace at Spalato included a rotunda—the mausoleum in which the cult of the emperor was to be celebrated after his apotheosis; in both cases it was later converted into a church. The colonnaded courtyards outside had their equivalents in the palace (no longer in existence) of Constantinople.

158. *Piazza Armerina, Roman Villa. Personification of Arabia or Egypt.*

The emperors and high dignitaries also had their country 'villas,' whose excavated ruins are in some cases very extensive, comparable in fact to a provincial palace of the Spalato type.

Some of these fourth-century residences, like the earlier ones in Rome, Pompeii and elsewhere, stood in the immediate vicinity of the city; others were in the open country. It is to one of the latter, only recently discovered, that we shall draw attention, in view of the variety and originality of its architectural features and wealth of mosaic pavements with figural themes. Architecture and mosaics form an aggregate of the highest interest, a signal example of secular art at its most sumptuous in the selfsame period when Christian art was producing its first major works.

This villa was brought to light at Piazza Armerina in central Sicily. Some archaeologists, for various reasons, see in it a villa of the emperor Maximianus Herculius and date it accordingly to the first years of the fourth century; others prefer to assign it to the middle of that century, or even to its latter half when the Senate reacted against the Christianity of the emperors.

As regards the mosaics anyhow, the later date would seem more likely, for they have parallels in the art of the Esquiline Treasure, which can be dated with fair accuracy to the end of the fourth century.

Whatever its date, the villa at Piazza Armerina is of the utmost interest and importance as a piece of architecture in the grand style erected by a great landowner in the province which still remained the granary of Italy. Beyond the monumental entrance gate was a colonnaded court giving on to a vestibule, then to the main colonnaded

154

159. *Piazza Armerina, Roman Villa. Capture of Wild Animals, detail.*

courtyard with a pool in the centre. Various rooms gave on to the main courtyard, beginning, on the north-west, with a long series of elaborate bathing rooms remarkable for the variety of their layouts (some having curved walls and exedrae). On the opposite side of the court was a spacious reception hall, apsed at the back, and in front of this hall was a very long vestibule. Other rooms, of various shapes, opened on the vestibule. South of the main courtyard was yet another colonnaded court, of a very unusual and ingenious layout; and on the east side of it was a large room of trefoil design, famed for its mosaics on mythological themes.

There is no building anywhere, whether intact or in ruins, which conveys so vivid an idea of what the palace architecture of the Roman emperors must have been like in the fourth century. Except of course as regards size—since for reasons of prestige the emperor's 'Sacred Palace' had to be built on a colossal scale.

Piazza Armerina thus provides us with an important piece of evidence for the history of architecture. The historical importance of its mosaics, however, is much less, being restricted in the main to the field of fourth-century pagan art. An extraordinary number

160-161. *Piazza Armerina, Roman Villa. Girls doing Physical Exercises.*

of mosaic pavements have come to light there, but most of them illustrate pagan themes; the most remarkable mosaics are devoted to Hercules, the overthrow of the Titans, and the legends of Lycurgus and Ambrosia. Other subjects, though of a more 'neutral' order, are also of pagan inspiration: Orpheus, the Seasons, the capture of wild animals. To the same group may perhaps be assigned the scenes with 'Bikini girls' engaged in various games and exercises, clad in the scantiest of bathing costumes, and without doubt the procession making its way towards the baths.

In view of their subject matter, these mosaics seem to rule out any possibility of regarding this luxurious residence as the home of a Christian; and we do best, no doubt, to accept the indications of its pagan ownership. For everything about it suggests that this remarkable monument evidences the senatorial 'reaction' against Christianity in the second half of the fourth century.

Even so, it should not be forgotten that in the late fourth century Christian artists had no qualms about including images from pagan mythology. Take for example the famous silver bridal casket of Projecta in the British Museum (part of the Esquiline Treasure found in Rome in 1793). Beside a Christian inscription naming the owner, we find not only a portrait of Projecta and her young husband but two series of scenes (in repoussé relief) which are also to be seen at Piazza Armerina: the procession on its way to the baths and a mythological cycle devoted to Venus. It is clear that the pagan goddess appears on the casket not as a divinity, but as an ornament customarily included in the decoration of wedding presents.

While the reliefs on the silver casket of Projecta are handled with a delicate touch, in the classical style (with no sign of its impending breakdown), the Piazza Armerina

156

162. *Rome. Bridal Casket of Projecta and Secundus, detail. British Museum, London.*

mosaics are notable for good intentions rather than high quality. They are the work of provincial craftsmen who did their best to imitate Roman models, but fell far short of them.

During the fourth century similar mosaic pavements were produced in large numbers for villas in the neighbourhood of Antioch, in Syria. Many of them, however, are of finer quality, showing not only technical skill but taste and a genuine artistic sense. The finest piece of all, now in the Louvre, stood in the central room of the so-called

164. *Silistra. Underground Mausoleum, detail: Deceased Couple.*

Constantinian Villa. Attributed to the early fourth century, this mosaic, intended perhaps to imitate a vault decoration, shows personifications of the four seasons, disposed along the four diagonals with hunting scenes between them. The four female personifications are in a thoroughly classical style and their amply moulded forms are on the whole successfully rendered. The work of less skilful mosaicists, the bucolic and pastoral scenes and those of the palestra do not have the same qualities of design and composition; but their delicate colouring, here as in all the Antioch mosaics, anticipates that of Byzantine art.

As always, sepulchral art was the last to abandon established practices. Until the close of the fourth century figure paintings continued to appear on the inner walls of tomb chambers. At Rome itself the tomb of Trebius Justus and the recently discovered tomb on the Via Latina contain groups of paintings; these will be discussed at a later page, because they bear a resemblance to certain Christian works. Something may be said here, however, of the mural paintings in a pagan tomb found near Silistra, on the Danube, in Bulgaria. Dating to the latter half of the fourth century, they depict a curious procession made up of the married couple buried in the tomb and their servants. These large sturdy figures, products of a vigorous local art, are far removed from the classical idealism of the Antioch mosaics, but they have much in common with the figures in fourth-century Roman frescoes. On close inspection, the faces are seen to foreshadow those in Carolingian miniature painting, and this is not a mere coincidence. They are fragments of an artistic language which might be equated to 'Low Latin'; from this style developed that of the Christian paintings of western Europe in the early Middle Ages.

159

163. *Daphne. Mosaic of the Seasons, detail: Personification of Spring. Louvre, Paris.*

We have passed in review these suggestive works of the fourth century in order to show how strong the pagan art tradition still was; despite the triumph of the Church and the conversion of the Empire, it remained a living force in many very different fields of art. Were the Christian works produced under Constantine and his immediate successors able to hold their own among these works in the pagan tradition? This must remain an open question, but it seems to me that there is room for doubt, in view of the very few Christian works that have come down to us for the period extending from

165. *Medal of Constantine the Great. Bibliothèque Nationale, Paris.*

the triumph of the Church to the reign of Theodosius. From Eusebius and the *Liber Pontificalis* we learn that Constantine himself founded several large churches in Rome: St John Lateran (312-319), St Peter's (after 326) and the oratory (?) of St Paul. Members of his family did likewise. Still other churches were founded in Jerusalem (Golgotha, Bethlehem, Mount of Olives, 325-337) and in Constantinople (St Sophia and Holy Apostles, 330-337). Some of these churches were left to be completed by Constantius II (who seemed to be in no hurry to do so), while others were built by popes and bishops in Rome and many other cities of the Empire. For the most part we know of their existence only from texts and inscriptions. A few, however, have survived in ruins or been discovered in the course of excavations: the church of the Ascension in Jerusalem; those of San Sebastiano, Sant'Agnese fuori le Mura, San Lorenzo fuori le Mura and SS. Marcellino e Pietro in the suburbs of Rome; the double cathedral of Trier, the cathedral of Gerasa in Palestine, the bishop's church at Epidaurus in Greece, and others in Syria and even

166. *Bust of Constantine the Great (?). Cabinet des Médailles, Bibliothèque Nationale, Paris.*

167-168-169. *Empress St Helena. Emperor Constantius II. Constantius II holding the Labarum. Cabinet des Médailles, Bibliothèque Nationale, Paris.*

in northern Mesopotamia (baptistery of Nisibis). Among the fourth-century churches of Syria and northern Mesopotamia several can be dated with precision thanks to a dedication.

Under Theodosius I and his sons, shortly before 400, information concerning the construction of new churches becomes more frequent and detailed.

In the domain of the figure arts, even fewer Christian works of the fourth century have survived, apart from the catacomb paintings and the sarcophagus reliefs, found above all in Rome, but also—as regards the sculptured sarcophagi—in Provence, Spain, North Africa and Constantinople. In Rome at least these paintings and carvings are a continuation of arts that had flourished before the triumph of the Church; they were not a product of that triumph. The only change is the introduction of some new iconographic themes towards the end of Constantine's reign, probably with a view to the adornment of the great churches founded by the emperor in Rome. Examples (in the form of copies) of these new themes can be seen in Santa Costanza, the only fourth-century church that has survived more or less intact, and above all in the funerary arts. By way of these copies we can see, too, that the repertory of historical subjects drawn from both the Old and the New Testament was being enlarged. But it seems safe to say that this enlargement only dates (like the first examples of certain picture cycles on the walls of churches) to the end of the fourth century and would thus belong to the second upsurge of Christian art in the Theodosian period.

Judging, then, by the works we have, the century that saw the great triumph and expansion of Christianity was not a great century of Christian art. This impression is due in part to the scarcity of surviving works, but it may well be the truth of the matter. The spread of Arianism and the relapse of Constantine's successors into paganism must have retarded or stopped the great projects undertaken by Constantine in the last years of his reign, and damped the ardour of any who were inclined to imitate him. After the short period of active church-building under Constantine (326-337), nearly half a century seems to have passed, from his death (337) to the accession of Theodosius I (379), without any notable undertakings in the field of Christian art. When a revival took place in the last decades of the century, this new burst of activity (which proved to be durable and definitive) was due on the one hand to the pro-Christian, anti-pagan and anti-Arian policy of Theodosius I and his sons; on the other to the no less vigorous and effective action of a whole group of Christian bishops, the highly cultivated and gifted men, both Greek and Roman, who came to be known as the Fathers of the Church: Basil, Gregory of Nyssa, Gregory Nazianzen, John Chrysostom, Ambrose, Augustine, Pope Leo I. The cult of relics encouraged by these great churchmen and the liturgy which they developed and standardized opened up a rich field of activity to Christian artists, who for centuries to come produced an unbroken succession of remarkable works.

The earliest Christian monuments of the fourth century go back to the reign of Constantine. Several buildings of this period mentioned in the previous chapter are a continuation of Christian art as it was before the triumph of the Church. But these are exceptions, leading nowhere. The real interest of this period lies in the Christian works initiated by Constantine himself and by those who seconded or followed him in the task of converting the Empire.

162

The Christian foundations of Constantine were probably motivated by the idea, given shape and currency in his time, of a world-wide Christian Empire. Thus he undertook the construction of large memorial churches on the 'holy places' of the religion which he had espoused: in Jerusalem, at various spots hallowed by the events described in Scripture, and above all at Golgotha, scene of Christ's resurrection; at His birthplace, Bethlehem (a foundation of the emperor's mother St Helena); and in Rome, then still the capital of the empire ruled by Constantine, vicegerent on earth of Christ triumphant over death. In Rome he founded churches at the places where Peter and Paul had suffered martyrdom, and perhaps on the tombs of other martyrs.

After founding the new capital at Byzantium (330), Constantine ordered the construction of Christian churches there, imposing buildings appropriate to an imperial capital. As in Rome (in the Lateran), he founded in Constantinople a cathedral beside the palace and—in addition to other places of worship of which little is known—a reliquary church (the Holy Apostles) which was the counterpart there of the churches erected in the 'holy places' of Jerusalem and Rome. At Antioch, at Mamre in Palestine, and very probably at Trier, close by the imperial palace, Constantine also had churches built on the same 'imperial' scale, as well as shrines for holy relics.

Judging by the descriptions of them and by the monuments themselves where they have been preserved, the Christian edifices founded by Constantine were designed on a monumental scale but always with an eye to the harmony of their proportions. Given the absence of vaulting, architects had little scope for technical feats, nor is there anything to suggest any innovations of an aesthetic order. This Christian architecture was only a branch of the Roman architecture of the period, the term 'Roman' being understood in its widest sense, for the Constantinian basilicas were not quite the same from one province to another.

The largest Constantinian foundation in Jerusalem was apparently the work of local architects: the Church (or Martyrium) of the Holy Sepulchre and the Church of the Resurrection at Golgotha (the Holy Sepulchre). Of this grandiose architectural complex only fragments of the walls and a few columns have survived. We shall probably never know for certain whether the rotunda enclosing the Holy Sepulchre was built under Constantine or a little later. Its existence is recorded in the time of Theodosius and the chances are—considering how little building was done in the period between these two emperors—that it was part of Constantine's original foundation. If his mother and daughter were honoured with mausolea in the form of a great rotunda (in Rome), he must have done more for the tomb of Christ than merely surround it with a colonnade. However that may be, the rotunda of the Holy Sepulchre undoubtedly dates to the fourth century. Too little remains for us to determine the original appearance of this small church, which for many centuries—from the fourth to the Persian invasion in the early seventh, and again during the Crusades from the eleventh century on—was the most hallowed shrine of Christendom. But from other Christian rotundas, built about the same time or shortly afterwards, and from ancient pictures of it, we can form an idea of certain features of its architecture. It was a circular church (like Santa Costanza in Rome), provided with niches, and with a ring of columns dividing the peripheral corridor from the round central room. Above the latter was a dome, and under this lay the Holy

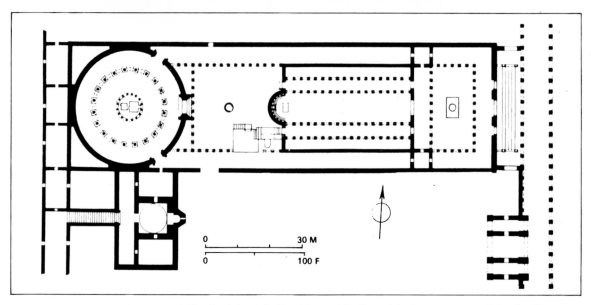

170. *Jerusalem. Round Church of the Holy Sepulchre and Basilica of the Resurrection at Golgotha: Plan.*

171. *Rome. Santa Costanza: Interior (after a print by Piranesi).*

172. *Rome. Santa Costanza: View of the Interior.*

Sepulchre itself. Hollowed out of the rock, it was covered over with a baldachin resting on four columns; within it could—and can still—be seen the 'sepulchre hewed in stone' in which the body of Christ was laid; outside it lay the stone which the Holy Women found rolled back when they came to anoint the body of the Saviour.

It is with this noble monument in mind, trying to imagine its original state, that one examines the round church of Santa Costanza in Rome. While the rotunda of the Holy Sepulchre was in proximity to the basilica of the Resurrection, Santa Costanza adjoined the contemporary basilica of Sant'Agnese (of the Constantinian basilica nothing survives except a curving stretch of wall in the choir and the foundations). The rotunda of Santa Costanza is entered by a vestibule, flanked by two niches, which leads into the circular aisle. Here, too, there are niches in the wall and two of them are adorned with contemporary mosaics. Over the aisle is a barrel vault buttressing the dome above the central rotunda. The latter is divided from the circular aisle around it by a ring of twelve pairs of twin columns, all exactly alike (none of them taken from other buildings) and crowned with handsome composite capitals. Large, elaborately wrought coussinets stand between the capitals and the springers of the semicircular arches supported by the columns. A straight polygonal wall pierced with windows rises over the columns and absorbs the thrust of the dome. A slight difference in the spacing of the columns discreetly introduces an axis into this building of circular plan—an axis marked furthermore by the slightly wider span of the arch in front of the entrance

165

174. *Rome. Ruins of the Mausoleum of St Helena.*

and the arch on the opposite side of the building. It was under the second of these arches that the massive, finely carved porphyry sarcophagus of Constantina, the emperor's daughter, was originally placed. Another rotunda was erected by Constantine as a mausoleum for his mother St Helena. Known by the name of Tor Pignattara, it stands at the gates of Rome near the cemeterial basilica of the martyr saints Marcellino and Pietro. It is an octagonal edifice covered with a dome of the same type as at Santa Costanza, but supported by only eight columns. An entablature replaces the arches between the columns. The barrel vaults are separated by transverse ribs. As at Santa Costanza, the rotunda is entered by a vestibule with exedrae on each side.

It had probably been customary for the emperors to build mausolea for members of their family. When Constantine became a Christian he continued the custom but linked these imperial mausolea with Christian churches, thus initiating a practice which

167

175. *Egypt.   Sarcophagus of Constantina : Vintaging Putti.   Museo Pio Clementino, Vatican City.*

lasted for centuries.   At Constantinople he erected a mausoleum for himself, in the form of a rotunda, and joined it up with the reliquary church of the Holy Apostles which he founded in his new capital.   Surrounded by cenotaphs of the twelve apostles, he was to be entombed there as a ruler 'equal to the apostles' (isoapostolic), as he was styled by a grateful Church which honoured him as the thirteenth apostle, the one who evangelized the Roman Empire.

There is another Christian rotunda which, whether erected under Constantine or later, may be one of the series of imperial mausolea which we have just described. This is a domed edifice, octagonal inside, square on the outside, at Centcelles, near Tarragona, in Spain.

It was in the time of Constantine that a bathing room in the Lateran palace, in Rome, was converted into a round baptistery. This was probably the ancestor of all the baptisteries in the form of a rotunda which, for centuries to come—until well into the Middle Ages—were to be built in Italy and all over western Europe.

After this series of Constantinian rotundas we come to the churches proper, all of which are basilicas. Before defining this term as used to designate an Early Christian church, it will be convenient here to mention the Constantinian churches which took this form.

Beside the Holy Sepulchre in Jerusalem stood an enormous church of basilical plan known as the Martyrium. It faced west—i.e. towards the Holy Sepulchre itself, from which it was separated by a small, unroofed atrium surrounded by porticoes. Its five-aisled nave was covered by a timber roof and entered through a vestibule which gave on the main street of Roman Jerusalem. This church was destroyed when the city was sacked by the Persians in 614. Just as the imperial mausolea in the form of a rotunda give us the best idea of what the round church of the Holy Sepulchre must have originally looked like, so in the case of the Martyrium we can only judge of its appearance in the light of the other basilicas founded by Constantine at Bethlehem, Rome and Trier.

Christian Basilicas

Near Jerusalem still stands the only Constantinian basilica that has survived almost intact: the Church of the Nativity of Christ at Bethlehem, founded in the reign of Constantine by his mother St Helena. Except for the ceilings, which have been replaced, and the whole chevet, rebuilt under Justinian in the sixth century, the fourth-century church is intact. The nave forms a vast rectangular hall, elongated yet fairly wide, which is divided into five aisles by four parallel rows of somewhat massive, sturdy columns. The shafts, bases and robust Corinthian capitals of each column are identical; shaped and carved with painstaking care, they must have been made by the craftsmen of a single imperial workshop. And that workshop must have had ample resources at its disposal, for unlike so many ancient churches, even famous ones, the Constantinian basilica at Bethlehem incorporated no ready-made materials taken from earlier buildings. The walls above the columns are high and smooth (their mosaic decorations are of later date), with wide and numerous windows which give the nave plenty of light. Still, these walls seem too high in proportion to the rather squat columns.

None of the fourth-century basilicas has survived in Rome, and the art historian has to make shift with the reconstructions of their plan and elevation pieced together by archaeologists from the ruins of these buildings and old drawings of them. These archaeological data have sufficed to prove one very important point (borne out by what we learn from the Church of the Nativity at Bethlehem): all the churches founded by Constantine and his mother in Rome, Constantinople and Palestine have the same structural characteristics. All correspond to what is known in Christian archaeology as a 'basilica' (a term applied even before Constantine to Christian places 'of worship, but used in Antiquity to designate churches of different forms): an oblong hall divided lengthwise by rows of columns into three, sometimes five parallel aisles. The broad central aisle is

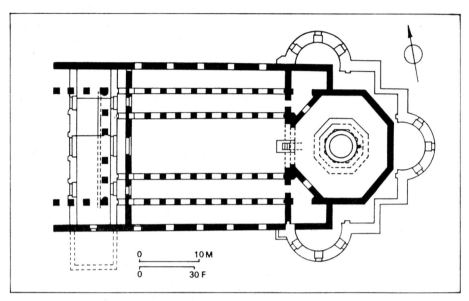

176. *Bethlehem. Plan of the Church of the Nativity.*

called the nave; the others are the side aisles. Lighting was provided by windows in all the outer walls and also by rows of windows in the clerestory (the side walls of the nave above the columns). Opening in one of the short sides of the edifice, the main door (or doors) usually faced an apse at the other end of the nave where the clergy officiated in front of the altar. From the fourth century on, what is known as a transept was sometimes added in front of the apse, but it only remotely foreshadowed the transept of medieval churches. It was often quite narrow, did not always project beyond the body of the church, and was sometimes traversed by the two rows of columns in the nave, which in that case continued up to the wall of the chevet.

Our knowledge of the Early Christian basilicas has grown considerably in the past few decades, especially as regards those of the fifth and sixth centuries. Recent research has revealed, for this period, both an unsuspected variety in the details of their ground-plan and internal arrangements, and a widespread adoption of the basilical plan in all the Christian lands of Europe, Asia and Africa. Fourth-century basilicas are rare, but already they show a variety of secondary features and cover a very wide area; for this type of Christian church, springing into existence with Constantine's earliest foundations, appeared simultaneously in Rome, Trier, Jerusalem and Constantinople. Commissioned by the emperor, master-builders with completely different backgrounds, in widely separated parts of the Empire, all had recourse to the same type of edifice. The similarity is striking and indeed fundamental, but it does not rule out considerable differences in the choice and treatment of certain structural features (apse, transept, entrance, atrium, etc.). One has the impression that, while there was a kind of tacit agreement as to the adoption of the basilical plan for large Christian churches, each builder was free to take up or reject many of the structural elements, and to vary them as he saw fit. Owing to this variety, these early churches cannot be classified according to any standard 'types.'

170

It used to be assumed, even quite recently, that the Christian basilica (meaning above all those in Rome) was the end-product of successive modifications and adaptations of the Roman private house, or the court of law, or the assembly hall of the palace, or the place of worship of other creeds. But the extant basilicas do not bear out any theory of progressive adaptation or systematic experimentation. The Constantinian architects, all of them, everywhere, gave the basilical form to the churches founded by Constantine and St Helena. None of them appears to have proposed anything else or given thought to different alternatives. Were they simply obeying the emperor's orders? No trace of such orders has been found, if they ever existed, and the variety of the secondary features (chevet, narthex and entrance taking different forms, presence or absence of transept and atrium, etc.) makes it seem unlikely that specific instructions were issued from the imperial palace.

Most probably the order to build a large church led each architect to adopt as a matter of course a common type of spacious hall, such as served for sittings of the tribunals and assemblies in the palace, also for large offices or meetings of the members of a society or the adepts of a creed. Such meeting halls were always in demand in every city and province, and the architectural design differed according to current practice, the available resources and of course the size of the fraternity or congregation for which they catered. The emperors built for the masses, and the great basilical halls of the imperial palaces and law courts, with colonnades separating the aisles and a raised gallery in the apse, must have seemed best suited to a Christian congregation. It is not known whether the Christians built any basilical churches before the time of Constantine, in the periods when they were left in peace.

The Constantinian architects may have been influenced in their choice of a design by the cult rooms of basilical plan which are known to have existed in Rome as early as the first century; for example the small basilical halls where the Pythagoreans and the worshippers of Mithras and the Cabiri celebrated their rites. The most famous of these halls is the underground basilica of the first century at the Porta Maggiore in Rome; it was used for the Neo-Pythagorean cult. At Maktar in Tunisia a basilica of the third century served as the meeting place of a youth fraternity. But undoubtedly a much more influential model was the synagogue.

Until recently the divorce between Jews and Christians seemed so complete and of such long standing that historians of Early Christian art took little or no account of Jewish antecedents. The discovery of Dura-Europos and its early third-century synagogue has shown this to be an error—an error the more surprising since students of Church history and the liturgy had always been aware of the frequent contacts between Jews and Christians until well into the fifth century, and of the profond influence exerted on the early liturgy by the Jewish ritual.

It is therefore only natural to look for a possible influence of synagogue architecture on the design of the first churches and—now that the frescoes in the Dura synagogue have proved the existence of a Jewish iconography in this early period—of Jewish imagery on the iconography of Early Christian art.

The Dura synagogue, as it so happens, is not a basilica. Excavations in Galilee, however, have brought to light several synagogues of the basilical type. The earliest of them go back to the time of the Severi (c. 200 A.D.). This is the case with the synagogue at Capernaum and a few others: already the building takes the form of an elongated rectangle divided lengthwise into three aisles. The Bible scroll was kept in a shrine at the far end. There is no apse (though it appears in later synagogues, perhaps under the influence of Christian churches) but, rather, a chevet. In the side aisles were pews for the congregation, but it would appear from other monuments and inscriptions of the period that the elders sat near the nave, more probably in the nave. Perhaps what chiefly differentiated these basilicas from Jewish churches was the absence of a clerestory (so that the elevation of nave and side aisles was the same) and the practice of joining the two colonnades marking the side aisles by a transversal portico (as in the Tell Hum synagogue). But all things considered these are only minor features which may have been peculiar to Galilee. This is an inference suggested by two great synagogues of the same period, one discovered at Ostia, the other at Tarsus. The latter was a fully developed basilica. The precocity of Jewish religious architecture as compared with that of the Christians was only to be expected in the circumstances: the Roman State, as pointed out earlier, officially recognized the Jewish religion and allowed the Jews to have their own places of worship, whereas Christianity was more or less outlawed until Constantine issued his edicts of toleration in 313.

In view of this state of affairs, and the fact that several pre-Constantinian synagogues were basilicas, it is reasonable to infer that these may have served as a model for the Christian basilicas. As soon as the laws of toleration were extended to Christians, their places of worship were given the same form as those of the Jews—this as a matter of course, since their religious rites were similar and, in many cities, Jews and Christians were related by blood. (This intermixing of races was noted by St John Chrysostom about 400.) The Christian basilica makes its appearance under Constantine, and the

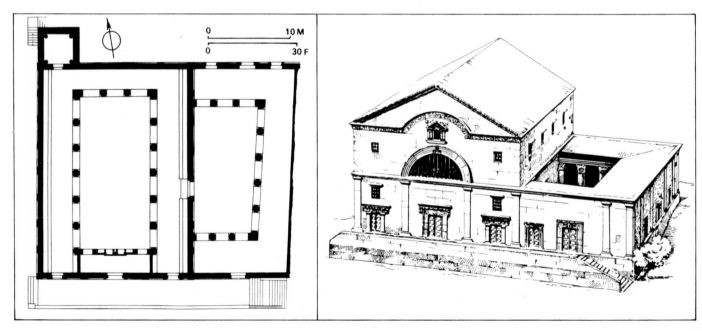

177. *Tell Hum. Plan of the Synagogue.*   178. *Tell Hum. Reconstruction of the Synagogue.*

direct link between these first Christian basilicas and the synagogues seems to be confirmed by the similar principle observed by the architects in orienting the building, the main door facing Jerusalem in the case of the synagogues of this period, and facing east in the case of the Constantinian basilicas. The basilica was equally well adapted to Jewish and Christian services, and that alone might have commended it to the Christians, the more so since, as we have seen, it was a kind of all-purpose building then in common use throughout the Empire. But it was its adoption in the reign of Constantine for the great churches he founded (beginning perhaps with the cathedral church of the Lateran, 312-319) that set the course of Christian architecture for centuries to come, wherever Christianity penetrated.

In many lands the forms adopted by Constantine's architects continued to be used with little change until the beginning of the Middle Ages; elsewhere, as in Constantinople, they remained in force until the sixth century.

Sponsored by the emperors, the basilica at once became the standard type of Christian church, to the exclusion of all other possible types of building (except for those serving a special purpose, like baptisteries and martyria).

Fourth-Century Churches

The Christian churches of the fourth century are known to us now only by a few ruins and a number of Renaissance drawings. Our information is thus too meagre for a thorough study of the regional peculiarities of these basilicas. Distinctive features can, however, be detected in some places, for example in Rome and in Syria. In both cases the idiosyncrasies we find in the Christian basilicas probably derive from the local, non-Christian buildings on which they were modelled. The first cathedral of Rome, the Lateran basilica, erected between 312 and 319 in the centre of one of the emperor's palaces, is known to have had five aisles and a transept. A mural painting of 1635-40 in which Gaspard Poussin had a hand enables us to form an idea of the triumphal arch, the main apse and the lofty arcades of this handsome Constantinian edifice before it was transformed a few years later (c. 1650).

The plan and drawings made by Alfarano in the sixteenth century show that old St Peter's in the Vatican (built after 326, perhaps after 333) was a five-aisled basilica, the two inner rows of columns in the nave carrying architraves, the two others arches. Set very high up, the clerestory had relatively small windows. A narrow transept divided the nave from the chevet and projected slightly beyond the outer walls of the nave. The back wall of the choir was flat, except for the projecting apse in the centre of it, behind the *confessio*. An atrium or open court, surrounded on all four sides by porticoes, stood in front of the entrance to the basilica, whose apse was at the west end, as in the Constantinian basilica of Golgotha in Jerusalem. This type of five-aisled basilica (other churches had only three aisles), with an atrium and a projecting transept, was adopted for other churches in Rome, beginning with San Paolo fuori le Mura, built in the time of Theodosius.

But there also existed in Rome another type of basilica which, after being temporarily in favour in the fourth century, was discarded. The four recorded examples of it

179. *View of St John Lateran (before reconstruction).   Attributed to G. Poussin.   San Martino ai Monti, Rome.*

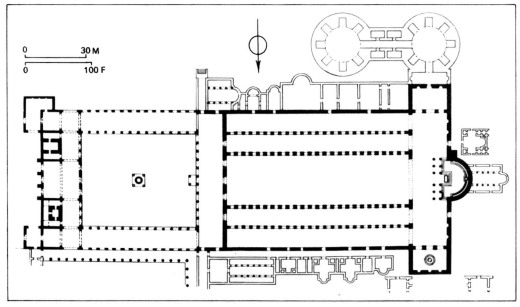

180.   *Vatican.   Plan of Old St Peter's (after Tiberio Alfarano).*

181. *Vatican. Interior of Old St Peter's (after Tiberio Alfarano).*

(known from ruins and excavations) stood *extra muros*, in Roman cemeteries. The most famous of them is the basilica of San Sebastiano, on the Via Appia, dating to the time of Constantine. The ruins of the first church of Sant'Agnese on the Via Nomentana are equally extensive, though representing only a fraction of the original basilica. The two other churches of this type are San Lorenzo in Campo Verano and SS. Marcellino e Pietro. Distinctive of all four is the design of the chevet, which spans the entire width of the building, the side walls of the nave joining at the back in a semicircle and the walls of the side aisles doing likewise to form a wider semicircle around the first. An ambulatory is thus created in the chevet, whose curving wall as seen from the outside resembled that of an amphitheatre or circus. This feature can be seen at a glance on the ground plan of San Sebastiano, and even more strikingly in the ruins of the immense chevet of Sant'Agnese (the ancient church, beside the rotunda of Santa Costanza; not to be confused with the later basilica of Sant'Agnese, which still stands).

175

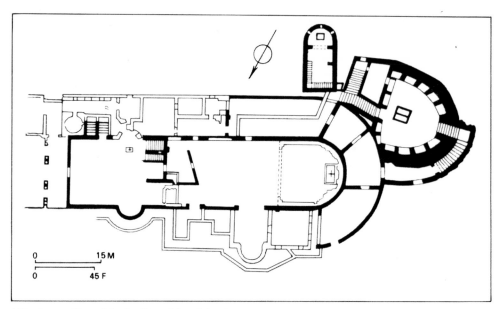

182. *Rome. Plan of the Basilica of San Sebastiano.*

183. *Rome. Sant'Agnese: Ruins of the Chevet of the Ancient Church.*

184. *Kharab Shems. Basilica: South Arcade of the Nave.*

A good deal of building was also done under Constantine in the imperial city of Trier. There, beside his palace, he had a large three-aisled basilica erected, with an atrium in front of it (the chevet appears to have been rebuilt at the end of the fourth century). Then a second three-aisled basilica, also with an atrium, was erected beside the first. This architectural complex repeats on a colossal scale the juxtaposition of two cathedral churches as we find it at Aquileia; even the location of the baptistery, between the two basilicas, is the same. The imposing churches at Trier cannot be dated with precision, but they must have been founded about 326.

In Syria a distinction has to be drawn between monuments in the north and south. Of the many ruined churches still to be seen in northern Syria, seven or eight may date back to the fourth century and even to the period before the new stimulus given to Christian architecture under Theodosius. One of these churches is dated by an inscription (Fafirtin, 372); others can be assigned to the same period in virtue of their forms and building techniques: Serjilla, Ruweiha, Simkhar, Kharab Shems, Brad. All are much alike: three-aisled basilicas with two arcades and a clerestory. The arches in the nave rest on columns and everywhere the roof was timbered. The fine masonry work is seen at its best in some of the façades with their carved door-frames and the triangular pediment on which the roof rested. But the distinguishing feature of these basilicas is the arrangement of the chevet, which seems to derive from the Roman buildings of Syria, for example the small pagan temples of the second and third centuries at Es-

177

185. *Ruweiha. South Church: South Arcade of the Nave.*

Sanamein, Slem, Kanawat and Mismiyeh. The central nave ends in a semicircular apse, as in Rome and elsewhere; here, however, the apse does not project beyond the building but is enclosed by the flat wall at the back (as at Fafirtin). Within the church the apse is flanked by two walls separating the side aisles from two small rooms at the far end of them, one on each side of the apse (these rooms being used as sacristies and reliquary chapels, and later, in the sixth century, as a diaconicon and prothesis). Thus the chevet of these Syrian basilicas formed what was in effect a self-contained unit. To this structural peculiarity, derived from earlier forms of local architecture, the Syrian type of Christian basilica owes its originality.

Of the ruined churches of this period in southern Syria two are dated by inscriptions: the church of Julianos at Umm El Jimal (344?) and the shrine at Der El Kahf (367-375). Three or four others also go back to the fourth century. With two exceptions (Nimreh and Tafha, which are three-aisled basilicas), the nave of these churches consists of a single, undivided hall. The arrangement of the chevet varies. There are several examples of a tripartite chevet, as in North Syria, and its adaptation to churches with

178

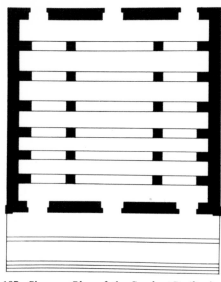

188. *Shaqqa. Cross-Section of the Secular 'Basilica.'*

187. *Shaqqa. Plan of the Secular 'Basilica.'*

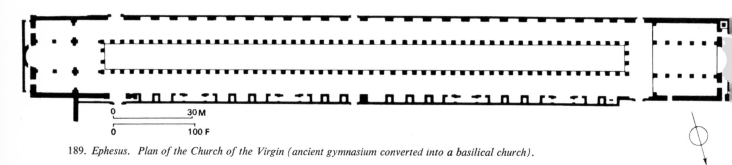

189. *Ephesus. Plan of the Church of the Virgin (ancient gymnasium converted into a basilical church).*

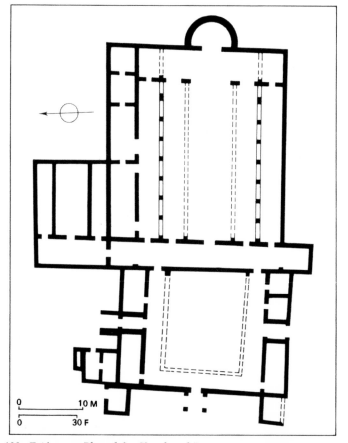

190. *Epidaurus. Plan of the Church and Baptistery.*

a single nave shows how easily this massive type of chevet could be treated as an independent unit (church of Masechos at Umm El Jimal). The church of Julianos has a projecting semicircular apse spanning the full width of the (single) nave; in this respect it resembles San Sebastiano in Rome. In both of the three-aisled basilicas (Nimreh and Tafha) we also find a projecting apse, but of a narrower span corresponding to the width of the central aisle—a characteristic feature of the churches of western Syria. For the art historian the chief interest of the early churches of southern Syria lies in their close resemblance to the third-century secular buildings of the same region. At Shaqqa, for example, two groups of pre-Christian civil edifices have survived, one of which, the so-called Quisariyeh group, includes several halls with a single nave and a three-aisled secular 'basilica' of the third century which have equivalents in some Christian churches of the fourth century (Julianos and Tafha). The continuity of an architectural tradition is demonstrated here better than anywhere else because of the structural peculiarities common to all these buildings, Christian and pre-Christian alike.

Characteristic of southern Syria, a region rich in basalt, is the unusual persistence of native building techniques. Walls and roofs are made of blocks of lava, the roofing slabs resting on projecting corbels. 'Rooms of unlimited length could thus be built, but their width was fixed once and for all by the size of the slabs' (ten feet long at most, according to Jean Lassus). During the Roman occupation the southern Syrians improved on this system by throwing a series of arches across the building breadthwise and resting the slabs of the flat roof on these. When it occurred to them to insert three successive arches in the same partition wall, they achieved a kind of three-aisled basilica; there is a second-century civil edifice of this type at Shaqqa and a Christian example at Tafha of uncertain date (Jean Lassus assigning it to the fifth century, while H. C. Butler groups it with the fourth-century Christian edifices: the latter date seems more likely). Here is a striking illustration of the continuity of architectural design in southern Syria; hence the special interest of this region. But though the three-aisled basilica made its appearance here as early as elsewhere, the Christian architecture of southern Syria never took effect beyond the frontiers of the province; indeed, from the fifth century on, the local tradition was deliberately abandoned in favour of basilicas imitating those of other provinces.

Of all the provinces of the Roman Empire, Syria alone has preserved, in various stages of decay, a series of fourth-century basilicas. But elsewhere too, at this time, the Christian communities were provided with large, handsome churches basilical in form. At Ephesus in the fourth century two parallel rows of columns were erected in the hall of a gymnasium, thus converting it into a large church. Evidently the basilical hall already seemed to answer best to the needs of Christian worship. Excavations at Corinth and Epidaurus have revealed the ground plan of very large five-aisled basilicas of a type similar to that of the Roman basilicas, yet distinct from it. The plan shows that the church itself was surrounded by a larger complex of secondary units, including (at Corinth) a trefoil chapel, built against a side aisle of the basilica, which must have served as a martyrium, where some holy relic was venerated. It was in the Theodosian period that the cult of relics first became widely popularized, and then that shrines began to be built in large numbers to house them. The finest of these martyria date from the

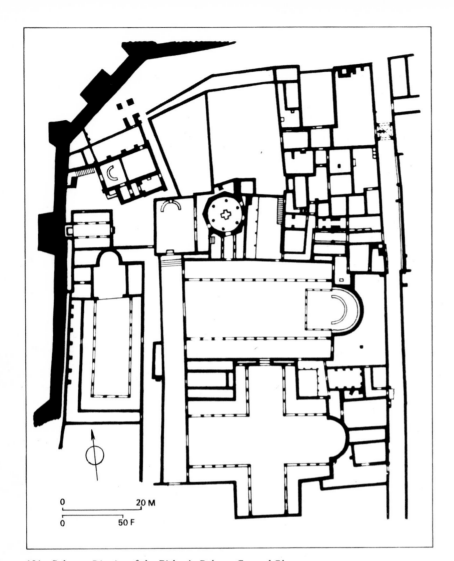

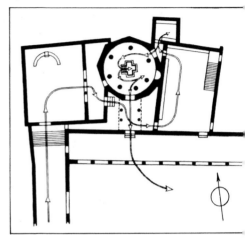

192. *Salona. District of the Bishop's Palace: Plan the Baptistery.*

191. *Salona. District of the Bishop's Palace: General Plan.*

fifth and sixth centuries, and it is for that period that the question of their influence on the development of Christian architecture arises. But already in the fourth century we find the first edifices on a central plan which were to be typical of the martyria, for example the rotunda of the Holy Sepulchre and the trefoil of Corinth. To these may be added the small, unpretentious shrine, given the shape of a cross, which was built at the gates of Antioch (Antioch-Kaoussieh) at the end of the fourth century to house the relics of St Babylas. It was in the fourth century, too, that some edifices having an unusual plan were transformed into basilicas (cf. the plans of Salona on the opposite page.)

In North Africa many spacious basilicas were erected in the course of the fourth century. All are in ruins, so that it is difficult now to imagine what they were originally like. We can, however, see their vast dimensions and variety of structural details— side aisles, vestibules, atria, baptisteries, and, notably, raised choirs advancing into the nave. Everywhere these basilicas are surrounded by secondary constructions, but these additions are not necessarily of the same period as the churches themselves.

If these fourth-century African basilicas have little to tell the historian of Christian architecture, this is because as yet not much is known about them. The most interesting

182

195. *Salona. Buildings of Unusual Plan around a Martyr's Tomb (first and second state).*

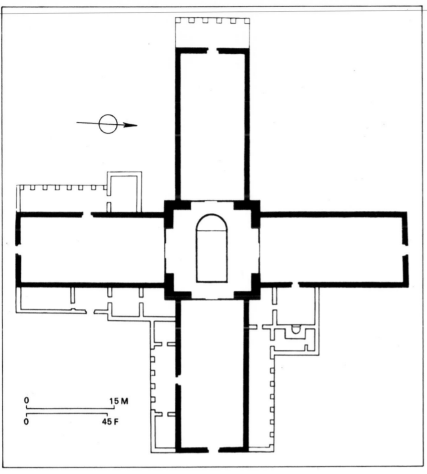

193. *Antioch-Kaoussieh. Cruciform Martyrium of St Babylas: Plan.*

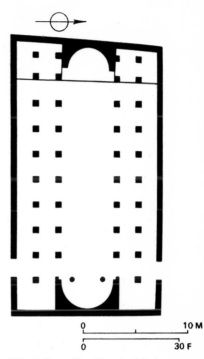

194. *Orléansville. Church of St Reparatus: Plan.*

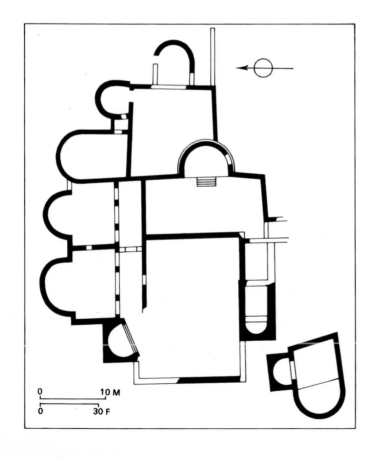

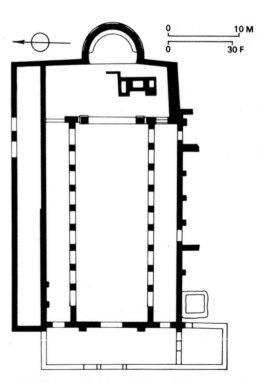

196. *Salona. Building of Unusual Plan converted into a Regular Basilica (third state).*

197. *Tebessa. Atrium of the Christian Basilica.*

198. *Tebessa. Nave of the Christian Basilica.*

examples of this period are the churches of Timgad (west basilica), Damous el-Karita (at Carthage), Hippo and Orléansville. But it is the church of Tebessa that gives us the best idea of the arrangement of a great complex of Christian architecture, with basilica, atrium and various dependencies; more will be said about Tebessa in the sequel to this volume.

184

199. *Tebessa. Christian Basilica, detail: Arcades in the Nave.*

The edicts of toleration and the emperors' conversion to Christianity seem to have had less effect on Christian painting and sculpture than on architecture. Figure sculpture had no place either in the larger or smaller Christian churches of the fourth century (except for the carvings on church furniture), and mosaics with religious imagery seem to have been rare. Two remarkable groups of mosaics have, however, been preserved in mausolea, one in Santa Costanza, Rome, the other in Spain at Centcelles, in the vicinity of Tarragona.

200. *Centcelles. Face of a Child.*

201. *Trier, Imperial Palace. Face of a Child. Bischöfliches Museum.*

202. *Rome. Santa Costanza, Annular Vault, detail: Birds amid Branches, Flowers, Fruit and Various Objects.*

The Santa Costanza Mosaics

At Santa Costanza the mosaics on a white ground in the vault of the circular aisle consist in part of purely ornamental designs and in part of motifs from the same cycle of vintaging putti that figure on many sarcophagi and in the catacombs. They appear also in the reliefs on the porphyry sarcophagus of Princess Constantina, and the layout of the mosaic panels matches that of the sarcophagus reliefs. The fact that these mosaics differ very little in style from Roman mosaic pavements lends support to the view that vault and floor mosaics were as a rule interrelated (at Santa Costanza the latter are not the original ones). A mosaic pavement recently discovered at Cherchel is an almost exact copy of the vault mosaics in Santa Costanza. The wall mosaics and those in the central dome of Santa Costanza no longer exist, but some Renaissance drawings give us an idea of their content: above a river peopled with putti and aquatic animals were Old Testament scenes with small figures. Little place was given as yet to Christian iconography in this Constantinian edifice; there were few Christian images, and those few on a small scale.

187

203. *Rome. Santa Costanza: Annular Vault, detail.*

It was in the fourth century, too, but presumably later, that the two symmetrical niches in the circular wall of the rotunda were adorned with mosaics representing large figures. The style of these works has no resemblance to that of the vault and dome mosaics and probably reflects the art of the great apse mosaics in the first Constantinian churches of Rome, St John Lateran and St Peter's in the Vatican. The two niche mosaics in Santa Costanza contain scenes which complement each other: Moses receiving the Tables of the Law, and Christ delivering the Law to St Peter in the presence of St Paul. But indifferent execution and unskilled restorations detract very seriously from the artistic value of these two theophanies, which resemble those of the sarcophagus reliefs and

188

204. *Rome. Santa Costanza, Annular Vault, detail: Bust of Constantina amid Vine-Shoots.*

205. *Rome. Santa Costanza, Annular Vault, detail: Medallions with Cupids, Figures, Birds and Animals.*

206. *Rome. Santa Costanza, Annular Vault, detail: Birds amid Branches and Various Objects.*

207. *Rome. Santa Costanza: The Lord delivering the Law to Moses.*

catacomb paintings of the fourth century; all alike render the divine majesty in the manner of Roman imperial art.

There exists only one other group of mosaics which can be assimilated to those in Santa Costanza. It decorates the dome of a fourth-century Christian mausoleum at Centcelles, near Tarragona, Spain, which may have been the burial place of Constantine's youngest son Constans I, who was murdered in 350 in the Pyrenees. The mosaics, however, are undoubtedly a work of the Constantinian period—unfortunately in a poor state of preservation. Arranged on superimposed registers, they combine a fine frieze of funerary subjects (both pagan and Christian) with several scenes from the salvation cycle (Daniel in the lions' den, the Three Children in the fiery furnace)—a cycle whose themes constantly recur in the sarcophagus reliefs and catacomb paintings. Local artists were probably responsible for the Centcelles mosaics, and very impressive works they are. Better perhaps than the Constantinian mosaics in Rome, they prefigure the subsequent evolution of the style.

192

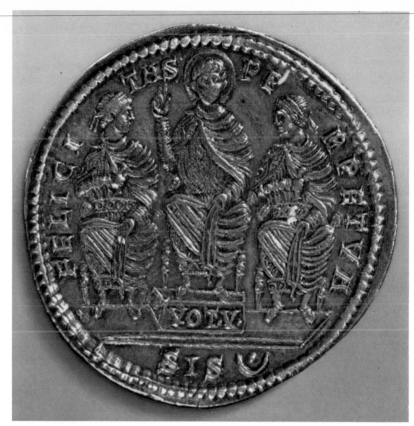

208. *Medal of Constans I: Constantine the Great and his Sons. Cabinet des Médailles,
Bibliothèque Nationale, Paris.*

The Triumphal Art of the Emperors

It was under the sons of Constantine and their immediate successors, and under
Theodosius, that the triumphal art of the emperors attained its most complete expression. This art was wholly pagan in origin and spirit. Yet it was the first Christian
emperors who, to enhance their prestige, drew freely on these pagan iconographic programmes—some of them antedating the conversion of the Empire, others offering a Christian reinterpretation of them, still others being newly invented Christian formulas. This
triumphal art must have flourished above all in the 'Sacred Palaces' at Rome, Constantinople, Trier and Antioch. But the mosaics, paintings, statues and reliefs which they
contained have all perished with the palaces themselves. We therefore have no alternative
but to fall back on replicas of these lost works: on the one hand copies of the statues
of emperors and empresses, on the other the small reliefs on imperial medals.

Abundant use was still being made in the fourth century of official statuary, above
all effigies of the emperor (and also, to a less extent, of the empress), life-size or larger
than life, standing or on horseback. Some of these works are justly famous, like the
statue of Constantine in front of the Lateran basilica, his head from Nish (in the National
Museum, Belgrade), the colossal head of Constantine II in the Palazzo dei Conservatori,
Rome, the over-lifesize statue of a Roman emperor at Barletta, near Bari, and also the
statue of Julian the Apostate in the Louvre, with its expressive face (hardened, however,
by the systematic application of frontal symmetry) and large eyes, everything about it
suggesting the superhuman grandeur of the ruler.

193

209. *Aphrodisias. Statue of the Emperor Valentinian II. Archaeological Museum, Istanbul.* ▶

211. *The Emperor Valentinian I (?), detail. Barletta.*

Other imperial portraits, often remarkable works, figure on the large gold medallions which the fourth-century emperors presented to their near relations and to the barbarian kings who submitted to and served the Empire. The reverse of these medals displays the symbolic imagery glorifying the emperor—an original iconography, half symbolic, half realistic, which in its essentials must have been familiar and readily comprehensible to everybody at that time, for it was taken up then and afterwards by the Church and adapted to Christian themes like the Majesty of God, the Resurrection of Christ and the dead, and the 'Parousia.'

196

◀ 210. *Head of Constantine the Great. National Museum, Belgrade.*

212. *Medal of Constans I: Bust of the Emperor.*   *Bibliothèque Nationale, Paris.*

213. *Medal with a Roman Emperor enthroned between Two Bodyguards.*
Koninklijk Kabinet, The Hague.

214. *Coin with the Apotheosis of Constantine.*   *Cabinet des Médailles, Bibliothèque Nationale, Paris.*

215-216. *Head of the Emperor Maximinus Daia.*   *Staatliche Museen, Berlin.*

217. *Medal: Constantine the Great crowned by the Hand of God. Kunsthistorisches Museum, Vienna.*

218-219. *Medal: Bust of Constantius Chlorus and his Triumphal Entry into London. Musée Municipal, Arras.*

200

220. *Medal: Conquering Emperor. Cabinet des Médailles, Bibliothèque Nationale, Paris.*

221. *Medal: The Emperor Valens. Kunsthistorisches Museum, Vienna.*

222. *Gaul. Medal: The Emperor Magnentius. Cabinet des Médailles, Bibliothèque Nationale, Paris.*

223.　*Rome.　Arch of Constantine, detail: Constantine making a Speech.*

Cameos and other engraved gems provide some notable examples of this same art, whose seminal centres were the imperial palaces and the craftsmen's workshops where they were executed. A particularly fine piece is the cameo in the National Museum, Belgrade, representing an emperor (possibly Constantine) on horseback. Another famous cameo is in the Cabinet des Médailles, Paris. A few years earlier than the Belgrade cameo, it carries a starkly realistic version of the theme of an imperial victory, the emperor's chariot rolling over the heaped-up corpses of Rome's vanquished enemies. The livid tint of the stone enhances the savagery of the scene. This conquering emperor is Licinius, one of Constantine's colleagues and, later, his pagan rival.

It is legitimate to compare the cameo of Licinius with the battle and victory scenes, triumphal processions and distributions of largesse that are represented on the Arch of Constantine in Rome and the Arch of Galerius at Salonica. In Rome, and even more at Salonica, the administration of the Senate and Court took the initiative of transforming the surfaces of these triumphal arches into chronicles in stone evoking the outstanding events of the reign of the glorified emperor. This is above all descriptive art, and the care taken to omit nothing has resulted in a laboured execution. With a heavy hand these sculptors, all very much alike and equally indifferent to classical tradition, have multiplied scenes and figures. What they show us is not the dramatic clash of battle, but the victory already won by the Romans under the leadership of Constantine or Galerius. For these sculptors the interest of the work of art lies in costumes, in weapons, in the exotic animals offered to the triumphant emperor by the Parthians—in material

202

224. *Medal: Two Co-regnant Emperors seated on the same Throne. Kunsthistorisches Museum, Vienna.*

225. *Rome. Arch of Constantine, detail: The Battle of the Milvian Bridge.*

and typological details rather than in the individual features of a face or the distinguishing peculiarities of a body. Men and events are subordinated to stereotyped themes, and the reliefs on these arches aim only at bringing together a suitable selection of such themes and applying them here to the glorification of Constantine or Galerius, whatever the battle or campaign concerned.

These two cycles of narrative reliefs occupy a significant place in the history of art because their rude, uncouth style is the best evidence we have of the decline of the classical aesthetic even in circles nearest the government of the Roman Empire; and because the handling of these reliefs implies the participation of artists from the provinces—a valuable indication of the influence exerted by the provincial workshops on the art of the capitals.

The part played by those workshops in the breakdown of the classical tradition of sculpture is well illustrated by the reliefs on these two arches.

A discovery made a few years ago on the site of the palace of Galerius at Salonica has provided us with another work equally characteristic of this type of sculpture, still pagan but contemporary with the beginnings of Christian sculpture. It is a sculptured arch which formed part of an unidentified monument. Among the figure reliefs on it are an emperor (Galerius?) and a personification of a city (Salonica?), both presented as *imagines clipeatae* held aloft by winged genii wearing Phrygian caps.

204

227-228. *Salonica. Arch of Galerius, details.*

229. *Rome. Catacomb of the Via Latina : Partial View of Room N.*

230. *Rome. Tomb of the Aurelii: Christ and the Apostles.*

Catacomb Paintings

It is in Rome that the largest number of fourth-century paintings have been preserved, most of them in the underground cemeteries (as was also the case with third-century paintings). The above-ground decorations have disappeared together with the buildings in which they figured.

Never were the Christian cemeteries of Rome and Naples so extensively utilized as in the fourth century, and along with the generalized use of subterranean galleries there was a parallel extension of the practices of burying the dead in carved sarcophagi and of decorating the walls of tomb chambers and arcosolia with religious paintings. Many of these paintings have survived, and most of them are unquestionably imitations of third-century prototypes.

To this period belong the wall and ceiling paintings in the cubicula of the Coemeterium Majus and the catacomb of SS. Pietro e Marcellino. This art shows no systematic evolution, and alongside admirably executed frescoes we find more or less rustic paintings; few of them depart from pre-Constantinian types. But now there was a frequent use of heavy painted frames (as in the early days of the Empire) in simulated relief and of larger figures, more fully modelled and more realistic than before. The customary Biblical scenes are peopled with lifelike figures, and portraits are convincingly individualized. Accentuating a trend that began in the third century, these painters arrived at such well-characterized portraits as those of the two girls in the Trasona

209

231.   *Rome.   Catacomb of Domitilla: Veneranda led into Heaven by St Petronilla.*

232. *Rome. Catacomb called Coemeterium Majus: Orant Virgin with half-length Child.*

catacomb and those in an arcosolium of the 'Coemeterium Majus' representing three half-length Orants: the husband and wife interred there and, between them, flanked by two monograms of Christ, a praying woman with a child partially visible in front of her. These last two figures may be a Virgin and Child, though the possibility that they represent a dead woman and her child cannot be excluded (for in the museums of Aquileia and Sofia there are second- and third-century grave stelae with half-length figures of a mother and child). In any case this is a fine piece of painting; the artist has been at pains to obtain a convincing likeness and to bring out the plastic volumes of the mother's head. We are leagues away from the hasty sketches of the third-century catacomb painters and their impersonal, almost evanescent Orants.

The lunette of a small arcosolium in the catacomb of Domitilla contains the famous scene of Veneranda being welcomed to the Other World by St Petronilla. Here again is a highly individualized portrait of the dead woman, a fine, full-length figure which, though actually quite small in size, produces a monumental effect. The presence of a saint welcoming the deceased marks the beginning of that cult of the saints which was to become so popular in the last quarter of the fourth century. This painting appears to date to shortly before that period, for an inscription of the year 356 was found in the same tomb chamber (it has now been placed beside the fresco).

211

233. *Rome. Catacomb of SS. Pietro e Marcellino, Crypt of the Saints: Christ.*

The monumental treatment of the figures of Veneranda and St Petronilla suggests that they may be copies of some mosaic or wall painting in an above-ground church. The same hypothesis has been put forward to explain the origin of a figure subject which does not appear in the catacomb paintings until the fourth century: Christ with the apostles. Sometimes all are standing, as in a famous ceiling in the catacomb of SS. Pietro e Marcellino; or else Christ is seated among the standing apostles (Commodilla); occasionally Jesus and his disciples are all seated (Domitilla, Giordani). Whatever the exact purport of these figure groups (Christ teaching, Christ and apostles sitting in judgment), all have a monumental character which is also found in the apse mosaics of the Early Christian basilicas (e.g. chapel of Sant'Aquilino in San Lorenzo, Milan), and these mosaics are thought to have served as models for the catacomb paintings. The apse mosaic of the Lateran basilica may have supplied such a model, and that of St Peter's may have inspired the mosaic of Christ delivering the Law in one of the small exedrae of Santa Costanza. In one particular case, that of the ceiling fresco in the catacomb of SS. Pietro e Marcellino, the imitation of an apse decoration is unmistakable, for we find the characteristic superimposition on two registers of symmetrical figure groups: Christ and the apostles, the Lamb and saints. The result is an impressive work which suggests that the apse decorations of the fourth-century basilicas must have been of a very high order.

212

234. *Rome. Catacomb of SS. Pietro e Marcellino, Crypt of the Saints: Christ between St Peter and St Paul above the Divine Lamb.*

235. *Rome. Catacomb of Panfilo: Partial View of a Painted Tomb Chamber.* ▶

237. *Rome. Catacomb of Commodilla: Bust of Christ.*

◀ 236. *Rome. Catacomb of SS. Pietro e Marcellino, Crypt of the Saints, detail: Two Saints.*

238. *Rome. Catacomb of Domitilla: Christ teaching among the Apostles.*

239. *Rome. Catacomb of the Giordani: Daniel in the Lions' Den.*

240-241. *Rome. Confessio under the Basilica of SS. Giovanni e Paolo: Standing Figures and Stag Drinking; Beheading of Three Saints.*

In another catacomb fresco, now destroyed (apse of the underground chapel of St Felicitas in the Massimo catacomb), this imitation was still more obvious. The complete apse decoration of a Roman basilica was exactly reproduced: not only the group of saints in Paradise, and the phoenix and figure of Christ in the conch, but also the Lamb and sheep set out in a frieze above the apse.

A third example is of more intrinsic interest, for this group of fourth-century paintings still decorates the walls of a *confessio*, a tiny subterranean shrine under the Early Christian basilica of SS. Giovanni e Paolo on the Caelian hill. As in the apse of a church, a saint is shown in the central panel as an Orant; two prostrate figures lie at his feet and others, one of them carrying a vase, are approaching him. Above are two standing figures and two symmetrical scenes: the beheading of three saints and a stag drinking the waters of life. The small size of these paintings relates them to the catacomb frescoes, but otherwise they reflect the new Christian painting which took form in the earliest basilicas, and reflect it better perhaps, and at a fairly early date (mid-fourth century?), than the replicas of it in the catacombs.

218

242. *Rome. Confessio under the Basilica of SS. Giovanni e Paolo: Saint as an Orant, deta[*

243. *Rome.   Confessio under the Basilica of SS. Giovanni e Paolo: Saint as an Orant.*

The destruction of the great figure compositions decorating the apse in fourth-century basilicas (St John Lateran, St Peter's, Golgotha, Bethlehem, etc.) is all the more regrettable since these major works would have given us a better understanding of the origins of the Christian apse paintings and mosaics, an essential and particularly stable feature of church decoration for centuries.

So far as can be judged from extant works, the apse decoration in civil basilicas and in temples devoted to the imperial cult may have been the source of the first apse decorations in Christian churches.

The apse paintings in a shrine of the imperial cult at Luxor in Egypt represented the four emperors of the Tetrarchy 'in majesty' (c. 310). As shown in a watercolour made a century ago, when this shrine was discovered, the four Tetrarchs were aligned along the curving wall of the apse, just as the saints were later aligned in Byzantine apses.

There was another example in Rome, in a temple of the Lupercalian cult erected in the late third century, the Basilica Creperia. Now destroyed, the ruins of this temple were described and drawn at the time of their discovery, in 1613, near the church of San Lorenzo in Panisperna. It was a three-aisled basilica with an apse. The apse decoration represented the she-wolf suckling Romulus and Remus, who were flanked by two Luperci with their thongs; a warrior, perhaps Mars, was represented in a disk at the summit of the arch.

Pagan Tomb Paintings

Irreparable as is the loss of the large-scale paintings of the fourth century at Rome and in every part of the Empire, we can form an idea of their general nature from the evidence provided both by Christian tomb paintings and by those in pagan tombs, which were still quite numerous during the fourth century.

The most famous of these paintings are in the arcosolium of a woman named Vibia, whose lot after death is depicted with an unusual wealth of detail. The most interesting part of this picture cycle is the central scene showing the dead woman being welcomed in the celestial paradise and invited to share in a banquet. The latter theme links this narrative painting with the pictures of Christian agapes in the after-world.

The parents of a young man named Trebius Justus had the walls of his tomb chamber adorned with descriptive paintings: a series of genre scenes, remarkable for their accurate and lifelike details, grouped around a portrait of the deceased under an arcosolium. These paintings have been thought to contain veiled allusions to the doctrines of the Gnostics.

But the subjects are taken directly from everyday life and handled in a monumental style that ranks them among the finest wall paintings of the fourth century. We see large buildings under construction with scaffolding set in place around them; workmen going about their tasks under the orders of the deceased; several large portraits of the young man's parents and other persons; and even some domestic animals. The entire wall surface is covered with these scenes, placed one above the other and peopled with boldly rendered figures whose names are inscribed beside them.

All this is far removed from the graceful sketches in the third-century catacombs, with their small figures caught up in a network of ornamental or architectural motifs. Here, as later in the churches and, from the third century on, in the wall paintings of pagan temples and those of the Dura synagogue, the painter was chiefly concerned with depicting large-scale figures and scenes in which they predominate. Whatever the religious group to which Trebius Justus may have belonged, his fellow-believers had a Good Shepherd represented in the vault of his tomb. We are reminded of the mixed character of the third-century paintings in the tomb of the Aurelii, and also those in the Via Latina tomb, for here too the religious affiliation of the pictures is difficult to determine.

244. *Rome. Tomb of Trebius Justus, detail: The Dead Man with his Parents.*

245. *Rome. Tomb of Vibia: Vibia led into Paradise.*

246. *Rome. Tomb of Trebius Justus: Masons working on a Building.*

LEPORIVS

248. *Rome. Catacomb of the Via Latina: Ascension of Elijah and the Good Shepherd.*

The Via Latina Paintings

Discovered in 1955 (but not published until 1962), an underground gallery of the middle or second half of the fourth century under the Via Latina formed a kind of private mausoleum belonging to a family or an unidentified fraternity. There are no inscriptions that might give a clue to its date or the names of the owners. But the quality of the wall paintings and the number and variety of the tomb chambers, imitating above-ground mausolea of rectangular and polygonal design, are such that only a wealthy patron could have afforded them. Curiously enough, among the dead interred in this hypogeum, while the majority were Christians, there were also pagans. With exemplary tolerance they were all buried together, although—judging by the paintings—in different cubicula. Christian and pagan paintings seem to be contemporary; so it is not a case of a pagan family subsequently converted to Christianity.

The discovery of the Via Latina hypogeum created a sensation because of this juxtaposition of pagan and Christian paintings and because, among the subjects represented, some are very rare, even unique. Art historians concur in admiring the high stylistic quality of some of these frescoes, peopled—sometimes thronged—with large figures whose expressive faces are beautifully delineated. This style has little in common with that of the catacomb paintings (except for some of the later frescoes in the catacomb of SS. Pietro e Marcellino and the Coemeterium Majus). Certain scenes, heretofore totally unknown in Early Christian painting in Rome, raise perplexing questions for the historian of religion: do they stem from a particular sect, from the cult of Hercules Soter ('Saviour'), or possibly from Jewish influences? The religious background of some of the paintings in the Via Latina hypogeum has still to be elucidated, but all agree that these are works of the highest interest from which much may be learned.

247. *Rome. Tomb of Trebius Justus: Servant leading a Horse.*

249. *Rome.   Catacomb of the Via Latina: Aristotle (?) with his Disciples.*

The style of all the Via Latina paintings being much the same, they may conveniently be considered as a series of self-contained picture cycles, each limited to a single tomb chamber.   In each room the decorations form a whole, ornamental motifs and figure paintings being assigned their respective places in accordance with a well-balanced decorative scheme.   Thus the octagonal Room I, obviously decorated in imitation of a

250. *Rome. Catacomb of the Via Latina: End of a Gallery with Closure Slabs.*

rich mausoleum, shows full- and half-length figures in the garb of philosophers. One of them, located in the centre of the ceiling and surrounded by four others, might be Jesus, the True Philosopher, with the four Evangelists. At the back of two of the arcosolia which open on this room, the same figure of Jesus appears again, enthroned and teaching, with Peter and Paul beside him. In one of the tympana is the scene which, more than any other, came as a surprise when the hypogeum was discovered: it shows another figure in the costume of a philosopher who, surrounded by other sages, is touching a small naked corpse with a wand. This scene is unique. According to the only satisfactory interpretation of it (given by Pierre Boyancé), it may represent Aristotle

227

251. *Rome. Catacomb of the Via Latina: Alcestis beside Hercules and Cerberus.*

demonstrating the presence of the soul in the human body. If so (as seems likely enough), this figure of Aristotle taken over by the Christians of the period would thus make a pair with that of Jesus, placed symmetrically in the same room.

Room N is decorated entirely with scenes from the myth of Hercules, and the choice of episodes proves that the mythological hero is evoked as a 'saviour' of men, with an emphasis on the belief in an after-life. Thus Hercules is represented leading Alcestis up from Hades, and Alcestis herself proposing to the doomed Admetus to die in his place.

But in most of the rooms, large and small, the picture cycles are entirely Christian; in them, indeed, the Christian faith is illustrated with a wealth of iconographic references which is unique of its kind. In the main this iconography is based on the salvation cycle from the Old and New Testaments—the same as that in the third-century catacombs. But here it is so much enriched by the addition of narrative scenes on Biblical subjects that the general purport of the cycle is modified. To take an example in Room B. In the vault we have the following scenes: the Flood, Absalom hanging by his hair, Samson and the lion; on the entrance wall: Phinehas (Aaron's grandson) slaying Zimri and the

228

252. *Rome. Catacomb of the Via Latina: Abraham's Sacrifice.*

253. *Rome. Catacomb of the Via Latina: Jacob's Dream of a Ladder reaching to Heaven.*

Midianitish woman Cozbi; in the right-hand arcosolium: Jacob's Ladder, the Vision of the three angels under the oak of Mamre, Jacob blessing Ephraim and Manasseh, Joseph's Dream, the Ascension of Elijah, Isaac's Meal, Balaam and the Angel. There are as many scenes again in the symmetrical arcosolium on the left, and still more on the tympanum at the back of the arcosolium. This will give some idea of the profusion of these narrative scenes and the variety of their subjects: there can be no doubt that they

230

254. *Rome. Catacomb of the Via Latina: Abraham entertaining the Three Angels under the Oak of Mamre.*

are straightforward evocations of the events depicted, some of which do not correspond to any case of a just man's deliverance. The existence has been suspected here of a more complex typology which had already been initiated by the Fathers of the Church at the time this catacomb was decorated but which (except for hints of it, first in the reliefs on the door of Santa Sabina, Rome, then in the choir mosaics of San Vitale, Ravenna) was not systematically adopted in art until the Middle Ages, chiefly in the West.

It is worth noting that there is an overwhelming majority of Old Testament scenes as against Gospel subjects. The same proportion obtains in the salvation cycles of the third century. The reason may lie in the Jewish origin of the Early Christian prayers for the dead. And the Via Latina frescoes prove that even after 350 Judaism, which of course revered only the books of the Old Testament, had lost none of its force. It is even possible that Roman painters could illustrate so many episodes from various books of the Old Testament because they had illustrated Hebrew Bibles to guide them.

255. *Rome.   Catacomb of the Via Latina: The Raising of Lazarus, detail.*

256. *Rome.   Catacomb of the Via Latina: The Raising of Lazarus.*

257. *Rome. Catacomb of the Via Latina: The Crossing of the Red Sea.*

Some of these subjects are treated here in a way found nowhere else. Such is the case with the wingless angels, the Flood scene (with God pouring down water from the top of a building), the Ascension of Elijah (with Elisha, wearing an *exomis*, with his yoke of oxen and a very large male personification), Abraham's vision of the three angels under the oak of Mamre, the Crossing of the Red Sea, the Raising of Lazarus. Here is an art which clearly had at its disposal an exceptionally rich thematic repertory and which but rarely found its way into the catacombs, its usual field of application being manuscript illuminations and decorations, all of which are now lost, in above-ground churches. The nave mosaics of Santa Maria Maggiore, made over half a century later, reveal here and there a similar inspiration, notably in the crowd scenes and in Abraham's vision of the three angels; when the difference of medium and later date are allowed for, the similarity is unmistakable. In the field of manuscript illumination, the tenth-century replicas in a Psalter (MS grec 139, Bibliothèque Nationale, Paris), based on Early Christian Greek originals, give a good idea of the fourth-century miniatures, which must have been quite as vivid and engaging as the scenes we can now admire in the Via Latina tomb, such as the Crossing of the Red Sea and the Raising of Lazarus.

258. *Rome. Catacomb of the Via Latina: Partial View of Room N.*

259. *Rome. Catacomb of the Via Latina: The Flood.*

260. *Rome. Catacomb of the Via Latina: Balaam and the Angel of the Lord standing in the Way.*

261. *Tabarka. Tomb Mosaic. Bardo Museum, Tunis.*

262. *Kelibia. Tomb Mosaic. Bardo Museum, Tunis.*

263. *Kelibia. Tomb Mosaic. Bardo Museum, Tunis.*

Mosaics on Individual Tombs

Excavations of Christian churches at Tarragona, Spain, and at Tabarka, at Uppenna, in the church of 'Priest Felix' near Kelibia and elsewhere in North Africa have revealed an Early Christian art form which seems to have been abandoned later on: mosaic coverings for individual tombs. These mosaics—which elsewhere and at other periods were replaced by tomb slabs—made their first appearance in the fourth century; and though, like most Early Christian art forms, they became even more popular in the following century, we have thought it more suitable to deal with them in this chapter, for a very definite reason.

These mosaics are virtually aniconic; such in any case are the oldest known examples of them. This reluctance to make use of images—understandable enough in the case of mosaics placed at ground level, or nearly so—probably reflects something of the initial attitude of the Christians towards figural imagery. Apart from the inscription, these mosaics represent simply a cross flanked by Alpha and Omega, floral motifs with birds evoking Paradise and a vase symbolizing its 'living waters' and the eternal freshness of its air. To the fourth century may perhaps also be assigned a mosaic slab, unique of its kind, from Tabarka in which the garden motifs are replaced by an architectural image: a basilica designated 'mother of churches' evokes the abode of believers in the after-life. But the believers themselves are not represented. The basilica is empty—unless the birds below the edifice may be taken to symbolize the congregation. If (as seems probable) this is so, we have here yet another example of the distaste for figural iconography in the—always extremely conservative—domain of sepulchral art.

265. *Sarcophagus of Curtia Catiana, detail: Portrait of a Child in a Medallion surrounded by Tritons. Museo di Pretestato, Rome.*

Sarcophagus Reliefs

Most of the Christian sarcophagi with decorations in relief undoubtedly date to the fourth century. There was still a mass production of them in Roman workshops which now were evidently more prolific than before the Peace of the Church. The same is true of the workshops in Provence, Spain and Africa, which generally followed Roman models. Carved sarcophagi were also made in Constantinople, probably in ateliers located near the white marble quarries of Proconnesus, an island in the Sea of Marmara.

We have already explained why any precise dating of the workshop reliefs on these sarcophagi seems impracticable. Exceptionally, a few of them can be dated by inscriptions naming the consuls of the year or alluding to contemporary events; and there are also several groups of sarcophagi which must have been made at different times.

Both the style of the sarcophagus of a child, Curtia Catiana (catacomb of Pretestato, Rome), and the presence on it of certain pagan motifs adapted to Christian usage assign it to the Constantinian epoch. One of these motifs is the journey oversea to the Islands of the Blest, to which the dead child (whose portrait figures in a medallion) is being conveyed by Nereids and Tritons.

239

264. *Sarcophagus of Junius Bassus, detail: Entry of Christ into Jerusalem. Grotte Vaticane, Vatican City.*

266. *Rome. Sarcophagus, detail: The Good Shepherd and a Female Musician. Museo Laterano, Rome.*

Sarcophagus 128 in the Lateran Museum belongs to the same period. The Good Shepherd and the herdsman of third-century sarcophagi reappear, but so do the winged genii of pagan art carrying baskets of fruit on either side of the dead man's portrait (in a rectangular frame resting on a pedestal, an arrangement anticipating that of icons), while female musicians evoke the harmony of the celestial spheres to which the dead man's soul is being transported. The composition is remarkable for its strict order and balanced rhythm, which differentiate this sculpture from third-century sarcophagus reliefs.

In the early fourth century it became the practice to decorate the front of the sarcophagus with a series of Old and New Testament scenes. Well before this, pagan sarcophagi had carried an unbroken succession of episodes or scenes. The Christians adapted this layout to the Biblical motifs now employed, most of which had been already used by the catacomb painters. It was a development of this schema that led at a later date to the arrangement in two superimposed zones of the same subjects (sometimes in larger numbers) on the front of a sarcophagus.

True, even in the third century small-scale scenes had been placed on the front at different levels. But at that time the whole frontal surface was treated as a single panel, whereas in the fourth century it was systematically divided into two separate horizontal registers, the only unifying element being the *imago clipeata* in the centre containing the half-length figure of the deceased.

240

267. *Rome. Sarcophagus: Portrait of the Deceased, Two Genii, Good Shepherd, Herdsman and Female Musicians. Museo Laterano, Rome.*

268. *Rome. Sarcophagus of Aurelius: Portrait of the Deceased, Jonah, Adoration of the Magi, Daniel, Adam and Eve, Healing of the Blind Man. Rome.*

A good example of the sarcophagus with a single frieze of juxtaposed scenes is that of young Aurelius in the cemetery of San Lorenzo fuori le Mura. Though a somewhat rustic work, it has artistic merits, notably in the rendering of the swaddled Child in the Virgin's arms, the anxious gaze of Eve and the distinctive lineaments of the dead youth.

241

D·VI·K·MAI·

269. *Rome. Sarcophagus, detail: Orant with Various Figures. Museo Laterano, Rome.*

Sarcophagus 161 in the Lateran Museum is similar but more expertly carved. The Orant occupies the centre of the front, on the right being scenes of Christ's miracles and on the left St Paul's arrest. As so often, the two scenes at the far ends of the front—Moses striking water from the rock and the Raising of Lazarus—form a matching pair. On the lid, another portrait is surrounded by hunting scenes (a pagan funerary theme taken over and 'converted' by the Christians). The style of the figures on the front of the sarcophagus is antiquizing, as on all the sarcophagi carved in high relief. The head

270. *Rome. Sarcophagus of the Two Brothers, detail: Portrait of the Dead Men. Museo Laterano, Rome.*

of the Orant, which has been left unfinished, reminds us that these workshop sarcophagi were generally prefabricated; only after they had been sold were the finishing touches added to the portraits.

The so-called Two Brothers sarcophagus from San Paolo fuori le Mura (Lateran Museum, No. 55) is an exceptionally fine work. It owes its name to the portraits of two men who look very much like each other (and also resemble St Paul) in the centre of the front, which combines signal examples of deliverance drawn from the Old and New Testaments with scenes of the Passion.

Framing the portraits, symmetrical figures of Moses and Abraham stand in front of the Hand of God, which delivers to Moses the Tables of the Law and stays Abraham's sword (sacrifice of Isaac). The gestures and movements of the small, elegantly draped figures have a rather studied dignity. Though this style is in the strict classical tradition, we find here, both in facial features and movements, an intensity of expression and a lofty seriousness which may well be of Christian inspiration.

243

271-272. *Rome. Sarcophagus of the Two Brothers: Old and New Testament Scenes, details. Museo Laterano, Rome.* ▶

A similar depth of feeling in the handling of classical forms can be sensed in another famous sarcophagus, that of Junius Bassus (Grotte Vaticane). (Bassus, Prefect of Rome, was, like Constantine, baptized on his deathbed.) The Two Brothers sarcophagus is probably slightly earlier than this magnificent work which, by rare good fortune (for we have only half a dozen dated sarcophagi of the mid-fourth century) bears the date 359. This naturally makes it a valuable piece of evidence. The inscription containing the date reminds us that Junius Bassus was a high Christian dignitary of the Empire and a former consul. After the sarcophagus and mosaics of Santa Costanza, works of imperial art, and the Calendar of 354, here is yet another example of the Christian art of Rome in the mid-fourth century, at its splendid best.

Following up other, less successful efforts in the same direction, the sculptor of the Junius Bassus sarcophagus (359) imposed a strict order on his reliefs. With this in mind he made use of structural elements such as columns, entablatures, arches and pediments. Each scene is set in an architectural frame, with an emphasis on the divisions between scenes (Christ is separated from Pilate by a column), somewhat in the manner of the pagan Sidamara sarcophagi of the second-third centuries, but with this difference: that whole scenes are located within each intercolumniation or tabernacle. Their placing reveals the same concern for orderly arrangement. In the centre of each register is Christ,

273. *Sarcophagus of Junius Bassus: Old and New Testament Scenes. Grotte Vaticane, Vatican City.*

274. *Sarcophagus of Junius Bassus, detail: Abraham's Sacrifice. Grotte Vaticane, Vatican City.*

275. *Sarcophagus of Junius Bassus, detail: The Arrest of Christ. Grotte Vaticane, Vatican City.*

enthroned or making his entry into Jerusalem, and the scenes on either side are set out symmetrically. On the upper register are two similar trimorphic groups (the arrest of Christ and that of St Peter); on the lower, two other matching groups. To ensure the symmetry of these two scenes, one of the Protoplasts in Eden, the other of Daniel in the lions' den, two unusual figures are added on either side of Daniel (that of the prophet no longer exists). The style of the figures—heads and bodies, drapery, attitudes— resembles that of the carvings on the Two Brothers sarcophagus; and there is the same high relief. Thus here again an addiction to classical forms is combined with relief carving that approximates to sculpture in the round.

Though the front of the sarcophagus is planned on new, more vigorous lines, the choice of images and the haphazardness of their arrangement remind us of earlier sarcophagi. However, instead of the customary scenes, two new ones were inserted in the middle of the composition. Both are christological and emphasize the royalty of Christ, drawing on motifs current in Roman Imperial art: the king enthroned with the cosmos at his feet (symbolizing worldwide sovereignty) and an *adventus*, the monarch's State entry into his city. These two new scenes were in the spirit of the new Christian *imperium* which Constantine had just founded and whose ruler was an earthly counterpart of the King of Heaven; conversely, the symbolic iconography of the emperors was transferred

248

to images of Christ. The first image of this nature—Christ enthroned between St Peter and St Paul—may have derived from an apse decoration in one of the Constantinian churches of Rome. This was imitated, but more markedly, on a ceiling in the catacomb of SS. Pietro e Marcellino. Here the Lamb, another image of Christ, but an allegorical one, is shown below Christ and the apostles. The sculptor of the Junius Bassus sarcophagus followed the curious practice of fourth-, fifth- and sixth-century Christian artists of reduplicating on the same object or the same wall images of Christ and the apostles. As in the apses, small allegorical scenes containing the Lamb and sheep were inserted in the spandrels of arches below the figure of Christ. This duplication was probably intended to remind the spectator of the Christian significance of the motifs represented; to provide against the possibility of his taking these allegorical images merely at their face value. (This practice, seen to be superfluous, was soon abandoned.)

Only a brief mention can be made of the so-called Bethesda group of sarcophagi on which reappear Christ's entry into Jerusalem and scenes framed in arcades. Less attractive than those on the Bassus sarcophagus, the Bethesda reliefs give more emphasis to the incidents in Christ's ministry, in the order in which they are described in the Gospels: the healing of the two blind men of Jericho, the miracle at Bethesda, the entry into Jerusalem. The grouping of the scenes is clearly purposeful and brings to mind the frescoes recently discovered in the Via Latina tomb.

But on the sarcophagi most representative of sculpture in Rome and throughout the West in the second half of the fourth century, the central theme is always that of the Junius Bassus sarcophagus: Christ in Majesty.

One of the finest (Lateran Museum 174) reproduces that scene in almost every detail; also several other scenes from the decorative colonnade of the Junius Bassus sarcophagus, but only those in the upper register. On the other hand the carvings extend over the two short sides which represent (in low relief as usual) Moses striking the rock, Christ healing the woman with an issue of blood and St Peter's denial. In the reliefs on the front we have

276. *Rome. Sarcophagus: Christ seated above a Personification of the Cosmos, with Old and New Testament Scenes. Museo Laterano, Rome.*

277. *Rome. Sarcophagus, detail. Museo Laterano, Rome.* ▶

279. *Rome. Sarcophagus, detail. Museo Laterano, Rome.*

the apogee of Christian classicism in Rome during the fourth century. As usual in such cases the style is somewhat stiff and lifeless—the classical elegance of heads and draperies seems overdone—but the high quality of the work is undeniable, and when we compare it with the uncouth reliefs on the Arch of Constantine, official though these are, we can gauge the progress that has been made.

The main figures in the scenes on the short sides of this sarcophagus stand out against an architectural background, possibly an evocation of the temples of Jerusalem. While this identification must remain an open question, these two reliefs deserve to be better known as precursors of medieval art. They anticipate it most markedly in the artist's evident uncertainty as to the rendering of space; all the figures are located in a space that is not only ill-defined but sometimes almost non-existent. The first man drinking at the spring tapped by Moses, the woman with an issue of blood, the column with the cock in the scene of St Peter's denial—all rest directly on the lower frame of the panel and each figure has only a tiny patch of ground to stand on. The very small size of the buildings, however, suggests a certain distance between them and the figures in the foreground, who look gigantic, backed as they are by Lilliputian churches. Even so, the composition as a whole is, in its way, harmonious and well-balanced.

252   280. *Rome. Sarcophagus, detail: Moses striking Water from the Rock. Museo Laterano, Rome.* ▶

◀ 278. *Rome. Sarcophagus, detail: The Judgment of Pilate. Museo Laterano, Rome.*

281. *Rome. Sarcophagus of Probus, detail: Two Apostles. Grotte Vaticane, Vatican City.*

On other sarcophagi of the same type Christ is represented standing, with his right arm uplifted and holding in his left the scroll of the Law, which he is delivering to St Peter (Sarcophagus of Probus, Vatican; Sant'Ambrogio, Milan; Verona). St Peter or Christ himself holds up the Cross, like a sceptre or trophy, while the apostles in a row acclaim their victorious Lord. The setting is either the heavenly Jerusalem or an arcaded portico. Possibly apse mosaics in St Peter's or elsewhere supplied the sculptors with this theme, clearly of imperial inspiration.

282. *Italy. Sarcophagus, detail: Daniel in the Lions' Den. San Giovanni in Valle, Verona.*

283. *Italy. Sarcophagus: Christ delivering the Law, with Various Scenes. San Giovanni in Valle, Verona.*

285. *Rome. Sarcophagus of Probus, detail: Christ delivering the Law. Grotte Vaticane, Vatican City.*

284. *Italy. Sarcophagus, detail: Christ delivering the Law, with the Two Deceased at his Feet. Cathedral of Saint-Sauveur, Aix-en-Provence.*

287. *Sarcophagus of the Good Shepherd. Museo Laterano, Rome.*

288. *Sarcophagus of the Good Shepherd, detail of one end: Vintaging Cupids. Museo Laterano, Rome.* 259

286. *Sarcophagus of the Good Shepherd, detail: The Good Shepherd. Museo Laterano, Rome.*

290. *Sarcophagus, detail: Christ delivering the Law, with the Apostles. Sant'Ambrogio, Milan.*

◀ 289. *Sarcophagus of the Good Shepherd, detail: Vintaging Cupids. Museo Laterano, Rome.*

291. *Sarcophagus, detail: Ascension of Elijah, Adam and Eve. Sant'Ambrogio, Milan.*

293. *Sarcophagus: Standing Christ delivering the Law in the presence of the Apostles. Sant'Ambrogio, Milan.* ▶

292. *Sarcophagus, detail: Portraits of the Deceased ('Imago clipeata'). Sant'Ambrogio, Milan.*

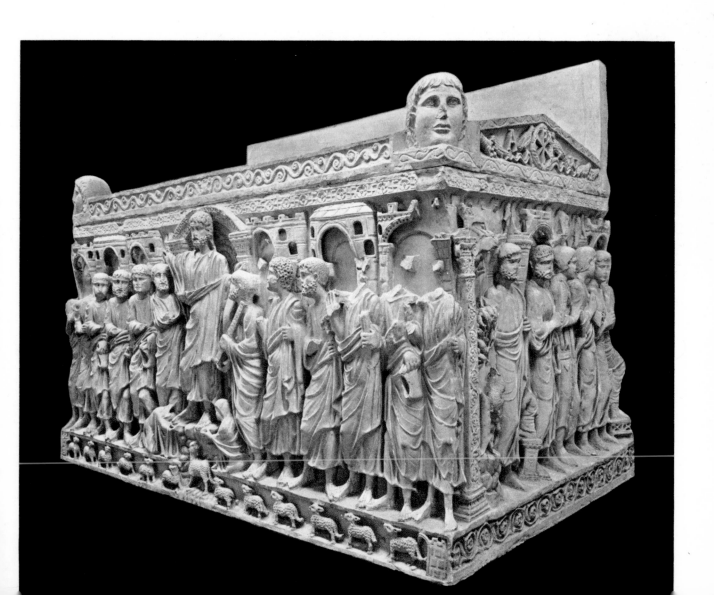

295. *Rome. Sarcophagus, detail: Symbolic Image of the Resurrection, Passion Scenes. Museo Laterano, Rome.*

296. *Rome. Sarcophagus: Passion Scenes. Museo Laterano, Rome.*

Of similar inspiration is another outstanding group of sarcophagi known by reason of their theme as the Passion sarcophagi, the Passion scenes being represented alone or with others relating to Peter and Paul. The setting usually consists of columns or tabernacles, but sometimes of a line of trees with their branches forming natural arches above the figures.

Both aesthetically and iconographically these reliefs are dominated by a symbol of the Resurrection (Arles, Lateran Museum 171, etc.): a cross surmounted by the monogram of Christ in a medallion flanked by two doves and two soldiers. The Roman guards of Christ's sepulchre are either keeping watch on it or sleeping at the foot of the cross. What we have here is a Christian derivative of the monumental Roman trophy, symbol of victory.

265

◀ 294. *Sarcophagus, detail: Monogram and Symbols, Sacrifice of Abraham, Four Figures. Sant'Ambrogio, Milan.*

297. *Rome. Sarcophagus, Passion Scenes, detail: The Judgment of Pilate. Museo Laterano, Rome.*

The unfinished sarcophagus (mid-fourth century) in San Sebastiano, Rome, was the work of a highly gifted sculptor with a feeling for plastic form and the beauty of classical Greek art. He did not hesitate, however, to juxtapose iconographic images of different origin, at times incongruous, in the five niches on the front. Thus Christ delivering the Law, in the centre, is given the face of an ancient Greek philosopher (with flowing hair and beard), while the Christ arraigned before Pilate is a young hero whom the Roman soldiers dare not touch. Judge and prisoner avoid looking at each other—nothing could better convey the 'apartness' of the leading figures in this scene. We

266

298. *Sarcophagus, detail: St Peter led out to Execution. San Sebastiano, Rome.*

may note another unusual iconographic detail in the decoration of this sarcophagus; on the left of Christ delivering the Law we see St Peter being led away to execution and the beheading of St Paul. The peculiarity here is that Christ gives his benediction to a St Peter who is going to his death.

Among the sarcophagi with triumphal themes which, originating in Rome, were imitated in Provence and Spain are some outstanding works of art; for example the one now used as the support of the ambo in Sant'Ambrogio, Milan. The reliefs of most aesthetic interest, in my opinion, are those which diverge most widely from the classical

299. *Sarcophagus with Passion Scenes, detail: The Arrest of St Peter. Musée Lapidaire, Avignon.*

norm and indicate a change of taste pointing the way to medieval art. Thus on the sarcophagus of Probus in St Peter's all the apostles, placed in a row, are making the same gestures and given the same attitudes. The figures are so disposed as to fill exactly the gaps between the columns, their forms being suitably adjusted (the bodies forming rectangles of varying width) or their proportions modified (e.g. the elongated figure of St Paul). The row of standing apostles clad in togas forms an apparently continuous, slightly undulating surface. This relief is a precursor of the Romanesque lintels, and the similarity of the theme—Christ and the apostles—heightens the resemblance. Certain works of the intervening period, such as the Aquitanian sarcophagi of the fifth and sixth centuries, on which the same themes appear, bridge the gap of time; though they differ in details, their sculptors faced and solved the same aesthetic problems. We exclude from this survey of fourth-century art the sarcophagi of Constantinople since, though quite possibly some of them are datable to the end of the fourth century, they can be studied best in the context of fifth-century art and in relation to the sarcophagi of Ravenna and Aquitaine.

The domain in which the triumph of Christianity is most conspicuous—if in a nega-

300. *Rome. Young Christ, detail. Museo delle Terme, Rome.*

tive sense—is that of sculpture in the round and, in particular, statuary. The new faith dealt the death blow to this form of art, hitherto preponderant throughout the Roman Empire. No written records explain the reason for its abandonment, which was, however, so general and so abrupt that there must have been some sort of prohibition, probably an unwritten one. This absence of any canonical ban may account for such exceptions as the silver *imagines* of Christ, the apostles and angels which Constantine set up on the entablature of a *tugurium* in the choir of St Peter's; also the two large seated statues traditionally ascribed to the fourth century and said to represent St Peter and St Hippolytus (the former is in St Peter's).

The fact of there being no official rule against statuary permitted the making of occasional statuettes of Christ such as the one in white marble of a young seated Christ (Museo delle Terme, Rome). This is an elegant, well-conceived piece of sculpture in the classical spirit, but it lacks vigour and in fact seems hardly worthy of its subject.

More genuinely Christian feeling can be seen in some of the Good Shepherd statuettes made in Rome and Constantinople, and above all perhaps in the small, more naive and rustic (and more poetic) statues most of which were probably used as supports

269

301. *The Good Shepherd. Louvre, Paris.*

302. *Young Christ. Museo delle Terme, Rome.*

for church furniture, but whose specific function has never been precisely determined.

During the fourth century the influence of Christianity spread to the industrial arts; this extension of its influence paralleled the rise in the social status of the Christian community. We have in mind techniques and categories of objects in current use in Rome and throughout the Empire, typified by the illuminated Calendar of 354 and the silver bridal casket of Projecta. These works show that well-to-do Christians of a certain standing in the social hierarchy of Rome were able to employ the most proficient craftsmen in the capital. But in cases of this kind the fact, vouched for by texts and inscriptions, that the persons who commissioned these works were Christians was not given any prominence, or even hinted at, in the works themselves. These are simply

270

303. *Greece. The Good Shepherd. Byzantine Museum, Athens.*

304. *North Italy. Reliquary Casket ('Lipsanotheca'). Museo dell'Età Cristiana, Brescia.*

de-luxe objects made for Christians, but with nothing specifically Christian about them. There are, however, other works whose Christian nature is unmistakable and though the great majority are semi-industrial products, and have little artistic merit, there are also brilliant exceptions.

Among the ivory carvings pride of place must be given to the box in the Museo dell'Età Cristiana at Brescia, usually described as a 'lipsanotheca,' i.e. a reliquary casket. It is an ivory box with a flat lid, entirely covered with elegant, finely executed reliefs representing Old and New Testament scenes. Themes regarded as of prime importance are treated on a larger scale and figure in the centre of the vertical sides of the box, also on the central part of the lid. Above and below the main scenes are secondary images;

272

305-306-307. *North Italy. Reliquary Casket ('Lipsanotheca'), details. Museo dell'Età Cristiana, Brescia.* ▶

those above representing themes from the New Testament, the others from the Old. Along the edge of the lid are medallions containing 'portraits' of Christ and the apostles.

For various and on the whole convincing reasons, the Brescia casket may be dated to the second third of the fourth century and (though this is much less certain) assigned to a Milanese workshop. In its iconography—the choice of subjects, the presence of unusual Biblical scenes—this casket has a certain kinship with Roman sarcophagi and the wall paintings of the Via Latina tomb. Here too we sense the presence of iconographic models and perhaps of Christian ideas drawn from Jewish sources. On the other hand, the Brescia craftsman keeps to a strictly classical tradition, so much so that we are reminded of ivories of the same period commissioned by members of the Roman senatorial opposition who disapproved of the christianizing policy of the emperors. Particularly striking are the heads of the apostles which, though they have the air of portraits, are actually versions of classical heads—a fact that belies the widespread notion that all the bearded men in Early Christian art are Orientals. Everywhere Christ is given the features of a classical ephebus; which shows that in Christian ideology God incarnate was envisaged as an 'ideal man' and that these artists, trained on classical lines, pictured the 'ideal man' as a youth of perfect beauty. There could scarcely be a more perfect realization of this ideal than on the Brescia casket. But the ivory-carver goes beyond the time-honoured formula and gives the face of Jesus a grave serenity.

The decline of the classical ideal, especially in the outlying provinces of the Empire, put an end to this way of interpreting a Christian ideal. Evidently there was some doubt as to whether a young, beardless face rendered to best advantage the concept of Man made perfect. Might it not be better expressed by a face whose features were of a distinctive ethnic type? The fact remains that already at the close of Antiquity the beardless Christ had become a symbol of the Logos, irrespective of the Incarnation, and His ideal youthfulness signified that He existed outside Time and that age could not affect His physical appearance.

The ivory diptych in the Bargello at Florence is similarly inspired. On one side is Adam in the Garden of Eden before the Fall, when the animals lived at peace among themselves and with him. Like the Christ of the Brescia casket, Adam, the perfect man, has the body of a handsome youth. On the other leaf of the diptych are episodes of a subject rarely illustrated: St Paul's sojourn on Malta. The apostle and his disciples have the grave demeanour of philosophers and in striking contrast to them are the islanders, represented with surprising realism (notably the emaciated sick man and the paralysed arm of another man led to Paul for healing).

Along with the ivories, the bronze lamps bearing Christian symbols call for mention. Excellent examples of these can be seen in all the great museums. They are finely executed, of various shapes, and, except for the chrism, the cross or some other Christian symbol, conform in every detail to the classical type, not omitting the dragon-head handles. We only slightly exceed the chronological limits of this volume when we associate with these fourth-century lamps the few instances, a little later in date, of lamps in the form of a boat with small figures in it—Christ, St Peter, the disciples. A sail is set and bellies in the wind. Here the symbolism is simple and convincing: the ship of the Church weathers

274

309. *North Africa. Cup: Two Apostles with Nets; Holy Sepulchre. Bardo Museum, Tunis.*

the storms of life and brings the Christian safe to port. The reliefs on earthenware lamps, if of a humbler order, are similarly inspired.

Fine glassware was produced all over the Empire and many factories in Italy, Cologne, on the Phoenician coast and in Africa catered for the Christian community. There was a special demand for drinking cups and goblets whose bases were adorned with images executed in goldleaf mounted between two layers of glass fused together. These were usually portraits of the owners, inscribed with their names and wishes for good health. This technique, current in Antiquity, was taken over by the Christians who, however, added to the portraits (or replaced them by) images of Christ, the apostles or other religious motifs. Many specimens of these, too, have survived, and some are unquestionably of high artistic merit. A striking instance is the bowl in the Cologne Museum, the bottom of which is adorned with medallions of different sizes. Some contain busts which have been identified as portraits of Constantine's sons; others are adorned with scenes of 'deliverances' similar to those figuring in Early Christian sarcophagus reliefs and also on the walls of catacombs.

276

310. *Rome. Two Figures. Museo Sacro, Vatican City.*

Lastly, there is a group of beautifully engraved glass vessels, many of them decorated with Christian themes. The finest example was found at Carthage and is now in the local Bardo Museum. The apostles Peter and Andrew are portrayed on it as fishermen, one holding a fishing-line, the other nets. This handsome work is of particular interest as illustrating the persistence of the classical tradition; here the Christians did not only keep to the time-honoured form of this type of vessel and the technique of deep, finely modulated incision, but also retained the ancient iconography. The two near-nude figures and their gestures are exactly like those of the many Roman images of fishermen whose type forms had long been established. Apart from the inscription of the apostles' names, only the motif of two crossed fishes placed on stones was a distinctively Christian element. This motif was in keeping with the general theme and lent itself to interpretation as a symbol of the Eucharistic meal. Here we have a revealing instance of the way the Christian artists proceeded when soon after the Peace of the Church they progressively extended the use of Christian themes to the industrial and sumptuary arts.

Conclusion

(icon   know)

We have seen how, with a surprising time-lag as regards the birth of the Christian religion, there arose an art of truly Christian inspiration. This first Christian art was of a highly discreet nature, especially in the period before the edicts of toleration of the early fourth century, a fact all the more remarkable in view of the spectacular developments in store for the arts inspired by Christianity.

We have studied a number of works and monuments, their religious programme, their iconography and the various forms employed in this very early period for the expression of Christian themes and as ancillary to the celebration of the appointed rites. The functions of this art were strictly limited and the place it occupied among the artistic achievements of the period within the Roman Empire was a modest one, as modest indeed as was the social status of those who utilized it. To begin with, the edicts of toleration did little to modify this state of affairs, less perhaps than might have been expected. The only considerable change took place in the domain of church architecture and its adornment, a change personally promoted by Constantine the Great, founder of the Christian Empire.

After covering the reigns of Constantine and his successors, this volume ends on the eve of the reign of Theodosius I, in the last third of the fourth century. For it was then that, with Christianity established as the State religion of the entire Roman Empire, a new phase in the history of Christian art began. The next volume in this series will be devoted to the great Christian art of Antiquity. Originating in the reign of Theodosius I and spanning the golden age of Justinian, this art flourished until the rise of Islam and the Arab invasions.

The first Christian art has bequeathed to us fewer masterpieces than works often of a touching quality, the first naive stirrings of an art destined to a glorious future. Here we have a phenomenon rarely to be observed: that of a new religion serving its apprenticeship in a domain hitherto outside its ken. As we have pointed out, everything goes to show that the interest in pictorial art began among the Christian lay community, not at the level of the clergy. On the other hand, we find that, from the third century onward, there is an evident kinship between the works of art made in widely separated parts of the Empire and this unification may well have been encouraged, perhaps enjoined, by the superior clergy.

Yet, though a certain unity of programme and iconography existed as early as the third century, the forms current in the Christian pictorial arts tended already to vary from place to place. Attention has been drawn to this in our account of the paintings and mosaics of Syria-Mesopotamia, Antioch, Sicily and Rome. The chief regions of the Empire seem to have given different inflexions to their respective styles, while ostensibly conforming to the classical tradition.

As regards the subsequent course of the Christian arts, so far as taste and style are concerned these are marked by a cleavage between three great regional families of works of art (a divergence that became still more pronounced in the Middle Ages): those of the Levant and Transcaucasia, those of the Greeks, and those of the Latin races. Only the Greeks, henceforth Byzantines, retained the graceful, noble style of the Hellenistic prototypes. The others, especially the Latins, aimed chiefly at expression and a resolutely concrete way of seeing. The works dealt with in this volume show something of the underlying origins of the clear-cut aesthetic differences that developed between the arts of the East and the West during the Middle Ages.

Documents

On the following pages, in English translation, are a number of Greek and Latin texts dating to the period with which this volume is concerned. They are witness-accounts, written by contemporaries, of Early Christian works of art and those who brought them into existence or made use of them.

These documents do not pretend to completeness; they are but a selection of extrasct which have seemed to us particularly suggestive. Some describe the early churches; others evoke the setting in which the first Christian art was created, and help us to understand the aesthetic which, beginning in Late Antiquity to supersede the classical aesthetic, came to maturity in the art of the Middle Ages.

We cite first of all the texts relating to architecture, then those concerned with images, and finally some extracts of a more general character: considerations on vision and the work of art, and, an account of a pilgrimage to Jerusalem.

I. ARCHITECTURE

The Christian churches of Golgotha, at Jerusalem, founded by Constantine.

Book III, Ch. 25. - After these things, the pious emperor addressed himself to another work truly worthy of record, in the province of Palestine... He judged it incumbent on him to render the blessed locality of our Saviour's resurrection an object of attraction and veneration to all. He issued immediate injunctions, therefore, for the erection in that spot of a house of prayer... Ch. 26. - For it had been in time past the endeavour of impious men... to consign to the darkness of oblivion that divine monument of immortality... This sacred cave, then, certain impious and godless persons had thought to remove entirely from the eyes of men... Accordingly they brought a quantity of earth from a distance with much labour, and covered the entire spot; then, having raised this to a moderate height, they paved it with stone, concealing the holy cave beneath this massive mound. Then... they prepared on this foundation a truly dreadful sepulchre of souls, by building a gloomy shrine of lifeless idols to the impure spirit whom they call Venus... Nevertheless, these devices of impious and wicked men against the truth had prevailed for a long time... But calling on the divine aid, [the emperor] gave orders that the place should be thoroughly purified... As soon, then, as his commands were issued, these engines of deceit were cast down from their proud eminence to the very ground, and the dwelling-places of error, with the statues and the evil spirits which they represented, were overthrown and utterly destroyed. Ch. 27. - [The emperor] gave further orders that the materials of what was thus destroyed, both stone and timber, should be removed and thrown as far from the spot as possible... The emperor... directed that the ground itself should be dug up to a considerable depth, and the soil which had been polluted by the foul impurities of demon worship transported to a far distant place. Ch. 28. - ...

But as soon as the original surface of the ground beneath the covering of earth, appeared, immediately and contrary to all expectation, the venerable and hallowed monument of our Saviour's resurrection was discovered. Then indeed did this most holy cave present a faithful similitude of his return to life... Ch. 29. - Immediately after the transactions I have recorded, the emperor sent forth injunctions... commanding that a house of prayer worthy of the worship of God should be erected near the Saviour's tomb on a scale of rich and royal greatness... He laid his commands, therefore, on the [Roman] governors of the Eastern provinces, that by an abundant and unsparing expenditure they should secure the completion of the work on a scale of noble and ample magnificence. He also despatched the following letter to the bishop... writing in these terms. Ch. 30. - 'Victor Constantius... to Macarius... I have no greater care than how I may best adorn with a splendid structure that sacred spot, which, under Divine direction, I have disencumbered as it were of the heavy weight of foul idol worship...' Ch. 31. - 'It will be well, therefore, for your sagacity to make such arrangements and provision of all things needful for the work, that not only the church itself as a whole may surpass all others whatsoever in beauty, but that the details of the building may be of such a kind that the fairest structures in any city of the empire may be excelled by this. And with respect to the erection and decoration of the walls, this is to inform you that our friend Dracilianus, the deputy of the Praetorian Praefects, and the governor of the province, have received a charge from us. For our pious directions to them are to the effect that artificers and labourers, and whatever they shall understand from your sagacity to be needful for the advancement of the work, shall forthwith be furnished by their care. And as to the columns and marbles, whatever you shall judge, after actual inspection of the plan, to be especially precious and serviceable, be diligent to send information to us in writing, in order that whatever quantity or sort of materials we shall esteem from your letter to be needful, may be procured from every quarter, as required...'

Ch. 32. - 'With respect to the ceiling of the church, I wish to know from you whether in your judgment it should be panel-ceiled, or finished with any other kind of workmanship. If the panel ceiling be adopted, it may also be ornamented with gold...'

Ch. 33. - Accordingly, on the very spot which witnessed the Saviour's sufferings, a new Jerusalem was constructed, over against the one so celebrated of old, which... had experienced the last extremity of desolation, the effect of Divine judgment on its impious people... Ch. 34. - This monument, therefore, first of all, as the chief part of the whole, the emperor's zealous magnificence beautified with rare columns, and profusely enriched with the most splendid decorations of every kind. Ch. 35. - The next object of his attention was a space of ground of great extent, and open to the pure air of heaven. This he adorned with a pavement of finely polished stone, and enclosed it on three sides with porticos of great length. Ch. 36. - For at the side opposite to the cave, which was the eastern side, the church itself was erected; a noble work rising to a vast height and of great extent both in length and breadth. The interior of this structure was floored with marble slabs of various colours; while the external surface of the walls, which shone with polished stones exactly fitted together, exhibited a degree of splendour in no respect inferior to that of marble. With regard to the roof, it was covered on the outside with lead, as a protection against the rains of winter. But the inner part of the roof, which was finished with sculptured panel work, extended in a series of connected compartments, like a vast sea, over the whole church; and, being overlaid throughout with the purest gold, caused the entire building to glitter as it were with rays of light. Ch. 37. - Besides this were two porticos on each side, with upper and lower ranges of pillars, corresponding in length with the church itself; and these also had their roofs ornamented with gold. Of these porticos, those which were exterior to the church were supported by columns of great size, while those within these rested on piles of stone beautifully adorned on the surface. Three gates, placed exactly east, were intended to receive the multitudes who entered the church. Ch. 38. - Opposite these gates the crowning part of the whole was the hemisphere, which rose to the very summit of the church. This was encircled by twelve columns (according to the number of the apostles of our Saviour), having their capitals embellished with silver bowls of great size... Ch. 39. - In the next place he enclosed the atrium, which occupied the space leading to the entrances in front of the church. This comprehended, first the court, then the porticos on each side, and lastly the gates of the court. After these, in the midst of the open market-place, the general entrance-gates, which were of exquisite workmanship, afforded to passers-by on the outside a view of the interior which could not fail to inspire astonishment.

EUSEBIUS, *Life of Constantine*, Book III, chapters 25-39. English translation by E.C. Richardson in *A Select Library of Nicene and Post-Nicene Fathers of the Christian Church*, edited by H. Wace and P. Schaff, Parker & Co., Oxford, and The Christian Literature Co., New York, 1890.

Church of the Nativity at Bethlehem founded by St Helena.

Book III, Ch. 41. - In the same country [Constantine] discovered other places, venerable as being the localities of two sacred caves: and these also he adorned with lavish magnificence. In the one case, he rendered due honour to that which had been the scene of the first manifestation of our Saviour's divine presence, when he submitted to be born in mortal flesh; while in the case of the second cavern he hallowed the remembrance of his ascension to heaven from the mountain top. And while he thus nobly testified his reverence for these places, he at the same time eternized the memory of his mother, who had been the instrument of conferring so valuable a benefit on mankind. Ch. 43. - [Helena] dedicated two churches to the God whom she adored, one at the grotto which had been the scene of the Saviour's birth; the other on the mount of his ascension... And farther, the mother of the emperor raised a stately structure on the Mount of Olives also, in memory of his ascent to heaven who is the Saviour of mankind, erecting a sacred church and temple on the very summit of the mount... Thus did Helena Augusta, the pious mother of a pious emperor, erect over the two mystic caverns these two noble and beautiful monuments of devotion, worthy of everlasting remembrance, to the honour of God her Saviour, and as proofs of her holy zeal, receiving from her son the aid of his imperial power...

Oration of Eusebius Pamphili in praise of the Emperor Constantine, Ch. 9. - In the same country he discovered three places venerable as the localities of three sacred caves; and these also he adorned with costly structures, paying a fitting tribute of reverence to the scene of the first manifestation of the Saviour's presence; while at the second cavern he hallowed the remembrance of his final ascension from the mountain top; and celebrated his mighty conflict, and the victory which crowned it, at the third. All these places our emperor thus adorned in the hope of proclaiming the symbol of redemption to all mankind [that is, the Cross].

EUSEBIUS, *Life of Constantine*, Book III, chapters 41 and 43, and Oration, chapter 9. English translation by E.C. Richardson in *A Select Library of Nicene and Post-Nicene Fathers of the Christian Church*, edited by

H. Wace and P. Schaff, Parker & Co., Oxford, and The Christian Literature Co., New York, 1890.

A Church at Tyre (Phoenicia) rebuilt
early in the reign of Constantine (c. 316-319).

The following extracts are from a festival oration addressed by Eusebius, Bishop of Caesarea in Palestine, to Paulinus, Bishop of Tyre, who had just finished rebuilding his cathedral church after the havoc wrought by the last persecutors of the Christians.

This oration is a good example of the Christian rhetoric in vogue at the time of the triumph of the Church; and it illustrates the method employed by orators (which has its counterparts in the Christian iconography of this period), who evoke at the same time a real church and an ideal architecture which it symbolizes—that of the City or Temple of Heaven.

And so we may raise our voices in a... hymn of victory and cry aloud: 'As we have heard, so also we have seen in the city of the Lord of Hosts, in the city of our God.' And in what city but this new-made city built by God? It is the Church of the Living God, the pillar and basis of truth, and of it another inspired saying joyously declares: 'Glorious things have been spoken of thee, O city of God.' And since in this city God the All-Gracious has brought us together through the grace of His Only-begotten, let each of the invited guests sing, nay shout, 'I was glad when they said to me, "Into the house of the Lord we will go"' and 'Lord, I have loved the beauty of Thy house, and the dwelling-place of Thy glory.'

...Accordingly, the whole area that he took in [for the church] was much larger [than before], and he gave the outer enclosure the protection of a wall surrounding the whole, to provide the maximum safety for the entire structure. Then he opened up a gateway, wide and towering high, to receive the rays of the rising sun, thus providing even those who stood outside the sacred precincts with an unlimited view of the interior, and as it were turning the eyes even of strangers to the Faith towards the first entrances, so that no one should hurry past without being profoundly moved by the thought of the former desolation and the miraculous transformation now: he hoped that perhaps emotion at the mere sight would turn people and propel them towards the entrance.

He does not permit a man who has passed inside the gates to go at once with unhallowed and unwashed feet into the holy places within; he has left a very wide space between the church proper and the first entrances, adorning it all round with four colonnades at right angles, so that the outer walls turn the site into a quadrangle and pillars rise on every side. The space between these he has filled with wooden screens of trellis work to a proportionate height. In the middle he left a clear space where the sky can be seen, so that the air is bright and open to the sun's rays. There he placed symbols of sacred purifications, constructing fountains exactly in front of the cathedral: these with their ample flow of fresh water enable those who are proceeding towards the centre of the sacred precincts to purify themselves. For all who enter, this is the first stopping-place, lending beauty and splendour to the whole and at the same time providing those still in need of elementary instruction with the station they require.

Passing beyond this wonderful sight, he opened passages to the cathedral through still more numerous gateways inside the court. In the full blaze of the sun once more, he sited three gates on one side: the centre one he dignified with height and breadth far exceeding those of the outside pair, and by providing bronze plates bound with iron, and elaborate reliefs, he gave it breathtaking loveliness, so that it looks like a queen between two humble bodyguards. In the same way he determined the number of the gateways to the colonnades along both sides of the whole edifice: over the colonnades, to admit still more light, he designed separate openings into the buildings; and these he ornamented elaborately with exquisite wood-carvings.

The basilica itself he built solidly of still richer materials in abundance, never for a moment counting the cost. This is not, I think, the time to state the precise measurements of the building, or to describe in full its dazzling beauty, the incredible vastness, the brilliant appearance of the workmanship, the towering walls that reach for the sky, and the costly cedars of Lebanon that form the ceiling. Even about them the inspired word has something to tell us. 'The trees of the Lord shall be glad, the cedars of Lebanon which He planted.'

I need not go into details now about the perfection of the overall design and the superlative beauty of the individual parts, for the evidence of our eyes makes instruction through the ears unnecessary. But I will say this: after completing the great building I have described, he furnished it with thrones high up, to accord with the dignity of the prelates, and also with benches arranged conveniently throughout. In addition to all this, he placed in the middle the Holy of Holies—the altar—excluding the general public from this part too by surrounding it with wooden trellis-work wrought by the craftsmen with exquisite artistry, a marvellous sight for all who see it.

Not even the floor was overlooked by him. This he made bright with marble laid in wonderful patterns, going on next to the outside of the building, where he constructed halls and chambers along both sides on a great scale, skilfully uniting them with the fabric of the basilica so that they share the openings that let light into the central building. These, too, were provided for those still in need of cleansing and sprinkling with water and the Holy Ghost, and were the work of our most peaceful Solomon, who built the temple of God, so that the prophecy I quoted earlier is no longer mere words but plain fact...

Building truly in righteousness, he equitably divided the whole people in accordance with their powers. With some, he walled round the outer enclosure—that was enough for them—making unwavering faith the protective barrier. This accounted for far the greater part of the people, who were not strong enough to support a greater edifice. To some he entrusted the entrances to the church proper, giving them the task of waiting at the doors to guide those entering, since he justifiably regarded them as gateways to the house of God. Others he made under-props to the first outer pillars that form a quadrangle round the court, bringing them for the first time into touch with the letter of the four gospels. Others he joined to the basilica along both sides, still under instruction and in process of advancing, but not very far removed from the divine vision that the faithful enjoy of what is innermost. From these last he chooses the undefiled souls, purified like gold by divine washing; these he makes under-props to pillars much grander than the outer ones, drawing on the innermost mystic teaching of Holy Writ, while others he illumines with openings towards the light. With one huge gateway, consisting of the praise of our Sovereign Lord, the one only God, he adorns the whole cathedral; and on both sides of the Father's supreme power he supplies the secondary beams of the light of Christ, and the Holy Ghost. As to the rest, from end to end of the building he reveals in all its abundance and rich variety the clear light of the truth in every man, and everywhere and from every source he has found room for the living, securely-laid, and unshakable stones of human souls. In this way he is constructing out of them all a great and kingly house, glowing and full of light within and without, in that not only their heart and mind, but their body too, has been gloriously enriched with the many-blossomed adornment of chastity and temperance.

There are also in this shrine thrones and an infinite number of benches and seats, all the souls, on which rest the Holy Spirit's gifts, just as in olden time they appeared to the holy apostles, and others with them, to whom were revealed dividing tongues like flames of fire, fire which rested on each one of them. In the ruler of them all we may say that the entire Christ Himself has found a resting-place, and in those who take second place to him proportionately, according to each man's capacity to receive the power of Christ and the Holy Spirit divided among them. The souls of some might be benches for the angels assigned to each man with a view to his instruction and protection. As to the solemn, great, and unique altar, what could it be if not the spotless Holy of Holies of the common Priest of them all—His soul? Standing beside it on the right-hand side, the great High Priest of the universe, Jesus Himself, the only begotten of God, receives with shining eyes and upturned hands the sweet-smelling incense of all the worshippers, and the bloodless and immaterial prayer-sacrifices, and transmits them to the Father in heaven, the God of the universe. He Himself first adores the Father, and alone renders Him the honour due; then He beseeches Him to continue favourable and propitious towards us for ever.

Such is the great cathedral which throughout the whole world under the sun the great Creator of the universe, the Word, has built, Himself again fashioning this spiritual image on earth of the vaults beyond the skies, so that by the whole creation and by rational beings on earth His Father might be honoured and worshipped. As for the realm above the skies and the patterns there of things here on earth, the Jerusalem above, as it is called, the heavenly Mount Zion and the celestial city of the Living God, in which countless hosts of assembled angels and the church of the first-born enrolled in heaven give glory with praises beyond our utterance or understanding to their Maker, the supreme Ruler of the universe—these things no mortal can worthily hymn; for indeed eye has not seen and ear has not heard, and into the heart of man there have not entered, these very things which God has prepared for those that love Him...

EUSEBIUS, *The History of the Church from Christ to Constantine*, Book 10, chapter 4, translated by G.A. Williamson, Penguin Books, Harmondsworth, 1965, by kind permission of the publishers.

A Church erected at Gaza in Palestine after the Destruction of a Pagan Temple, in the early fifth century.

Now when the Marneion [pagan temple at Gaza, Palestine] was wholly burned, and the city was set in order, the blessed bishop [Porphyry] took counsel with the holy clergy and the Christ-loving lay-folk, to found a holy church in the place that was burned, as it had been revealed unto him when he was in Constantinople; for which reason also he received the money from the Empress Eudoxia [wife of the Emperor Arcadius and mother of Theodosius II], most beloved of God... Some then counselled that it should be built after the fashion of the temple of the idol; for the shape of it was sound, being set about with two porticos, one within the other; but the midst of it was a dome spread out and stretching up on high; and it had also other things becoming unto idols... After this fashion, then, some said that the holy church should be built, but others said the contrary, saying that the very remembrance of the fashion thereof should be destroyed...

When, therefore, the ashes were carried away and

all the abominations were destroyed, the rubbish that remained of the marble work of the Marneion, which they said was sacred, and in a place not to be entered, especially by women, this did the holy bishop resolve to lay down for a pavement before the temple outside in the street, that it might be trodden under foot not only of men, but also of women and dogs and swine and beasts. And this grieved the idolaters more than the burning of the temple...

MARK THE DEACON, *The Life of Porphyry, Bishop of Gaza*, chapters 75 and 76, translated by G.F. Hill, Clarendon Press, Oxford, 1913.

The Basilica of St Peter's in Rome in the sixth century.

The apostle St Peter was buried in the church called from ancient times the Vatican. This church stands on four rows of admirable columns, ninety-six in number; at the altar are four more, which makes a hundred in all, not including the ones which carry the canopy of the baldachin [ciborium] beneath which is the tomb. This tomb, placed under the altar, is of the rarest workmanship. He who wishes to address a prayer to it opens the grating enclosing it, approaches the sepulchre and, passing his head through a small window in it, prays for the thing he desires. At once his prayers are answered, only provided they be righteous... Many of the faithful bring golden keys to open the grating, taking those which were there and thus replacing them; they avail themselves of them to heal various infirmities... Above the tomb are four columns, admirably graceful and white as snow, which, they say, support the ciborium that stands over the tomb.

GREGORY OF TOURS, *De gloria martyrum*, I, XXVIII.

The Basilica at Lyons in the fifth century

...High stands the church in splendour, extending neither to right nor left, but with towering front looking towards the equinoctial sunrise. Within is shining light, and the gilding of the coffered ceiling allures the sunbeams golden as itself. The whole basilica is bright with diverse marbles, floor, vaulting and windows all adorned with figures of most various colour, and mosaic green as a blooming mead shows its design of sapphire cubes winding through the ground of verdant glass. The entrance is a triple portico proudly set on Aquitanian columns; a second portico of like design closes the atrium at the farther side, and the mid-space is flanked afar by columns numerous as forest stems. On the one side runs the noisy highway, on the other leaps the Saône; here turns the traveller who rides or goes afoot, here the driver of the creaking carriage; here the towers, bowed over the rope, raise their river-chant to Christ till the banks re-echo Alleluia...

From a letter of SIDONIUS APOLLINARIS to his friend Hesperius, in *The Letters of Sidonius*, Book II, Letter X, translated by O.M. Dalton, Clarendon Press, Oxford, 1915.

II. FIGURAL ARTS

First Mention of an Image of Christ.

...In the early morning hours he [the emperor Severus Alexander] would worship in the sanctuary of his Lares, in which he kept statues of the deified emperors —of whom, however, only the best had been selected— and also of certain holy souls, among them Apollonius [of Tyana] and, according to a contemporary writer, Christ, Abraham, Orpheus, and others of this same character and, besides, the portraits of his ancestors...

Scriptores Historiae Augustae: AELIUS LAMPRIDIUS, *Severus Alexander*, chapter XXIX, translated by David Magie, Loeb Classical Library, William Heinemann, London, and G.P. Putnam's Sons, New York, 1922.

The Earliest Christian Symbols

And let our seals be either a dove, or a fish, or a ship scudding before the wind, or a musical lyre, which Polycrates used, or a ship's anchor, which Seleucus got engraved as a device; and if there be one fishing, he will remember the apostle, and the children drawn out of the water. For we are not to delineate the faces of idols, we who are prohibited to cleave to them; nor a sword, nor a bow, following as we do, peace; nor drinking-cups, being temperate.

CLEMENT OF ALEXANDRIA, *The Instructor*, Vol. I, Book III, chapter XI, translated by W. Wilson, Vol. IV in the *Ante-Nicene Christian Library: Translations of the Writings of the Fathers*, edited by A. Roberts and J. Donaldson, T. and T. Clark, Edinburgh, Hamilton & Co., London, John Robertson & Co., Dublin, 1867, 1869.

Description of a Mosaic or Wall Painting representing the Martyrdom of St Euphemia.

The judge is seated on his bench; with fierce displeasure he looks at the maiden. For art, when it chooses, can depict wrath, even on an inanimate material. Close by are the henchmen, the throng of soldiers.

The clerks have their tablets and styles; one of them has paused and turned sharply towards the maiden, as if admonishing her to answer in a louder voice, lest he should fail to hear and make some mistake in the records. Euphemia is attired in the plain dark pallium which was the garment of philosophers. She is portrayed with all that beauty and grace which distinguished her in her lifetime, yet with that modesty and gravity which showed her inward spirit. We see her brought before the judge by two soldiers, one of whom drags her forward; the other pushes her from behind. But though from modesty her eyes are cast down, there is an expression in her face which shows it is not fear. We see her, in another part of the picture, tortured by two executioners, one of whom has seized her long hair and pulls back her head, to force her to raise it; the other strikes her on the mouth with a wooden mallet; the blood flows from her lips; and at the piteous sight, tears flow from the eyes of the spectators. In the background is seen the interior of a dungeon. St Euphemia, seated on the ground, raises her hands to heaven, and prays for mercy, and for strength to bear her sufferings. Over her head, behold! the cross appears, symbol of her martyrdom and sign of redemption. Then, near the prison, we see a pile of faggots kindled, and in the midst stands the beautiful and courageous martyr. She extends her arms towards heaven; her countenance is radiant with hope, with faith, with joy.

ASTERIUS OF AMASIA, *Homily on St Euphemia*, Migne, *Patrologiae cursus completus*, Greek series, XL, 355.

Plotinus and Art

We give below some passages from the Enneads *of Plotinus which describe his way of contemplating a work of art and the philosophical and religious value he assigns to vision. In his account of the manner in which a work of art should be approached, all visual experience evaluated and enjoyed, and in particular in his theory of the proper mode of contemplation, Plotinus anticipates the viewpoint of both artist and beholder in the Middle Ages. Indeed, in virtue of their anticlassical elements, the forms of medieval art seem to answer best to the new programme whose outlines Plotinus was the first to adumbrate.*

For our main quotations from Plotinus we use Stephen Mackenna's translation, accompanied by explanatory extracts from our article Plotinus and the Origins of Medieval Aesthetic, *published in* Cahiers Archéologiques, *I, 1945.*

'I think, therefore, that those ancient sages, who sought to secure the presence of divine beings by the erection of shrines and statues, showed insight into the nature of the All; they perceived that, though this Soul is everywhere tractable, its presence will be secured all the more readily when an appropriate receptacle is elaborated, a place especially capable of receiving some portion or phase of it, something reproducing it, or representing it, and seeming like a mirror to catch an image of it' (*Ennead IV*, 3, 11, Mackenna's translation).

The image is a mirror of the thing represented, which therefore participates in its model in virtue of the Stoic theory of universal sympathy. This mirror serves not only to reflect the appearance of material things but also, and above all, to capture the world soul; that is, the spiritual essence of these things and even the Divine. For Plotinus holds that the *nous* (the Reason Principle) binds together all the realities of the cosmos, while the phenomenon of sympathy, which links together the various parts of the visible world, is a weakened image of this perfect union. Everything that exists has a soul, the entire universe is a living being, and this soul, present in every material thing, is nothing other than a reflection of the supreme Intelligence, the *nous*. Indeed this reflection of the *nous*, the spiritual element, is the only truly real thing in the universe; all the rest is pure matter, in other words sheer non-being.

Thus animated, the material world is justified and even given a value; through it we become aware of the supreme Intelligence. But the Intelligence it reflects is the only reality in matter. Therefore the work of art should reflect this matter, as in a mirror. Nevertheless it is useful only as an instrument for acquiring knowledge of the *nous* (an imperfect instrument, but serviceable all the same); here indeed is the *raison d'être* of the work of art. What it gives us, what we should look for in it, is a reflection—weakened but genuine all the same—of the supreme Intelligence, sole reality.

It is easy to gauge the effect that theories of this kind were likely to have on the practice of figural art. They tended to throw doubts on the value of representations whose only aim was to imitate the appearances of Nature. In the long run they might well diminish the artist's sensibility, and that of the spectator, with respect to the characteristics of a material world fallen into disrepute. In their quest of the inner reality of things, both artists and public might get into the habit of merely glancing at external appearances and be inclined less than in the past to concentrate on data worthy of attention. Their powers of observation were liable to decline now that the search for the 'true' image, that of the intelligible, obliged them to subordinate direct observation to a more or less drastic interpretation of its data. If it was to be in any way intelligible this more abstract art language needed to conform to definite conventions. Plotinus himself was aware of this.

For if the purpose of the work of art was the one Plotinus assigned to it (and not a simple joy in the beauty it achieved, an imitation of the outward aspects of material things, or the imparting of moral or intellectual instruction), the beholder could not decipher its message without special training. Above all he needed clearly to understand the physical nature of the process of seeing.

'Seen from a distance, objects appear reduced and close together, however far apart they be: within easy range, their sizes and the distances that separate them are observed correctly.

'Distant objects show in this reduction because they must be drawn together for vision and the light must be concentrated to suit the size of the pupil; besides as we are placed further and further away from the material mass under observation, it is more and more the bare form that reaches us stripped so to speak of magnitude as of all other quality.

'Or it may be that we appreciate the magnitude of an object by observing the salience and recession of its several parts, so that to perceive its true size we must have it close at hand...

'Still (it will be objected) the columns seen from a distance are faint; but they are not small as the masses are.

'True; but there is the common fact of diminution. There is colour with its diminution, faintness; there is magnitude with its diminution, smallness; and magnitude follows colour diminishing stage by stage with it.

'But the phenomenon is more easily explained by the example of things of wide variety. Take mountains dotted with houses, woods and other land-marks; the observation of each detail gives us the means of calculating, by the single objects noted, the total extent covered: but, where no such detail of form reaches us, our vision, which deals with detail, has not the means towards the knowledge of the whole by measurement of any one clearly discerned magnitude. This applies even to objects of vision close at hand; where there is variety and the eye sweeps over all at one glance so that the forms are not all caught, the total appears the less in proportion to the detail which has escaped the eye; observe each single point and then you can estimate the volume precisely' (*Ennead II*, 8, 1, Mackenna's translation).

What Plotinus had in mind was true magnitude, true distance and, with a view to ascertaining these, the presence in the image of all details and distinct colours (the true or 'local' colours), since these reveal the extent of the 'real' in the void of matter. Obviously true magnitude and true distance are recognizable only if all details are present and none of the colours is shaded off (this rules out foreshortening and geometric or aerial perspective). Ideally then, according to Plotinus, every image which is to lend itself to fruitful contemplation should be set out in the foreground and the component parts of the image arranged side by side on a single plane.

Moreover Plotinus asserts that this way of seeing 'on a plane surface' can even, in certain conditions, safeguard us against the perception of matter. 'The depth [of beings and things] is matter, and that is why matter is dark. The light illuminating it is form; the mind perceives the form and, seeing the form of a being, assumes that the depth of this being is a darkness placed below the light. Similarly the eye, a luminous body, fixing itself on light and colours (which are species of light), discerns the existence of the dark, material substratum hidden beneath the coloured surface' (*Ennead II*, 4, 5).

From this it would follow that an image purporting to reflect the Reason Principle must ignore, indeed reject, any representation of 'depth' and 'darkness' (the figuration of space, Plotinus notes, generally entails a distinction between more or less brightly illuminated parts) and confine itself to the 'coloured surface,' presumed to be lit up everywhere and thus devoid of shadows. This programme was more or less systematically carried out in the paintings of Late Antiquity and the following centuries. Plotinus may have seen them (or sensed this tendency in the painters of his day) and approved of them as being attempts to render luminous, chromatic form, image of the *nous*.

To make the contemplation of an image efficacious, other preconditions, at once physical and 'mystical,' were requisite. 'The eye must be adapted and assimilated to what it sees. Never could an eye see the sun unless it had become like the sun, or the soul see the beautiful without itself being beautiful. Therefore let each man who wishes to contemplate God and beauty, begin by becoming godlike and beautiful himself' (*Ennead I*, 6, 9). Elsewhere Plotinus says that beauty should be contemplated 'not with the eyes of the body' but 'with the inner eye'—an important point, since it follows, then, that we do not see an image in the same way with our ordinary eyes and with the inner eye. This remark has a special interest for the historian, for he often finds it reiterated by medieval theologians and sermon-writers in connection with Christian images. Plotinus was not the first to notice this phenomenon; the idea and the expression 'the inner eye' go back to the days of earlier mystics who bade initiates contemplate godhead 'with the eyes of believers' (1).

Elsewhere Plotinus wonders where exactly does the phenomenon of sight take place? In the eye and soul of him who sees, or at the place where the thing seen

---

(1) PLUTARCH, too, knew of these mystical practices. 'On the faces of statues of deities they perceive, as in a dream, facts revealed by the gods. Beyond the image of Isis the worshipper glimpses the goddess herself and his soul is refreshed by her ineffable beauty' (*Isis and Osiris*, ch. 78). APULEIUS (*Metamorphoses*, XI, 24) describes in much the same way the sensations of the worshipper of Isis, who in a state of ecstasy gazes at her statue. 'He enjoys an inexpressible pleasure emanating from the effigy of the goddess.'

is located, and where the 'light of the eye' contacts it? 'Perceptions are not figures or imprints made on the soul for, in our opinion, no imprint on the soul, delineating the perceptible object, takes place. When we perceive an object with our eyes, it is clear that we always see it at a distance and we contact it by means of sight; therefore the impression takes place at the spot where the object is and the soul does not see it by reason of some mark made on it [the soul], like that made on wax by a seal. For the soul would not need to look outside itself if it had within it the form of the object which it sees' (*Ennead IV*, 6, 1).

This passage has a direct bearing on the art of Late Antiquity and the early Middle Ages, in which we find so many instances of a conventional perspective of two equally curious types. One of them is the 'inverted' perspective in which the object represented (or certain parts of it) is shown larger, the further it is removed from the spectator. The other is the 'radiating' perspective in which certain curious images seem to be viewed from above and the foreshortenings of all the objects represented converge on a central focus. Both procedures have precedents in arts previous to Late Antiquity; they were often employed in the archaic arts of the East—and similar procedures are often found in child art.

For Plotinus the function of the image was to supply an apprehension, an intellectual apprehension, of the *nous*. For here we have a form of contemplation, the only form of it which makes it possible to disregard pure matter (non-being), and to elicit the spiritual order reflected in matter and informing it. It is indeed this very act of contemplation of the intelligible that creates this order and makes the perceptible world a reflection of the *nous*. Emile Bréhier (1) describes it as a 'spiritualistic physics' as opposed to the normal 'mechanistic physics.' The basic principle of this 'spiritualistic physics' is that the parts are not elements but products of the whole (in contemplating the *nous*, we introduce it into matter), and the idea of the whole is thus more real than its parts.

This is what Plotinus means when he says that 'the world becomes transparent to the mind.' As Emile Bréhier points out (2), Plotinus sums up in this remark the mental operation which he describes in the *Fifth Ennead*, using a Platonic thesis as his point of departure. Plato's theory is that sight is the result of a contact between the inner light of the eye and the light of the outside world. Plotinus, however, assumes that this separation between the two lights is done away with, that they become transparent *inter se* and interpenetrate. Ordinarily this light is impeded and reflected by solid objects. Plotinus also assumes that this solidity, too, is done away with and so the transparency of objects becomes absolute; all objects interpenetrate without losing any of their qualities and without limiting the light (IV, 4-11). He goes further: in the visible world objects limit and obstruct each other reciprocally, or intermingle. But it is possible to conceive that this limitation and this obstruction, due solely to the resistances of visible things, are suppressed; in which case we have Ideas in their pure state: movement that never ceases, stability truly stable, the beautiful without admixture of the ugly (IV, 11-15). Normal vision presupposes a distance between him who sees and his surroundings. Plotinus bids us negate this and assume that his environment is absorbed in the man, the man in his environment; this is 'seeing with the mind' (IV, 15-18). Lastly we distinguish between light and the source from which it emanates (notably the celestial bodies). Suppress this distinction, let all be equally a source of light and we shall have a way of seeing in which there is no longer any differentiation between parts, all forms an organic whole (IV, 18-27). 'There is no point at which one can fix one's own limits and say, "Up to that point and no further it is I"' (VI, 5, 7). In other words the state of contemplating the intelligible is not accompanied by consciousness of one's self, for all our mental activity is directed to the contemplated object; we become that object, we surrender ourselves to it as matter for it to shape, we are only potentially ourselves. 'To see, one must lose consciousness of oneself and, to have consciousness of what is seen, one has to cease, to some extent, to see. If, then, we wish to see, having consciousness of what is seen, we must detach ourselves from it sufficiently, but not so much as not to return to it and plunge ourselves into it when we so desire. It is in this sort of to-and-fro movement, of union and separation, that we develop a consciousness of the absorption of ourselves in the All' (XI, 1-13)—the supreme aim of an ideal intellectual contemplation.

A similar—or identical—method leads to perfect knowledge. 'For us the true consists only in a series of propositions which we enounce regarding things; but let us picture to ourselves a knowledge that attains directly the things about which these propositions are enounced. In that case it does not follow its object but contains it, in its entirety, within itself and is identical with it' (IV, 40-56). A phenomenon of this kind is to be found in art, in which according to Plotinus (V, 3-4) resides 'a wisdom containing the very model that it imitates.' 'That wisdom is not composed of theorems but forms a single whole; its unity is not composed of many items that it brings together but, rather, starting out from this unity, this wisdom is broken up into a plurality' (V, 8, 5).

Plotinus attaches much importance to this conception of knowledge, a self-contained, immediate know-

---

(1) BRÉHIER, *La Philosophie de Plotin*, Paris, 1928, pp. 56-57.
(2) The rest of this paragraph is based on BRÉHIER's commentary on *Ennead V*, ch. 8, pp. 129 ff. (Plotinus, Vol. V, Budé series).

ledge that is not made up of successive accretions, and he sees it as superior to the other kind of knowledge: the wisdom of the gods and the blessed is not expressed by propositions but by beautiful images (V, 8, 5). The Egyptians understood this when they wrote, not with letters forming vocables and phrases, but by signs 'each of which constituted in itself a science, a wisdom, a reality apprehended instantaneously, not by a train of reasoning' (V, 8, 6). The writing of the Greco-Romans gives us nothing of the sort but, here as always, art in Plotinus' opinion has the great advantage that it enables this immediate and total knowledge. For this knowledge is acquired by means of the intellectual 'inner' eye described above. This mode of knowledge 'is not thought but an ineffable, non-intellectual contact, a touching of the primeval Being that exists before the birth of the intellect; touching is not thinking' (V, 3, 10).

All historians of philosophy agree that Plotinus did nothing less than call in question the value of the thinking mind; that he ceased to treat it, like Plato and Aristotle, as an instrument of knowledge or the starting point of a progressive synthesis (Emile Bréhier); and that in the system of Plotinus knowledge is transformed into an undefined emotion, a vague sense of life, an elusive *Stimmung* (Rudolf Eucken).

The two extracts from Mackenna's translation are taken, by permission of the publishers, from *Plotinus: The Ethical Treatises*, translated by Stephen Mackenna in *The Library of Philosophical Translations*, Medici Society, London, and Hale, Cushman & Flint, Boston, 1917-30.

A Pilgrim from Gaul, St Silvia of Aquitaine
(also called Etheria),
visits the Holy Land in the late fourth century.

Sinai. It was late on the Sabbath when we came to the mountain, and arriving at a certain monastery, the kindly monks who lived there entertained us, showing us all kindliness; for there is a church there with a priest. There we stayed that night, and then early on the Lord's day we began to ascend the mountains one by one with the priest and the monks who lived there. These mountains are ascended with infinite labour, because you do not go up gradually by a spiral path (as we say, 'like a snail shell'), but you go straight up as if up the face of a wall, and you must go straight down each mountain until you arrive at the foot of that central one which is strictly called Sinai. And so, Christ our God commanding us, we were encouraged by the prayers of the holy men who accompanied us; and although the labour was great—for I had to ascend on foot, because the ascent could not be made in a chair—yet I did not feel it. To that extent the labour was not felt, because I saw that the desire which I had

was being fulfilled by the command of God. At the fourth hour we arrived at that peak of Sinai, the holy Mount of God, where the law was given, i.e., at that place where the majesty of God descended on the day when the mountain smoked. In that place there is now a church—not a large one, because the place itself, the summit of the mountain, is not large; but the church has in itself a large measure of grace.

When therefore, by God's command, we had arrived at the summit, and come to the door of the church, the priest who was appointed to the church, coming out of his cell, met us, a blameless old man, a monk from early youth, and (as they say here) an *ascetic*; in short, a man quite worthy of the place. The other priests met us also, as well as all the monks who lived there by the mountain; that is, all of them who were not prevented by age or infirmity. But on the very summit of the central mountain no one lives permanently; nothing is there but the church and the cave where holy Moses was. Here the whole passage having been read from the book of Moses, and the oblation made in due order, we communicated; and as I was passing out of the church the priests gave us gifts of blessing from the place; that is, gifts of the fruits grown in the mountain. For although the holy mount of Sinai itself is all rocky, so that it has not a bush on it, yet down near the foot of the mountains —either the central one or those which form the ring— there is a little plot of ground; here the holy monks diligently plant shrubs and lay out orchards and fields; and hard by they place their own cells, so that they may get, as if from the soil of the mountain itself, some fruit which they may seem to have cultivated with their own hands. So, then, after we had communicated and the holy men had given us these gifts of blessing, and we had come out of the door of the church, I began to ask them to show us the several localities. Thereupon the holy men deigned to show us each place. For they showed us the famous cave where holy Moses was when for the second time he went up to the Mount of God to receive the tables [of the law] again after he had broken the first on account of the sin of the people; and the other places also which we desired to see or which they knew better they deigned to show us...

Jerusalem. But when the first cock has crowed, forthwith the bishop descends and enters inside the cave to the Anastasis. All the doors are opened, and the whole crowd streams into the Anastasis. Here innumerable lights are shining; and when the people have entered, one of the priests says a psalm, and they all respond; then prayer is offered. Again one of the deacons says a psalm, and again prayer is offered; a third psalm is said by one of the clergy, and prayer is offered for the third time, and the commemoration of all men is made. Then these three psalms having been said, and these three prayers offered, behold censers are brought into the cave of the Anastasis, so that the whole Basilica of the Anastasis is filled with odours. Then where the bishop stands inside the rails, he takes the Gospel and advances to the door, and himself reads of the Lord's resurrection. And when he has begun to read this, there is such a moaning and groaning of all the people, and such weeping, that the most obdurate person would be moved to tears, for that the Lord endured such grievous things for us. Then the Gospel having been read, the bishop comes forth, and is led to the Cross with hymns, and all the people with him. There again one psalm is said and a prayer offered. Again he blesses the faithful, and the dismissal is given. As the bishop comes forth they all approach [to kiss] his hand; and presently the bishop betakes himself to his own house. From that hour all the monks return to the Anastasis, and psalms and antiphons are said until daylight; and after each psalm or antiphon prayer is offered. For every day in turn the priests and deacons keep vigil at the Anastasis with the people. If any of the laity, either men or women, wish it, they stay there till it is light; but if they do not wish to do so, they return to their houses and go to sleep again.

Good Friday in Jerusalem. A chair is placed for the bishop in Golgotha behind the Cross, which stands there now [since A.D. 326]; the bishop sits down in the chair, there is placed before him a table covered with a linen cloth, the deacons standing round the table. Then is brought a silver-gilt casket, in which is the holy wood of the cross; it is opened, and the contents being taken out, the wood of the cross and also its inscription [the *titulus* which Pilate had fixed to the cross] are placed on the table. When they have been put there, the bishop, as he sits, takes hold of the extremities of the holy wood with his hands, and the deacons, standing round, guard it. It is thus guarded because the custom is that every one of the people, faithful and catechumens alike, leaning forward, bend over the table, kiss the holy wood, and pass on. And as it is said that one time a person fixed his teeth in it, and so stole a piece of the holy wood, it is now guarded by the deacons standing round, so that no one who comes may dare to do such a thing again...

Dedication Festival in Jerusalem. Those days are called the days of Dedication, on which the holy church

in Golgotha, called the Martyrium, and the holy church at the Anastasis, where the Lord rose after His passion, were consecrated to God. The dedication festival of these holy churches is observed with the greatest honour, since the Cross of the Lord was found on that day. For so it was ordained that the day on which first the above-mentioned holy churches were consecrated should be the day on which the Cross of the Lord was found, that it should be thus observed with all manner of joy. And this, too, we find in the Holy Scriptures, for that was the day of dedication on which holy Solomon, when the house of God which he had built was completed, stood before the altar of God, and prayed as it is written in the books of Chronicles.

When, then, the dedication festival has come, eight days are observed; for many days before they begin to assemble from every quarter, not only monks and Renuntiants from the different provinces of Mesopotamia, Syria, Egypt, or the Thebaid, where there are a number of monks, but from all sorts of different places and provinces. For there is no one who does not for that day wend his way to Jerusalem for such great rejoicing and so honourable a festival; even secular persons, both men and women, with faithful hearts, for the sake of this festival, collect at this time at Jerusalem from all the provinces. The bishops at fewest are in Jerusalem at this time to the number of forty or fifty, and with them come many of their clergy. In short, a man thinks he has committed a grievous sin if he is not present on so solemn an occasion, provided that no necessity has prevented him, such as may keep one from a good design. During these days of the dedication, the decoration of all the churches is the same as at Easter and Epiphany; and on the several days they proceed to the different places as at those seasons. For on the first and second day they proceed to the Great Church—the Martyrium; on the third day to Olivet, to the church on the mountain itself, from which the Lord ascended into heaven after His Passion, below which church is that cave in which the Lord taught the Apostles on the Mount of Olives. And on the fourth day...

The Pilgrimage of S. Silvia of Aquitania to the Holy Places, Vol. I (pp. 13-14, 47-48, 63-64, 76-77) of *The Library of the Palestine Pilgrims' Text Society*, translated by J.H. Bernard, London, 1897.

Chronological Table

	MEN		EVENTS
200	Septimius Severus (193-211) Plotinus, philosopher (204-269)		
220	Alexander Severus (222-235)		
	Maximinus (235-240)	235	Persecution of the Christians.
240	Philip the Arabian (244-249)		
	Decius (248-251)	250	Persecution of the Christians.
260	Gallienus, sole emperor (260-268)	262	Last celebration of the secular games.
	Aurelian (270-275) Probus (276-282)	273	Death of Mani, founder of Manichaeism.
280	Diocletian (284-305)		
	St Pachomius (c. 292-346), founder of coenobitical monasticism	293	Beginning of the Tetrarchy.
300	Constantine I, Augustus (306-324)	303-304	Persecution of the Christians.
		312	Constantine's victory over Maxentius at the Milvian Bridge, near Rome.
	Pope Sylvester (314-335)	315	First monastery founded by St Pachomius.
320	Constantine I, Emperor (324-337) St Gregory of Nyssa (c. 335-c. 395) St Gregory Nazianzen (329-c. 390) St Basil (c. 330-379) Constantius II (337-361)	320	Sunday henceforth observed as a day of rest in all courts of justice.
		324	Constantine's victory over Licinius.
		325	First œcumenical council of the Church.
340	St Ambrose (340-397) St John Chrysostom (344/347?-407) St Jerome (c. 348-420) Pope Liberius (352-366) St Augustine (354-430)	330	Inauguration of Constantinople.
360	Julian the Apostate (361-363)		
380	Theodosius I (379-395)	380	Imperial edict establishing Christianity as the State religion.
	Pope Siricius (384-399)	391	Imperial edict prohibiting pagan worship.
		394	Olympic Games abolished.
	Arcadius I, Emperor of the West (395-408) Honorius I, Emperor of the East (395-423)	404	Ravenna becomes the capital of the Western Empire (until 476).
400		405	Gladiatorial combats forbidden.
	Theodosius II, Emperor of the East (408-450)	410	Capture of Rome by Alaric.
420			
	Pope Sixtus III (432-440)	430-431	Council of Ephesus: Mary proclaimed 'the Mother of God.'
440	Pope Leo the Great (440-461)		

c. 200   Dura-Europos, on the Euphrates, 'Christian House.'

c. 200-230   Rome, first catacomb paintings.
            First sarcophagi with reliefs on Christian themes.

245-256   Dura-Europos, wall paintings in the synagogue.
249-261   Rome, parish church on the Esquiline *(Titulus Equitii)*.

271-283   Rome, construction of Aurelian's wall.

308-319   Aquileia, church of Bishop Theodore.
c. 310   Luxor, wall paintings in the temple of the imperial cult.
            Rome, Arch of Constantine.
315   Bethlehem, Church of the Nativity founded by St Helena.
            Jerusalem, churches of Golgotha founded by Constantine.
319 (?)   Rome, church and baptistery of the Lateran founded by Constantine.

after 326   Vatican, St Peter's founded by Constantine.

c. 350   Tiberias, synagogue.
354   Roman calendar illustrated for a Christian.
356   Rome, paintings with St Petronilla in the Catacomb of Domitilla.

c. 370   Rome, paintings in the new catacomb of the Via Latina.
372   Syria, church of Fafirtin.
c. 378   Jerusalem, Church of the Ascension on the Mount of Olives.

382   Milan, Church of San Nazzaro (SS. Apostoli).
384-399   Rome, Church of Santa Pudenziana founded by Pope Siricius.
385-386   Milan, Basilica of the Martyrs (Sant'Ambrogio).
386   Rome, Church of San Paolo fuori le Mura founded by Valentinian II.

c. 400   Salonica, mosaics in St George and Christ Latomos.
            St Menas, near Alexandria, second basilica, founded by Arcadius.
            Sohag, Egypt, two basilicas.
between 400 and 640   Monasteries of Bawit and Sakkara, Egypt, and their wall paintings.
413-440   Constantinople, construction of the city walls.
418   Syria, Church of Dar Kita.

Glossary-Index

Bibliography

GENERAL WORKS

1. Handbooks, Dictionaries, Bibliographies.

L. BRÉHIER, *L'Art Chrétien. Son développement iconographique des origines jusqu'à nos jours*, Paris, 1918; 2nd edition, 1928.

F. CABROL, H. LECLERCQ and H.-I. MARROU, *Dictionnaire d'archéologie chrétienne et de liturgie*, 15 vols., Paris, 1908-1953.

E. COCHE DE LA FERTÉ, *L'Antiquité chrétienne au Musée du Louvre*, Paris, 1958.

O. M. DALTON, *Byzantine Art and Archaeology*, Oxford, 1911; reprinted, 1961.

O. M. DALTON, *East Christian Art. A Survey of the Monuments*, Oxford, 1925.

F. J. DÖLGER, *Antike und Christentum*, 6 vols., Münster (Westphalia), 1929-1950. Surveys of monuments and of writings on early Christianity and its art. Cf. KLAUSER.

R. GARRUCCI, *Storia dell'arte cristiana nei primi otto secoli della Chiesa*, 6 vols., Prato, 1873-1880.

J. HUBERT, *L'Art pré-roman*, Paris, 1938.

J. HUBERT, *L'Architecture religieuse du haut Moyen Age en France*, Paris, 1951. Collection of plans.

K. M. KAUFMANN, *Handbuch der christlichen Archäologie*, Paderborn, 3rd edition, 1922.

T. KLAUSER, *Reallexikon für Antike und Christentum* (in course of publication since 1950, 4 volumes available).

F. X. KRAUS, *Geschichte der christlichen Kunst*, I, Freiburg-im-Breisgau, 1896.

H. LECLERCQ, *Manuel d'archéologie chrétienne depuis les origines jusqu'au VIIIe siècle*, 2 vols., Paris, 1907.

Lexikon für Theologie und Kirche, edited by M. BUCHBERGER, 10 vols., Freiburg-im-Breisgau, 1930-1938.

O. MARUCCHI, *Eléments d'archéologie chrétienne*, 3 vols., Paris, 1889-1892; 2nd edition, 1900-1909.

C. R. MOREY, *Early Christian Art. An Outline of the Evolution of Style and Iconography in Sculpture and Painting from Antiquity to the Eighth Century*, Princeton, 1941.

W. NEUSS, *Die Kunst der alten Christen*, Augsburg, 1926.

H. PEIRCE and R. TYLER, *Byzantine Art*, London, 1926; *L'Art byzantin*, 2 vols., Paris, 1932-1934.

J. PIJOAN, *Arte cristiano primitivo y bizantino*, in *Summa artis, Historia general del Arte*, VII, Madrid, 1940; 3rd edition, 1954.

Reallexikon für Antike und Christentum, edited by T. KLAUSER. See KLAUSER.

Reallexikon zur deutsche Kunstgeschichte, founded by O. SCHMITT, edited by L. H. HEYDENREICH (in course of publication since 1937).

D. T. RICE, *The Beginnings of Christian Art*, London, 1957.

J. P. RICHTER, *Quellen der byzantinischen Kunstgeschichte*, Vienna, 1897.

A. RIEGL, *Die spätrömische Kunstindustrie nach den Funden in Österreich-Ungarn*, new edition, Vienna, 1927.

A. RUMPF, *Stilphasen der spätantiken Kunst*, Cologne, 1957.

H. SCHLUNK, *Kunst der Spätantike im Mittelmeerraum*, Berlin, 1939. Collections of the Kaiser Friedrich Museum, Berlin.

V. SCHULTZE, *Grundriss der christlichen Archäologie*, Munich, 1919; second edition, 1934.

J. STRZYGOWSKI, *Der Ursprung der christlichen Kirchenkunst*, Leipzig, 1920; *Origin of Christian Church Art*, Oxford, 1923.

L. VON SYBEL, *Christliche Antike. Einführung in die altchristliche Kunst*, 2 vols., Marburg, 1906-1909.

P. TOESCA, *Storia dell'arte italiana: I, Il Medioevo*, Turin, 1927.

W. UNGER, *Quellen der byzantinischen Kunstgeschichte*, Vienna, 1878. The source books of Unger and Richter (see above) complement each other. They bring together extracts from texts relating to the monuments of Constantinople (in German translation).

A. VENTURI, *Storia dell'arte italiana*, 22 vols., Milan, 1901-1936.

W. F. VOLBACH and M. HIRMER, *Frühchristliche Kunst. Die Kunst der Spätantike in West- und Ostrom*, Munich, 1958. The English edition of this book *(Early Christian Art*, Thames and Hudson, London) is to be recommended for its wealth of illustrations and its concise, informative text.

O. WULFF, *Altchristliche und byzantinische Kunst*, in *Handbuch der Kunstwissenschaft*, 2 vols., Berlin, 1914-1915.

Bibliographical information is given regularly in the following periodicals: *Bonner Jahrbücher*, *Byzantinische Zeitschrift*, *Revue des études byzantines*, *Rivista di archeologia cristiana*, *Theologische Literaturzeitung*. For the war years and the post-war period up to 1952, a bibliographical survey with commentaries is given by A. M. SCHNEIDER, in: F. DÖLGER and A. M. SCHNEIDER, *Byzanz*, Berne, 1952 (this bibliography covers all Early Christian art).

2. Catalogues and Inventories.

Actes du Ve Congrès international d'archéologie chrétienne à Aix-en-Provence, 1954, Vatican City, 1957. Miscellany of articles constituting an inventory of Early Christian monuments in all countries.

Atti del III (and *del IV) Congresso internazionale di archeologia cristiana* (in 1932 and 1938), Vatican City, 1934-1940. Same remark as for the previous item.

R. DE LA BLANCHÈRE and P. GAUCKLER, *Catalogue du Musée Alaoui* [Carthage], 2 vols., Paris, 1891-1910.

C. CECCHELLI, *Monumenti cristiani eretici di Roma*, Rome, n.d. [1944].

F. CUMONT, *Les Fouilles de Doura-Europos (1922-1923)*, text and atlas, Bibliothèque archéologique du Haut-Commissariat de Syrie et du Liban, IX, Paris, 1926.

O. M. DALTON, *Catalogue of Early Christian Antiquities... in the British Museum*, London, 1901; *A Guide to the Early Christian and Byzantine Antiquities*, British Museum, London, 1921.

C. DIEHL, *L'Afrique byzantine. Histoire de la domination byzantine en Afrique (533-709)*, Paris, 1896.

J. FICKER, *Die altchristlichen Bildwerke im christlichen Museum des Laterans*, Leipzig, 1890.

S. GSELL, *Les Monuments antiques de l'Algérie*, 2 vols., Paris, 1901.

S. GSELL, *Atlas archéologique de l'Algérie*, Paris, 1912.

O. MARUCCHI, *I monumenti del Museo Cristiano Lateranense*, Rome, 1910.

G. MENDEL, *Catalogue des sculptures grecques, romaines et byzantines du Musée de Brousse*, Athens, 1908.

G. MENDEL, *Catalogue des sculptures grecques, romaines et byzantines des musées impériaux ottomans*, I-III, Constantinople, 1912-1914.

M. I. ROSTOVTZEFF, *Dura-Europos and its Art*, Oxford, 1938.

M. I. ROSTOVTZEFF and others, *The Excavations at Dura-Europos..., Preliminary Reports*, I to IX, New Haven, 1929-1946.
An account of the discoveries, which included several monuments of capital importance for the history of art in the second and above all in the early third century: Mithraeum, Temple of the Palmyrene Gods, Synagogue, Christian House, and a great many wall paintings.
See below (p. 313) for Jewish art in Antiquity.

O. WULFF, *Beschreibung der Bildwerke der christlichen Epochen*, III, Berlin, Königliches Museum, 1909-1910.

See also the catalogues of works given below in the special bibliographies, under: Painting, Sculpture, and Ivories.

3. Field Work.

A. MATTERN, *A travers les villes mortes de haute Syrie*, Mélanges de l'Université Saint-Joseph, XVII, Beirut, 1934.

A. POIDEBARD, *La Trace de Rome dans le désert de Syrie : le limes de Trajan à la conquête arabe. Recherches aériennes*. Text and atlas. Bibliothèque archéologique du Haut-Commissariat de Syrie et du Liban, XXIII, Paris, 1934.

4. Monuments by Countries.

Africa, North.

Y. ALLAIS, *Djemila*, Paris, 1938.

A. BALLU, *Les Ruines de Timgad (antique Thamugadi)*, Paris, 1897.

A. BALLU, *Les Ruines de Timgad. Nouvelles découvertes*, Paris, 1903.

A. BALLU, *Guide illustré de Timgad (antique Thamugadi)*, Paris, 2nd edition, 1911.

A. BALLU, *Guide illustré de Djemila (antique Cuicul)*, Algiers, 1926.

R. CAGNAT, *Carthage, Timgad, Tébessa et les villes antiques de l'Afrique du Nord*, Paris, 1909.

C. COURTOIS, *Timgad (antique Thamugadi)*, Algiers, 1951, and Paris, 1955.

P. GAUCKLER, *Basiliques chrétiennes de Tunisie*, Paris, 1913.

L. LESCHI, *Tipasa de Maurétanie*, Algiers, 1951.

L. LESCHI, *Djemila (antique Cuicul)*, Algiers, 1954.

E. MAREC, *Monuments chrétiens d'Hippone*, Paris, 1958.

P. MONCEAUX, *Timgad chrétien*, Paris, Annual Reports of the Ecole Pratique des Hautes Études, 1910-1911.

Egypt.

W. DE BOCK, *Matériaux pour servir à l'archéologie de l'Egypte chrétienne*, 2 vols., St. Petersburg, 1901.

Greece.

E. DYGGVE, F. POULSEN and K. RHOMAIOS, *Das Heroon von Kalydon*, Copenhagen, 1964.
A Hellenistic heroum.

G. SOTIRIOU, *The Early Christian Churches of Greece* (in Greek), Athens, 1931.

G. SOTIRIOU, *Christian and Byzantine Archaeology* (in Greek), Athens, 1942.

Italy.

G. BRUSIN and P. L. ZOVATTO, *Monumenti paleocristiani di Aquileia e di Grado*, Udine, 1957.

Naples :

H. ACHELIS, *Die Katakomben von Neapel*, Leipzig, 1936.

Rome :

C. CECCHELLI, *La vita di Roma nel Medio Evo*, Rome, 1951-1952.
A wealth of information on the arts and crafts in Rome both in medieval and pre-medieval times.

F. W. DEICHMANN, *Frühchristliche Kirchen in Rome*, Basel, 1948.

P. A. FÉVRIER, *La Catacombe de Priscille et l'origine des catacombes*, in *Cahiers archéologiques*, XI, 1960, pp. 1-14.

L. HERTLING and E. KIRSCHBAUM, *Die römischen Katakomben und ihre Märtyrer*, Vienna, 1955.

O. MARUCCHI, *Le catacombe romane*, Rome, 1933.

P. STYGER, *Die römischen Katakomben*, Berlin, 1933.
One of the few books on the catacombs which have filled in the historical background and advanced the study of the subject.

R. VIELLIARD, *Les Origines du titre de Saint-Martin-aux-Monts à Rome*, Mâcon, 1931.

Palestine.

J. W. CROWFOOT, *Early Churches in Palestine*, Schweich Lectures 1937, London, 1941.

Syria.

Antioch-on-the-Orontes. Publications of the Committee for the Excavation of Antioch and its Vicinity: I, *The Excavations of 1932*, edited by G. W. ELDERKIN.

G. TCHALENKO, *Villages antiques de la Syrie du Nord, la région de Bélus à l'époque romaine*, 3 vols., Paris, 1957-1959.

M. DE VOGÜÉ, *Syrie centrale. Architecture civile et religieuse du Ier au VIIe siècle*, 2 folio vols., Paris, 1865-1877.

T. WIEGAND, *Baalbek, Ergebnisse der Ausgrabungen und Untersuchungen in den Jahren 1898 bis 1905*, 3 vols., Berlin-Leipzig, 1921-1925.

T. WIEGAND, *Palmyra, Ergebnisse der Expeditionen von 1902 und 1927*, Archäologisches Institut des deutschen Reiches, Istanbul-Berlin, 1932.

K. WULZINGER and C. WATZINGER, *Damaskus*: I, *Die antike Stadt*, Berlin, 1921; II, *Die islamische Stadt*, Berlin-Leipzig, 1924.

Tripolitania.

J. B. WARD PERKINS and R.G. GOODCHILD, *The Christian Antiquities of Tripolitania*, in *Archaeologia*, XCV, Oxford, 1953, pp. VIII and 1-158.

Turkey.

R. JANIN, *Constantinople byzantine. Développement urbain et répertoire topographique*, Paris, 1950.

Yugoslavia.

E. DYGGVE, *History of Salonitan Christianity*, Oslo, 1951.

5. General Studies bearing on Art Forms and Techniques.

D.V. AINALOV, *The Hellenistic Basis of Byzantine Art* (in Russian), St. Petersburg, 1900-1901; English translation, *The Hellenistic Origins of Byzantine Art*, New Brunswick, 1961.

A. ALFÖLDI, *Zur Ausgestaltung des monarchischen Zeremoniells am römischen Kaiserhofe*, in *Römische Mitteilungen*, 34, 1934, pp. 1-118.

C. BAYET, *Recherches pour servir à l'histoire de la peinture et de la sculpture chrétiennes en Orient avant la querelle des Iconoclastes*, Paris, 1879.

S. BETTINI, *L'arte alla fine del mondo antico*, Padua, 1948.

R. BIANCHI-BANDINELLI, *Storicità di arte classica*, Rome, 2nd edition, 1950.

R. BIANCHI-BANDINELLI, *Continuità ellenistica nella pittura di età medio e tardo-romana*, in *Rivista dell'Istituto Nazionale dell'Archeologia e Storia dell'Arte*, new series, II, 1953 (in 1954), pp. 1-85.

L. BUDDE, *Die Entstehung des antiken Repräzentationsbilder*, Berlin, 1957.

R. BULTMANN, *Zur Geschichte der Lichtsymbolik im Altertum*, in *Philologus*, 97, 1948.

L. COURAJOD, *Leçons de l'Ecole du Louvre*, Paris, 1891.

W. ELLIGER, *Die Stellung der alten Christen zu den Bildern in der ersten vier Jahrhunderten*, Leipzig, 1930.

A. GRABAR, *L'Empereur dans l'art byzantin. Recherches sur l'art officiel de l'Empire d'Orient*, Paris, 1936.

A. GRABAR, *Martyrium. Recherches sur le culte des reliques et l'art chrétien antique*, 2 vols. and album, Paris, 1943-1946.

W. DE GRÜNEISEN, *Le Portrait (études comparatives). Traditions hellénistiques et influences orientales*, Rome, 1911.

A. HEISENBERG, *Grabeskirche und Apostelkirche*, 2 vols., Leipzig, 1908.
Studies of two famous churches no longer in existence: the Holy Sepulchre at Jerusalem and the Holy Apostles in Constantinople.

T. KLAUSER, *Die Cathedra im Totenkult der heidnischen und christlichen Antike*, Münster (Westphalia), 1927.

R. KRAUTHEIMER, *Early Christian and Byzantine Architecture*, London, 1965.

H. KRUSE, *Studien zur offiziellen Geltung des Kaiserbildes im römischen Reiche*, Paderborn, 1934.

E. MALE, *Rome et ses vieilles églises*, Paris, 1942.

E. MALE, *La fin du paganisme en Gaule et les plus anciennes basiliques chrétiennes*, Paris, 1950.

A. MALRAUX, *La Métamorphose des Dieux*, Paris, 1957; *The Metamorphosis of the Gods*, London and New York, 1959.

K. MICHEL, *Gebet und Bild in frühchristlicher Zeit*, Strasbourg, 1902.

E. MÜNTZ, *Etudes sur l'histoire de la peinture et de l'iconographie chrétiennes*, Paris, 1882.

G. RODENWALDT, *Eine spätantike Kunstströmung in Rome*, in *Römische Mitteilungen*, XXXIII, 1918.
On the battle pictures carried in triumphal processions and their influence on the sculpture of Roman triumphal monuments.

C. ROHAULT DE FLEURY, *La Messe ; études archéologiques sur ses monuments*, 3 vols., Paris, 1882-1883.

B. SCHWEITZER, *Die spätantike Grundlage der mittelalterlichen Kunst*, Leipzig, 1939.
Observations on monuments in Italy.

E. H. SWIFT, *Roman Sources of Christian Art*, New York, 1951.
A rather one-sided view of Roman influences.

R. VIELLIARD, *Recherches sur les origines de la Rome chrétienne. Essai d'urbanisme chrétien*, Mâcon, 1941.

F. WIELAND, *Mensa und Confessio*, Munich, 1906.

F. WIELAND, *Altar und Altargrab der christlichen Kirchen im IV. Jahrhundert*, Munich, 1912.

ARCHITECTURE

1. The Monuments.

D. AINALOV, *Christian Monuments of the Chersonese* [Crimea] (in Russian), Moscow, 1905.

B. M. APOLLONJ-GHETTI, A. FERRUA, S. J., E. JOSI and E. KIRSCHBAUM, S. J., with preface by Mgr L. KAAS, *Esplorazioni sotto la Confessione di San Pietro in Vaticano*, I-II, Vatican City, 1951.
On the excavations carried out under St Peter's during the war.

A. BADAWY, *Les Premières Eglises d'Egypte*, in *Kyrilliana*, Seminarium Franciscanum Orientale, Cairo, 1947. Texts.

P. B. BAGATTI, *Gli antichi edifici sacri di Betlemme*, Jerusalem, 1952.

W. DE BOCK, *Matériaux pour servir à l'archéologie de l'Egypte chrétienne*, 2 vols., St. Petersburg, 1901.

J. BOUBE, *La Nécropole paléochrétienne de Martres-Tolosane*, in *Pallas*, III, 1955. Publications de la Faculté des Lettres de Toulouse.

H. C. BUTLER, *American Archaeological Expedition to Syria in 1899-1900*. Part II: *Architecture and Other Arts*, New York and London, 1903.

H. C. BUTLER, *The Tychaion at es-Sanamein and the Plan of the Early Christian Churches in Syria*, in *Revue archéologique*, VIII, 1906, p. 413 ff.

H. C. BUTLER, *Syria. Publications of the Princeton University Archaeological Expeditions to Syria in 1904-1905 and 1909*. Part II : *Architecture*. Section B : *Northern Syria*, Leyden, 1910-1920.

H. C. BUTLER, *Early Churches in Syria, Fourth to Seventh Centuries*, edited and completed by E. BALDWIN SMITH, Princeton, 1929.

R. CAGNAT, *Carthage, Timgad, Tébessa et les villes antiques de l'Afrique du Nord*, Paris, 1909.

A. CAPITANI D'ARZAGO, *Architettura dei secoli quarto e quinto in alta Italia*, Milan, 1944.

C. DELVOYE, *Recherches récentes sur les origines de la basilique paléochrétienne*, in *Annuaire de l'Institut de philologie et d'histoire orientale et slave*, XIV, Brussels, 1954-1957, pp. 205-228.

G. B. DE ROSSI, *La Roma sotterranea cristiana*, 4 vols., Rome, 1864-1898.
The classic work on the catacombs of Rome, still indispensable.

E. DYGGVE, *Forschungen in Salona*, III, Vienna, 1939.

E. DYGGVE, *Probleme des altchristlichen Kulthauses*, in *Festschrift für Kirchengeschichte*, 59, 1940.

E. EGGER, *Frühchristliche Kirchenbauten im südlichen Norikum*, Vienna, 1916.

W. ELTESTER, *Die Kirchen Antiochias im IV. Jahrhundert*, in *Zeitschrift für die neutestamentliche Wissenschaft*, 38, 1937, p. 251 ff. (in 1938).

J. FINK, *Der Ursprung der ältesten Kirchen am Domplatz von Aquileia*, Münster-Cologne, 1954.

P. GAUCKLER, *Basiliques chrétiennes de Tunisie*, Paris, 1913.

W. GERBER and R. EGGER, *Forschungen in Salona*, I, II, III, Vienna, 1917, 1926, 1939.

C. HUELSEN, *Le Chiese di Roma nel medio evo*, Rome, 1927.

K. M. KAUFMANN, *Die Ausgrabung der Menasheiligtümer...*, 3 vols., Cairo, 1906-1908.

K. M. KAUFMANN, *Die Menasstadt...*, Leipzig, 1910.

C. KRAELING and others, *Gerasa, City of Decapolis*, New Haven, 1938.
Several churches of the 4th-7th centuries.

R. KRAUTHEIMER, *Corpus basilicarum christianarum Romae*, I et seq., Vatican City, in course of publication since 1937.

R. KRAUTHEIMER, *Mensa-Coemeterium-Martyrium*, in *Cahiers archéologiques*, XI, 1960, pp. 15-40.

D. KRENCKER and W. ZCHIETZSCH-MANN, *Römische Tempel in Syrien*, 2 vols., Berlin-Leipzig, 1938.

K. G. LANCKORONSKI, *Der Dom von Aquileia*, Vienna, 1906.

J. LASSUS, *Sanctuaires chrétiens de Syrie*, Paris, 1947.

P. LAUER, *Le Palais de Latran, étude historique et archéologique*, Paris, 1912.

A. MADER, *Altchristliche Basiliken und Lokaltraditionen in Süd-Judäa*, Paderborn, 1918.

F. MAYENCE, *La Première Campagne de fouilles à Apamée*, in *L'Antiquité classique*, I (1931), p. 33 ff., IV (1935), p. 199 ff., V (1936), p. 405 ff.

M. MESNARD, *La Basilique de Saint-Chrysogone à Rome*, Rome-Paris, 1935.

F. MILTNER, *Ephesos, Stadt des Artemis und des Johannes*, Vienna, 1958.

R. NETZHAMMER, *Die christlichen Altertümer der Dobrudscha*, Bucarest, 1918.

P. DE PALOL SALELLAS, *Tarraco hispanovisigoda*, Tarragona, 1953.

V. PARVAN, *Cetatea Tropaeum*, Bucarest, 1912.

W. M. RAMSAY and G. L. BELL, *The Thousand and One Churches*, London, 1909. Group of ancient churches in Asia Minor.

S. SALLER, *The Memorial of Moses on Mount Nebo*, Jerusalem, 1941.

M. SALMI, *La Basilica di S. Salvatore di Spoleto*, Florence, 1951.
I do not deal with this church in the present work, because I believe it to date from a later period.

F. SARRE and E. HERZFELD, *Archäologische Reise im Euphrat- und Tigrisgebiet*, 2 vols., Berlin, 1911-1920.
Description of the church of St Sergius at Resafa.

A. M. SCHNEIDER, *Die Brotvermehrungskirche von Et-Tabgha am Genesarethsee und ihre Mosaiken*, Paderborn, 1934.

W. SESTON and C. PERRAT, in *Revue des Etudes anciennes*, XXXXIX, 1947.
On the early constructions around the tomb of St Irenaeus at Lyons; the term 'basilica' in a funerary inscription.

J. STRZYGOWSKI, *Kleinasien, ein Neuland der Kunstgeschichte*, Leipzig, 1903.

J. VAULTRIN, *Les Basiliques chrétiennes de Carthage*, in *Revue africaine*, 73, 1932, p. 188 ff.

L. H. VINCENT and F. M. ABEL, *Bethléem, le sanctuaire de la Nativité*, Paris, 1914.

L. H. VINCENT and F. M. ABEL, *Jérusalem: II, Jérusalem nouvelle*, Paris, 1914.

L. H. VINCENT and F. M. ABEL, *Emmaüs, sa basilique et son histoire*, Paris, 1932.

J. B. WARD PERKINS and R. G. GOODCHILD, *The Christian Antiquities of Tripolitania*, in *Archaeologia*, XCV, Oxford, 1953, pp. VIII and 1-158.

J. B. WARD PERKINS and M. H. BALLANCE, *The Caesareum at Cyrene and the Basilica at Cremna*, in *Papers of the British School at Rome*, XXVI (new series XIII), 1958, pp. 137-194.

C. WATZINGER. *Denkmäler Palästinas*, II, Leipzig, 1935.

E. WIEGAND, *Das sogenannte Praetorium von Phaena-Mismije*, in *Würzburger Studien zur Altertumswissenschaft*, 13. Heft, Stuttgart, 1938.

2. Studies

W. ALTMANN, *Die italischen Rundbauten*, Berlin, 1906.

C. CECCHELLI, *Mausolei imperiali e reali di tardo impero e dell'alto medioevo*, Rome, 1940.

A. CHOISY, *L'Art de bâtir chez les Romains*, Paris, 1873.

A. CHOISY, *L'Art de bâtir chez les Byzantins*, Paris, 1883.

C. DELVOYE, *Les Basiliques paléochrétiennes*, in *Corsi*, Ravenna, 1959.
Summary of a course of lectures, with select bibliography.

J. DURM, *Die Baukunst der Etrusker und der Römer*, Stuttgart, 1905.

N. DUVAL, *Les Origines de la basilique chrétienne*, in *L'Information d'histoire de l'art*, 1962, No. 1, pp. 1-19.

E. DYGGVE, *Basilica discoperta, un nouveau type d'édifice cultuel paléochrétien*, in *Atti del IV congresso internazionale di archeologia cristiana*, I, Vatican City, 1940, pp. 415-431.

P. FRANKL, *Die frühmittelalterliche und romanische Baukunst*, in *Handbuch der Kunstwissenschaft*, Berlin, 1926.

G. GIOVANNONI, *La Tecnica della costruzione presso i Romani*, Rome, 1924.

H. GLUCK, *Ursprung des römischen und abendländischen Wölbungsbaues*, Vienna, 1933.

L. HAUTECŒUR, *Mystique et architecture. Le symbolisme du cercle et de la coupole*, Paris, 1954.

J. HUBERT, *Les Eglises à rotonde orientale*, in *Actes du IIIᵉ Congrès international pour l'étude du Haut Moyen Age (1951)*, Olten-Lausanne, 1954.

T. KLAUSER, *Vom Heroon zur Märtyrer-Basilica*, Bonn, 1942.

H. KÖTHE, *Frühchristliche Nischen-Rundbauten*, Marburg, 1925.

H. KÖTHE, *Das Konstantins Mausoleum und verwandte Denkmäler*, in *Jahrbuch des deutschen archäologischen Instituts*, XLVIII, 1933.

R. KRAUTHEIMER, *The Beginnings of Christian Architecture*, in *Review of Religion*, 1932.

R. KRAUTHEIMER, *S. Pietro and the Tripartite Transept in the Early Christian Basilica*, in *Proceedings of the American Philosophical Society*, LXXXIV, 1941, pp. 353-595.

R. KRAUTHEIMER, *Introduction to an Iconography of Mediaeval Architecture*, in *Journal of the Warburg and Courtauld Institute*, V, 1942, pp. 1-33.
The problem of typology in Christian architecture: what defined an edifice in the eyes of the Ancients?

E. LANGLOTZ and F. DEICHMANN, article BASILIKA in *Reallexikon für Antike und Christentum*, I, 1950.

P. LEMERLE, in *Bulletin de la Classe des Lettres... de l'Académie royale de Belgique*, 1948.

G. LEROUX, *Les Origines de l'édifice hypostyle en Grèce, en Orient et chez les Romains*, Paris, 1913.

U. MONNERET DE VILLARD, *L'architettura romana negli ultimi secoli dell'Impero*, in *Collegio degli ingegneri ed architetti*, XLVIII, 9-10, 1915.
Domed edifices of Rome and the Near East.

A. ORLANDOS, *The Timber-roofed Basilica* (in Greek), 2 vols., Athens, 1952-1954.

W. RAVE, *Trompe und Zwickel*, in *Festschrift für Hans Jantzen*, Berlin, 1951.

M. RUMPLER, *La Coupole dans l'architecture byzantine et musulmane*, Strasbourg, 1956.

310

E. B. SMITH, *Architectural Symbolism of Imperial Rome and the Middle Ages*, Princeton, 1956.

A. STANGE, *Das frühchristliche Kirchengebäude als Bild des Himmels*, Cologne, 1950.

P. STYGER, *Nymphäen, Mausoleen, Baptisterien*, in *Architectura*, I, 1933.

J. B. WARD PERKINS, in D.T. RICE, *The Great Palace of the Byzantine Emperors*, II, Edinburgh, 1958. Important study of the construction of Byzantine walls.

3. Secular Architecture.

K. O. DALMAN, *Der Valens-Aquädukt in Konstantinopel*, Bamberg, 1933.

N. DUVAL, *La Place de Split dans l'architecture antique du Bas-Empire*, in *Urbs*, Split, 1961-1962, pp. 67-95.

N. DUVAL, in *Bulletin de la Société nationale des Antiquaires de France*, 1961, pp. 76-117.

E. DYGGVE, *Ravennatium Palatium sacrum*, in *Medd. Dansk. Vid. Selsk.*, III, No. 2, Copenhagen, 1941, 63 pp.

E. DYGGVE, *La Région palatiale de Thessalonique*, in *IIᵉ Congrès international des Etudes classiques*, Copenhagen, 1954.

J. EBERSOLT, *Le Grand Palais de Constantinople et le livre des cérémonies*, Paris, 1910.

H. P. L'ORANGE, *Il palazzo di Massimiano Erculeo di Piazza Armerina*, in *Studi in onore di A. Calderini e R. Paribeni*, III, 1956.

F. OELMANN, *Hilani und Liwanhaus*, in *Bonner Jahrbuch*, 127, 1922.

A. M. SCHNEIDER and W. KARNAPP, *Die Stadtmauer von Iznik (Nicäa)* Berlin, 1938.

J. STRZYGOWSKI and P. FORSCHHEIMER, *Die byzantinischen Wasserbehälter von Konstantinopel*, Vienna, 1893.

K. M. SWOBODA, *Römische und romanische Paläste*, Vienna, 1919.

T. WIEGAND and E. MAMBURY, *Die Kaiserpaläste von Konstantinopel*, Berlin, 1934.

PAINTING

R. BIANCHI-BANDINELLI, *Continuità ellenistica nella pittura di età medio e tardo-romana*, in *Rivista dell'Istituto Nazionale dell'Archeologia e Storia dell'Arte*, new series, II, pp. 1-85, 1953 (in 1954).

M. BORDA, *La pittura romana*, Milan, 1958.

L. DE BRUYNE, in *Rivista di archeologia cristiana*, XXVII, 1951, pp. 195-216.

A. FERRUA, *Le pitture della nuova catacomba di via Latina*, Vatican City, 1960.

E. R. GOODENOUGH, *Jewish Symbols in the Greco-Roman Period*, 8 vols., New York, 1953 et seq.

A. GRABAR, *Le Thème religieux de la synagogue de Doura (245-246 après J.-C.)*, in *Revue de l'histoire des religions*, 123, 1941, pp. 143-192, and 124, 1941, pp. 5-35.

E. JOSI, various articles in *Rivista di archeologia cristiana*, in particular V, 1928, pp. 167-217, and X, 1933, pp. 7-16.

G. P. KIRSCH, in *Rivista di archeologia cristiana*, VII, 1930, pp. 203-234.

C. KRAELING, *The Synagogue* [of Dura-Europos], in *The Excavations at Dura-Europos*, VIII, New Haven, 1958.

A. G. MARTIMORT, in *Rivista di archeologia cristiana*, XXV, 1949, pp. 106-114.

O. MARUCCHI, *Le catacombe romane*, Rome, 1933.

G. MATTHIAE, *Pittura romana del medioevo*, Rome, 1965.

B. PACE, *I mosaici di Piazza Armerina*, Rome, 1955.

K. PFISTER, *Katakombenmalerei*, Potsdam, 1924.

G. C. PICARD, *Mosaici greci e romani*, in *Enciclopedia Universale dell'Arte*, Vol. X, pp. 676-683, Venice-Rome, 1963.

M. I. ROSTOVTZEFF, *The Excavations at Dura-Europos. Preliminary Report of the Fifth Season of Work*, New Haven, 1934.

A. M. SCHNEIDER, *Die Brotvermehrungskirche von Et-Tabgha am Genesarethsee und ihre Mosaiken*, Paderborn, 1934.

H. STERN, in *Dumbarton Oaks Papers*, XII, 1958, pp. 157-218.

H. STERN, in *Cahiers archéologiques*, XII, 1962, pp. 99-113.

M. VAN BERGHEM and E. CLOUZOT, *Mosaïques chrétiennes du IVᵉ au Xᵉ siècle*, Geneva, 1924.

J. WILPERT, *Le pitture delle catacombe romane*, Rome 1903.

J. WILPERT, *Die römischen Mosaiken und Malereien der kirchlichen Bauten vom IV. bis XIII. Jahrhundert*, 4 vols., Freiburg-im-Breisgau, 1916.

F. WIRTH, *Römische Wandmalerei vom Untergang Pompejis bis ans Ende des 3. Jahrhunderts*, Berlin, 1934.

SCULPTURE

G. BECATTI, *La colonna coclide istoriata*, Rome, 1960.

B. BERENSON, *The Arch of Constantine, or The Decline of Form*, London, 1954.

C. CECCHELLI, in *Actes du VIᵉ Congrès international d'Etudes byzantines*, II, Paris, 1951.

R. DELBRUCK, *Antike Porphyrwerke*, Berlin, 1932.

C. DELVOYE, *La Sculpture byzantine*, in *Corsi*, Ravenna, 1961. Summary of a course of lectures, with select bibliography.

A. GIULIANO, *Arco di Costantino*, Milan, 1955.

A. GRABAR, *Sculptures byzantines de Constantinople (IVᵉ-Xᵉ s.)*, Paris, 1963.

J. KOLLWITZ, *Die oströmische Plastik der Theodosianischen Zeit*, Berlin, 1941.

H. P. L'ORANGE, *Studien zur Geschichte des spätantiken Porträts*, Oslo, 1933.

H. P. L'ORANGE, *Apotheosis in Ancient Portraiture*, Oslo, 1947.

H. P. L'ORANGE and A. VON GERKAN *Der spätantike Bilderschmuck des Konstantinbogens*, Berlin, 1935.

H. PEIRCE and R. TYLER, *Byzantine Art*, London, 1926; *L'Art byzantin*, 2 vols., Paris, 1932-1934.

E. WILL, *Le Relief cultuel gréco-romain*, Paris, 1956. Cf. D. SCHLUMBERGER, in *Syria*, 1958.

O. WULFF, *Altchristliche und mittelalterliche byzantinische und italienische Bildwerke*, Berlin Museum, 1909.

O. WULFF and F. VOLBACH, *Beschreibung der Bildwerke der christlichen Epochen*: III, *Ergänzungsband*, Berlin, 1923.

Sarcophagi.

F. BENOIT, *Sarcophages paléochrétiens d'Arles et de Marseille*, Paris, 1954.

J. BOUBE, *Les Sarcophages paléochrétiens de Martres-Tolosane*, in *Cahiers archéologiques*, IX, 1957, pp. 33-72.

G. BOVINI, *I sarcofagi paleocristiani, determinazione della loro cronologia mediante l'analisi dei ritratti*, Rome, 1949.

H. VON CAMPENHAUSE, *Die Passionssarkophage*, in *Marburger Jahrbuch für Kunstwissenschaft*, 1929.

F. GERKE, *Die christlichen Sarkophage der vorkonstantinischen Zeit*, Berlin, 1940.

F. GERKE, *Christus in er spätantiken Plastik*, Berlin, 1941.

M. LAWRENCE, *The Sarcophagi of Ravenna*, College Art Association Studies, No. 2, New York, 1945.

E. LE BLANT, *Les Sarcophages chrétiens de la ville d'Arles*, Paris, 1879.

E. LE BLANT, *Les Sarcophages chrétiens de la Gaule*, Paris, 1886.

H. U. VON SCHONEBECK, *Der Mailander Sarkophag und seine Nachfolge*, Vatican City, 1935.

E. S. STRONG, *Roman Sculpture from Augustus to Constantine*, London and New York, 1907; revised edition : *La scultura romana da Augusto a Costantino*, 2 vols., Florence, 1923-1926.

O. THULIN, in *Römische Mitteilungen*, 1929.
Statuette of the seated Christ, Museo delle Terme, Rome.

J. B. WARD PERKINS, in *Archaeologia*, 87, London, 1938, pp. 79-128.
Sarcophagi of Aquitaine.

J. WILPERT, *I Sarcofagi cristiani antichi*, 5 vols., Vatican City, 1929-1936.

IVORIES

G. BOVINI and L. B. OTTOLENGHI, *Catalogo della mostra degli avori dell'alto medioevo*, Ravenna, 2nd edition, 1956.

O. M. DALTON, *Catalogue of Early Christian Antiquities ... in the British Museum*, London, 1901.

O. M. DALTON, *Catalogue of the Ivory Carvings of the Christian Era ... of the British Museum*, London, 1909.

R. DELBRÜCK, *Probleme der Lipsanothek in Brescia*, Bonn, 1952.

H. GRAEVEN, *Frühchristliche und mittelalterliche Elfenbeinwerke in photographischer Nachbildung*, 2 vols., Rome, 1898-1900.
Collections in England and Italy.

J. KOLLWITZ, *Die Lipsanothek zu Brescia*, Berlin, 1933.

M. LAURENT, *Les Ivoires prégothiques conservés en Belgique*, Brussels-Paris, 1912, new edition, 1927.

M. H. LONGHURST, *Victoria and Albert Museum. Catalogue of Carvings in Ivory*, Part I, London, 1927.

E. P. DE LOOS-DIETZ, *Vroeg-christelijke ivoren*, Assen, 1947.

E. MOLINIER, *Catalogue des ivoires du Musée national du Louvre*, Paris, 1896.

C. R. MOREY, *Gli oggetti di avorio e di osso. Catalogo del Museo Sacro Vaticano*, I, Vatican City 1936.

C. R. MOREY, *Early Christian Ivories of the Eastern Empire*, in *Dumbarton Oaks Papers*, I, pp. 41 ff., Washington, 1941.

J. NATANSON, *Early Christian Ivories*, London, 1953.

W. NEUSS, *Die Anfänge des Christentums im Rheinlande*, Bonn, 3rd edition, 1933.

J. SAUER, *Die altchristliche Elfenbeinplastik*, Leipzig, 1922.

G. STUHLFAUTH, *Die altchristliche Elfenbeinplastik*, Leipzig, 1896.

W. VÖGE, *Beschreibungen der Bildwerke der christlichen Epochen. Die Elfenbeinwerke. Katalog des königlichen Museum zu Berlin*, 2nd edition, Berlin, 1900.

W. F. VOLBACH, *Elfenbeinarbeiten der Spätantike und des frühen Mittelalters*, 2nd edition, Mainz, 1952.

INDUSTRIAL ARTS

In addition to the catalogues and surveys listed above under General Works (Garrucci, Peirce and Tyler, Volbach and Hirmer), consult the following:

J. LABARTE, *Histoire des arts industriels au Moyen Age et à l'époque de la Renaissance*, 2nd edition, 3 vols., Paris, 1872-1875.

E. MOLINIER, *Histoire générale des arts appliqués à l'industrie, du Ve à la fin du XVIIIe siècle*, 6 vols., Paris, 1896-1912.

A. RIEGL, *Die spätrömische Kunstindustrie nach den Funden in Osterreich-Ungarn*, Vienna, 2 vols., 1901-1923.

GOLD AND JEWELRY

W. DENNISON, *A Gold Treasure of the Late Roman Period from Egypt*, New York, 1918.

M. C. ROSS, *Early Christian and Byzantine Art*, Baltimore, 1947.
Includes many pieces from American collections exhibited at the Walters Art Gallery, Baltimore, in 1947.

MEDALS

The great Roman medals in gold, of the 4th, 5th and 6th centuries, are genuine works of art.
In addition to Peirce and Tyler, I and II, consult the following for their fine plates:

W. FRŒHNER, *Les Médaillons de l'empire romain depuis le règne d'Auguste jusqu'à Priscus Attale*, Paris, 1878.

G. GNECCHI, *I medaglioni romani*, 3 vols., Milan, 1912.

F. KENNER, in *Jahrbuch der kunsthistorischen Sammlung des allerhöchsten Kaiserhauses*, IX, 1889.
The best reproductions of the Vienna collection, the richest of all collections in large 4th century medals.

J. MAURICE, *Numismatique constantinienne*, 3 vols., Paris, 1908-1912.
Mediocre reproductions, but the best repertory of the iconographic types of Constantinian coins and medals.

GLASS

Apart from Peirce and Tyler, I and II, and catalogues of isolated objects, there are very few studies of glassware.
The following works all deal with 'gold glasses,' i.e. the Early Christian bowls and drinking vessels in which gold leaf was applied to the base of the cup and etched with patterns, inscriptions and pictures.

R. GARRUCCI, *Vetri ornati di figure in oro trovati nei cimiteri cristiani*, Rome, 2nd edition, 1864.

C. R. MOREY, in *Festschrift für P. Clemen*, Düsseldorf-Bonn, 1926.

H. VOGEL, *Die altchristlichen Goldgläser*, Freiburg-im-Breisgau, 1900.

ICONOGRAPHY

General Iconographic Surveys

No special publication of this kind exists but many books dealing with painting and sculpture, and with certain aspects of the industrial arts, offer a more or less extended treatment of iconographic imagery. See above under General Works, Painting, Sculpture, and Industrial Arts.
There are innumerable books and articles dealing with one or several iconographic themes. In the selection given below we distinguish between pagan, imperial, Jewish and Christian themes. We would also emphasize the multiplicity of the iconographic programmes—a characteristic trait of the art dealt with in this volume.

Pagan Themes

A. ALFÖLDI, *The Festival of Isis at Rome under the Christian Emperors of the IVth Century*, in *Dissertationes Pannoniae*, II, 7, Budapest, 1937.

A. ALFÖLDI, *Die Kontorniaten*, Budapest, 1941-1943.

F. CUMONT, *Recherches sur le symbolisme funéraire des Romains*, Paris, 1942.

F. WIRTH, *Römische Wandmalerei vom Untergang Pompejis bis ans Ende des 3. Jahrhunderts*, Berlin, 1934.

See also Stern and Kollwitz, listed above under Painting and Sculpture respectively.

Imperial Roman and Byzantine Themes

In addition to the studies of coins, see above the works by Grabar (under General Works, 5), Kollwitz and L'Orange (under Sculpture), Delbrück (under Ivories), and also the following:

A. ALFÖLDI, two lengthy studies in *Römische Mitteilungen*, 49, 1934, pp. 1-118 and 50, 1935, pp. 1-171.

P. G. HAMBERG, *Studies in Roman Imperial Art*, Uppsala, 1945.

H. P. L'ORANGE, *Studies in the Iconography of Cosmic Kingship in the Ancient World*, Oslo, 1952.

Jewish Themes

E. R. GOODENOUGH, *Jewish Symbols in the Greco-Roman Period*, 8 vols., New York 1953 et seq.
An exhaustive and valuable corpus.

H. KOHL and C. WATZINGER, *Antike Synagogen in Galiläa*, Leipzig, 1916.

Sculptures of a religious character :

A. GRABAR, *Le Thème religieux de la synagogue de Doura (245-246 après J.-C.)*, in *Revue de l'histoire des religions*, 123, 1941, pp. 143-192, and 124, 1941, pp. 5-35.

H. L. HEMPEL, *Zum Problem der Anfänge der A.T. Illustration*, in *Zeitschrift für die alttestamentliche Wissenschaft*, 69, 1957, pp. 103-131.

C. KRAELING, *The Synagogue* [of Dura-Europos], in *The Excavations at Dura-Europos*, VIII, New Haven, 1958.
This important but inadequately illustrated monograph does not supersede previous publications.

J. LEVEEN, *The Hebrew Bible in Art*, London, 1944.

R. DU MESNIL DU BUISSON, *Les Peintures de la synagogue de Doura-Europos*, Vatican City, 1939.

C. NORDSTRÖM, *Some Jewish Legends in Byzantine Art*, in *Byzantion*, XXV-XXVII, 1958, pp. 457-508.

C. ROTH, *Jewish Antecedents of Christian Art*, in *Journal of the Warburg and Courtauld Institute*, 16, 1953.

K. WEITZMANN, *Die Illustration der Septuaginta*, in *Münchener Jahrbuch der bildenden Kunst*, III-IV, 1954, pp. 96-120.

Christian Themes

In addition to the general surveys listed above under General Works, consult the art and archaeological journals, the monographs on various monuments and works of art (under Painting, Sculpture, Ivories, and Industrial Arts), and the many studies of iconographic themes.

L. DE BRUYNE, *L'Imposition des mains dans l'art chrétien ancien*, in *Rivista di archeologia cristiana*, XV, 1943, p. 113 ff.

C. CECCHELLI, *Il trionfo della croce*, Rome, 1954.

F. CUMONT, *L'Adoration des Mages et l'art triomphal de Rome*, in *Atti della Pontificia Accademia romana di archeologia*, Series III, Memorie, 3, pp. 81-105, Rome, 1932.

P. A. FÉVRIER, *Les Quatre Fleuves du Paradis*, in *Rivista di archeologia cristiana*, XXXII, pp. 179-199, 1956.

J. FINK, *Noe der Gerechte in der frühchristlichen Kunst*, Münster (Westphalia), 1955.

F. GERKE, *Christus in der spätantiken Plastik*, Mainz, 1938.
Cf. K. WESSEL, in *Archäologischer Anzeiger*, 1950-1951, p. 300; 1953, p. 168 ff.; and F. VAN DER MEER, *Majestas Domini*, Rome, 1938.

E. H. KANTOROWICZ, *The Kings Advent* in *The Art Bulletin*, XXVI, 1944, p. 267 ff.

H. KEHRER, *Die heiligen drei Könige in der Literatur*, 2 vols., Leipzig, 1908-1909.

N. P. KONDAKOV, *Iconography of the Mother of God* (in Russian), 3 vols., St. Petersburg, 1914-1915.

C. LEONARDI, *Ampelos. Il simbolo della vite nell'arte pagana e paleocristiana*, in *Ephemerides liturgicae*, Ser. historica, XXI, 1947.

A. G. MARTINIER, *L'Iconographie des catacombes et la catéchèse antique*, in *Rivista di archeologia cristiana*, XXV, 1949, p. 105 ff.

K. MICHEL, *Gebet und Bild*, in *Studien über christliche Denkmäler*, new series, I, Strasbourg, 1902.

F. NOACK, *Die Geburt Christi in der bildenden Kunst...*, Darmstadt, 1894.

C. H. PUECH, *Le Cerf et le serpent*, in *Cahiers archéologiques*, IV, 1949, p. 20 ff.

J. QUASTEN, *Der Gute Hirt in frühchristlicher Totenliturgie und Grabeskunst*, in *Miscellanea in honorem Giovanni Mercati*: I, *Studi e testi*, No. 121, Vatican City, 1946, p. 37 ff.

J. REIL, *Die frühchristlichen Darstellungen der Kreuzigung Christi*, Leipzig, 1904.

E. SCHLEE, *Die Ikonographie der Paradiesflüsse*, Leipzig, 1937.

M. SIMON, *Sur l'origine des sarcophages chrétiens du type Bethesda*, in *Mélanges d'archéologie et d'histoire*, LV, 1938, p. 201 ff.

E. B. SMITH, *Early Christian Iconography and the School of Provence*, Princeton, 1918.
Now out of date. On a similar theory put forward by Volbach, who assigns certain Early Christian ivories to Gaul, see his book on ivory carvings (above under Ivories).

F. SÜHLING, *Die Taube als religiöses Symbol im christlichen Altertum*, in *Römische Quartalschrift*, Suppl. 24, 1930, pp. 1-399.

J. WILPERT, *Fractio panis*, Freiburg-im-Breisgau, 1895.

Baptismal Iconography

L. DE BRUYNE, in *Miscellanea liturgica in honorem C. C. Mohlberg*, I, Rome, 1948.

L. DE BRUYNE, in *Actes du Ve Congrès international d'archéologie chrétienne*, *Aix-en-Provence, 1954*, Vatican City, 1957.
Cf. H. STERN in the same volume of proceedings.

Iconography in Churches

Rome.

(In addition to monographs on churches listed above under General Works.)

K. LEHMANN, in *The Art Bulletin*, XXXVII, 1955, pp. 193-196, 291-292.
On the iconography of Santa Costanza.

H. STERN, in *Dumbarton Oaks Papers*, Vol. XII, pp. 157-218, 1958.
On the same subject.

Ravenna.

C. O. NORDSTRÖM, *Ravennastudien*, Stockholm, 1953.

O. S. VON SIMSON, *Sacred Fortress. Byzantine Art and Statecraft in Ravenna*, Chicago, 1948.

See also several studies in *Felix Ravenna*.

313

List of Illustrations

The descriptive notices in the List of Illustrations
have been compiled with the assistance of Madame Clémence DUPRAT,
scientific advisor to the Arts of Mankind series.

The present volume deals with a period in which many of the surviving works of art cannot be dated with precision. In the main text of the book we have indicated or suggested the chronological limits within which a given work or group of works may be situated. To do more would be to distort the evidence we have and run the risk of serious errors. For this reason, in the descriptive notices that follow, we have purposely refrained from assigning conjectural dates to works or monuments which cannot be dated with any certainty.

In many cases, too, the size of the object is not indicated in the descriptive notice. The exact measurements of a fragmentary textile or a necklace may have a certain commercial interest, but for the historical and aesthetic study of such objects—and this is the purpose of the present work—they are generally irrelevant. The reader will have no trouble imagining the approximate size of objects in common use (furniture, books, arms, vases) and of others whose scale is defined either by the dimensions of their constituent materials (ivory plaques, coloured stones and glass) or by their architectural setting (scale plans of the buildings will give a sufficient idea of the size of the mosaics and wall paintings contained in them).

A.G

FRONTISPIECE. *Antique Christian Art.* Rome, S. Costanza, vault of the ambulatory. *Figure Medallions alternating with Floral Motifs.* 4th century. *In situ.* Mosaic. (Photo Scala)

1. Rome. *Aerial View.* (Photo Fotocielo)

2. Constantinople. *Aerial View.* (Museum of St Sophia Photo)

3. Jerusalem. *Panoramic View.* (Photo Roger Viollet)

4. *Roman Art.* Rome, Forum of Trajan. *Trajan's Column, detail: Dacian Peasants before the Emperor.* Cast. Early 2nd century. *In situ.* Marble. (Archi-

vio fotografico, Gallerie e Musei vaticani)

5. *Roman Art. Medal of Septimius Severus.* 3rd century. Paris, Bibliothèque Nationale, Cabinet des Médailles. Gold. (Photo Bibliothèque Nationale)

6. *Roman Art.* Rome. *Column of Marcus Aurelius, detail: Execution of Barbarian Prisoners.* Late 2nd century. *In situ.* (Photo Anderson)

7. *Roman Art.* Sabratha, Libya, Theatre. 'Pulpitum,' Central Niche, detail: *Septimius Severus sacrificing to the African Gods.* 2nd century. *In situ.* (Photo Dr Pierre Guiraud, Service of Antiquities of the Libyan government)

8. *Roman Art. Medal of Diocletian, Persecutor of the Christians.* Early 4th century. Paris, Bibliothèque Nationale, Cabinet des Médailles. Gold. (Photo Bibliothèque Nationale)

9. *Roman Art.* Salonica. *Arch of Galerius, detail: Triumph of the Emperors.* About 300. *In situ.* (Photo Hassia)

10. *Roman Art.* Rome. *Arch of Constantine, detail: The Emperor distributing Largesse.* Before 315. *In situ.* (Gabinetto fotografico nazionale, Rome)

11. *Roman Art. Medal of Constantine and his Ideal Model Alexander the Great.* 324-337. Paris, Bibliothèque Nationale, Cabinet des Médailles. Gold. (Photo Bibliothèque Nationale)

12. *Roman Art. Consular Diptych of Stilicho: Stilicho, Serena and Eucherius.* About 395. Monza, Cathedral Treasury. Ivory. (Photo Alinari)

13. *Antique Christian Art.* Rome. *Sarcophagus, detail: Portraits of Husband and Wife.* 5th century. Rome, S. Sebastiano, Museum. Marble. (Photo Pontificia Commissione di archeologia sacra)

14. *Roman Art.* Rome. *Roman Calendar of 354. Portrait of Constantius II as Consul (after a drawing by Peiresc).* 354. Copy of the 17th century. Rome, Vatican Library. (Library Photo)

15. *The Emperor Valentinian I (?) in Military Costume, detail.* 4th century. Barletta, South Italy. Bronze, overall height 16 ft 9 in. (Hirmer Fotoarchiv, Munich)

16-17. *Roman Art.* Rome. *Medal of the Emperor Valens, obverse and reverse.* 364-378. Vienna, Kunsthistorisches Museum. Gold. (Museum Photo)

18. *Roman Art. Statuette of an Empress.* Late 4th century. Paris, Bibliothèque Nationale, Cabinet des Médailles. Marble. (Photo Bibliothèque Nationale)

19. *Antique Christian Art.* Aquileia, North Italy, Cathedral of Bishop Theodore. *Jonah.* Early 4th century. *In situ.* Mosaic pavement. (Photo Mauro Marocco)

20. *Antique Christian Art.* Rome. *Jonah.* 4th century. Vatican, Museo Cristiano. Gold-painted glass. (Photo Held)

21. *Antique Christian Art.* Provence. *Sarcophagus, detail.* 3rd century. Brignoles (Var), Church of Saint-Sauveur. Marble. (Photo U.D.F.-La Photothèque)

22. *Antique Christian Art.* Rome, Catacomb of SS. Pietro e Marcellino, Chamber XIII. *The Raising of Lazarus.* Late 3rd century. *In situ.* Wall painting, 31 1/2 by 43 in. (Photo Held)

23. *Antique Christian Art.* Rome, Catacomb called Coemeterium Majus, Chamber II, ceiling. *Adam and Eve.* 4th century. *In situ.* Wall painting, 27 1/2 by 39 1/2 in. (Photo Held)

24. *Antique Christian Art.* Rome, Catacomb of the Via Latina, Cubiculum B, left-hand arcosolium. *Adam and Eve grieving.* Mid-fourth century. *In situ.* Wall painting, 33 by 45 in. (Photo Held)

25. *Antique Christian Art.* Sfax, Tunisia. *Funerary Mosaic: Orant.* 4th-5th century. Bardo Museum, Tunis. Mosaic. (Atlas-Photo, Charles Lenars, Nice)

26. *Antique Christian Art.* Rome. *Sarcophagus, detail: Orant flanked by Trees.* Early 3rd century. Rome, Museo Torlonia. Marble. (Photo Pontificia Commissione di archeologia sacra)

27. *Antique Christian Art.* Aquileia, North Italy, Cathedral of Bishop Theodore. *The Good Shepherd.* Early 4th century. *In situ.* Mosaic pavement. (Photo Antonello Perissinotto, Padua)

28. *Antique Christian Art.* Rome, Catacomb of Callisto, Crypt of Lucina, chamber near the tomb of Cornelius. *The Good Shepherd.* Early 3rd century. *In situ.* Wall painting, diameter 28 in. (Photo Held)

29. *Antique Christian Art.* Rome. *The Raising of Lazarus.* 4th century. Vatican, Museo Cristiano. Gold-painted glass. (Photo Held)

30. *Antique Christian Art.* Rome, Catacomb of Pretestato. *Sarcophagus with Vintaging Cupids, short side.* 4th century. Rome, Museo Laterano. Marble. (Hirmer Fotoarchiv, Munich)

31. *Antique Christian Art.* Rome, Syncretic Tomb of the Aurelii, side of an arcosolium. *Jonah thrown overboard from a Boat with a Square Sail.* 4th century. *In situ.* Wall painting, 39 1/4 by 28 1/4 in. (Photo Held)

32. *Antique Jewish Art.* Dura-Europos, Synagogue, west wall, lower register. *The Triumph of Mordecai (Purim), detail.* Between 245 and 256. Damascus Museum. Wall painting, height of the register 51 in. (University of Michigan Photo)

33. *Antique Christian Art.* Rome. *Sarcophagus, Front, detail: Christ seated above a Personification of the Cosmos.* 4th century. Rome, Museo Laterano. Marble. (Photo Pontificia Commissione di archeologia sacra)

34. *Roman Art.* Rome, Underground Basilica of Porta Maggiore. *Mythological Scene.* First century. *In situ.* Stucco. (Photo De Antonis)

35. *Antique Christian Art.* Rome, Catacomb of the Via Latina, Room N, right-hand niche. *Hercules in the Garden of the Hesperides.* Mid-4th century. *In situ.* Wall painting, 33 1/2 by 33 1/2 in. (Photo Held)

36. *Antique Christian Art.* Rome, Catacomb of the Via Latina, Cubiculum B, left-hand arcosolium, lunette. *Jacob and his Sons arriving in Egypt.* Mid-4th century. *In situ.* Wall painting, 33 by 66 in. (Photo Held)

37. *Antique Christian Art.* Rome, Catacomb of the Via Latina, Cubiculum B, left-hand arcosolium. *Cain and Abel bringing Offerings.* Mid-4th century. *In situ.* Wall painting, overall size 33 by 45 in. (Photo Held)

38. *Antique Jewish Art.* Dura-Europos, Synagogue, west wall, middle register. *Head of a Prophet, detail.* Between 245 and 256. Damascus Museum. Wall painting, height of this register 59 in. The mural decoration of the Synagogue was reconstituted by H.F. Pearson. (University of Michigan Photo)

39. *Antique Christian Art.* Rome (?). *Sarcophagus: Christ and the Apostles, detail.* 4th-5th century. Paris, Louvre. Marble. (Photo U.D.F.-La Photothèque)

40. *Antique Christian Art.* Rome (?). *Sarcophagus, detail: Head of an Apostle.* 4th-5th century. Paris, Louvre. Marble. (Photo U.D.F.-La Photothèque)

41. *Antique Christian Art.* Rome. *Sarcophagus of Junius Bassus: Cycle of Old and New Testament Subjects and Christ delivering the Law, detail.* About 359. Rome, Grotte Vaticane. Marble. (Photo De Antonis)

42. *Antique Christian Art.* Rome. *Sarcophagus, Front, detail: A Head.* 4th century. Rome, S. Sebastiano. (Photo German Archaeological Institute, Rome)

43. *Antique Christian Art.* Rome, Catacomb of Commodilla. *Virgin and Child enthroned between St Felix and St Adauctus with the Donatrix Turtura, detail: Head of Turtura.* 528. *In situ.* Icon fresco. (Photo Pontificia Commissione di archeologia sacra)

44. *Antique Christian Art.* Rome, S. Maria Maggiore. *View of the Interior.* Double colonnade and mosaics of 432-440; ceiling and marbles later. *In situ.* (Photo Alinari)

45. *Pagan Syrian Art.* Dura-Europos. *Cult Relief: The Syrian God Aphlad and a Priest sacrificing, detail.* First century A.D. Present whereabouts unknown. Limestone, overall size 20 by 12 in. (Photo General Directorate of Antiquities and Museums, Damascus)

46. *Pagan Palmyrene Art.* Palmyra. *Relief: Procession of Women.* Early first century A.D. Palmyra Museum. Soft limestone, 20 by 16 in. (Photo French Institute of Archaeology, Beirut)

47. *Roman Art. Heads of Two Tetrarchs, detail.* Early 4th century. Venice, Piazza San Marco, at the south-west corner of St Mark's. Porphyry. (Photo Osvaldo Böhm)

48. *Pagan Palmyrene Art.* Palmyra, Tomb of the Three Brothers (Magharat-el-Djelideh), south wall, detail. *Funerary Portrait.* 160. *In situ.* Wall painting. (After C.H. Kraeling, *Color Photographs of the Paintings in the Tomb of the Three Brothers at Palmyra,* in *Annales archéologiques de Syrie,* XI, XII, 1961-62, Damascus, pl. VIII)

49. *Antique Pagan Syrian Art.* Edessa, Hill of Djebel Adhar. *Funerary Mosaic of Moqimu (copy by Mrs Seton Lloyd).* 3rd century. *In situ.* Mosaic pavement, 98 1/2 by 100 1/2 in. (Photo J.-B. Ségal)

50. *Roman Christian Art.* Rome, Villa Torlonia. *Sarcophagus, detail: Plotinus (?) surrounded by Female Figures and Disciples.* About 270. Rome, Museo Laterano. Marble. (Photo German Archaeological Institute, Rome)

51. *Antique Christian Art.* Rome, SS. Pietro e Marcellino, lunette of an arcosolium, detail. *Christ healing the Woman with an Issue of Blood.* Late 3rd century. *In situ.* Wall painting, 24 1/2 by 21 1/4 in. (Photo Held)

52. *Antique Christian Art.* Dura-Europos. *'Christian House': Isometric View.* 3rd century. (After Jean Lassus, *Sanctuaires chrétiens de Syrie,* Paris, 1947, fig. 5, p. 11)

53. *Antique Christian Art.* Dura-Europos. *'Christian House': Plan.* 3rd century. (After *The Excavations at Dura-Europos, Preliminary Report of the Fifth Season of Work,* October 1931-March 1932, New Haven, Yale University Press, 1934, pl. XXXIX)

54. *Christian Art.* Rome, S. Martino ai Monti. *Isometric View of the Original Church.* 3rd century. (After René Vieilliard, *Les Origines du titre de Saint-Martin-aux-Monts à Rome,* in *Studi di antichità cristiana,* IV, Rome-Paris, 1931, fig. 4, p. 26)

55. *Christian Art.* Aquileia, North Italy. *Cathedral of Bishop Theodore: Plan.* Early 4th century. (After Paolo Verzone, *L'architettura religiosa dell'alto medio evo nell'Italia settentrionale,* Milan, 1942, fig. 12, p. 32)

56. *Antique Christian Art.* Salona, Dalmatia. *Basilica and Martyrium of St Anastasius (reconstruction by E. Dyggve).* 4th century. (Photo E. Dyggve)

57. *Antique Christian Art.* Salona, Dalmatia. *Martyrium of St Anastasius (reconstruction by E. Dyggve).* 4th century. (Photo E. Dyggve)

58. *Antique Christian Art.* Rome, Catacomb of the Giordani, detail. *Orant.* 4th century. *In situ.* Wall painting, 36 1/4 by 26 1/4 in. (Photo Held)

59. *Antique Christian Art.* Dura-Europos, 'Christian House,' Baptistery. *Overall View of Apse and North Wall.* Early 3rd century. Yale University Art Gallery, New Haven, Conn. (Museum Photo)

60. *Antique Christian Art.* Dura-Europos, 'Christian House,' Baptistery, apse above the baptismal font. *The Good Shepherd and his Flock.* Early 3rd

century. Yale University Art Gallery, New Haven, Conn. (Museum Photo)

61. *Antique Christian Art.* Dura-Europos, 'Christian House,' Baptistery, north wall, detail. *Healing of the Paralytic.* Early 3rd century. Yale University Art Gallery, New Haven, Conn. Wall painting. (Museum Photo)

62. *Antique Christian Art.* Dura-Europos, 'Christian House,' Baptistery, north wall, detail. *Christ and St Peter walking on the Water.* Early 3rd century. Yale University Art Gallery, New Haven, Conn. Wall painting. (Museum Photo)

63. *Antique Christian Art.* Dura-Europos, 'Christian House,' Baptistery, detail. *The Woman of Samaria at the Well.* Early 3rd century. Yale University Art Gallery, New Haven, Conn. Wall painting. (Museum Photo)

64. *Pagan Syrian Art.* Dura-Europos, Mithraeum, detail. *Mithras Hunting.* 2nd century. Yale University Art Gallery, New Haven, Conn. Wall painting. (Museum Photo)

65. *Pagan Syrian Art.* Dura-Europos, Mithraeum, detail. *Portrait of Zoroaster (?).* 2nd century. Yale University Art Gallery, New Haven, Conn. Wall painting. (Museum Photo)

66. *Antique Jewish Art.* Dura-Europos, Synagogue, back wall. *Overall View of the Wall Paintings, with the Torah Shrine.* First third of 3rd century. Damascus, National Museum. Wall painting. (University of Michigan Photo)

67. *Antique Jewish Art.* Dura-Europos, Synagogue, west wall, detail. *The Crossing of the Red Sea; The Abandoned Temple, detail.* 3rd century. Damascus, National Museum. Wall painting. (University of Michigan Photo)

68. *Antique Jewish Art.* Dura-Europos, Synagogue, west wall, detail. *The Temple of Dagon devastated by the Ark; The Childhood of Moses, detail.* 3rd century. Damascus, National Museum. Wall painting. (University of Michigan Photo)

69. *Antique Jewish Art.* Dura-Europos, Synagogue, west wall, detail. *The Miracle of the Well; Elijah resurrecting the Son of the Widow of Zarephath.* 3rd century. Damascus, National Museum. Wall painting. (University of Michigan Photo)

70. *Pagan Syrian Art.* Dura-Europos, House of the Scribes, ceiling, detail.

Portrait of the Roman Official Heliodorus. 2nd or 3rd century. Yale University Art Gallery, New Haven, Conn. Wall painting. (Museum Photo)

71. *Antique Jewish Art.* Dura-Europos, Synagogue, west wall, detail. *Figure of a Man: Abraham.* 3rd century. Damascus, National Museum. Wall painting. (University of Michigan Photo)

72. *Roman Art.* South Italy. *Votive Relief of Cassia Priscilla: Hercules and Omphale with Scenes of the Labours of Hercules.* 2nd century. Naples, Museo Nazionale. (Photo Alinari)

73. *Roman Art.* Rome, Barberini 'Mithraeum.' *Mithras, Scenes of the Cosmogony, and Other Images of his Cycle, detail.* 3rd century. *In situ.* Wall painting. (Photo De Antonis)

74. *Antique Christian Art.* Rome, Cemetery under St Peter's, Tomb of the Julii, vault. *Vine-Shoots and Christ as the Sun God.* 3rd or 4th century. *In situ.* Mosaic. (Photo Held)

75. *Antique Christian Art.* Rome, Catacomb of Domitilla, Flavian Hall, detail. *Birds beside a Vase.* Mid-3rd century. *In situ.* Wall painting, 29 1/2 by 31 1/2 in. (Photo Held)

76. *Antique Christian Art.* Rome, Catacomb of Domitilla, detail. *Ceiling Painting: The Good Shepherd.* Late 2nd-early 3rd century. *In situ.* Wall painting. (Photo Pontificia Commissione di archeologia sacra)

77. *Antique Christian Art.* Rome, Catacomb of Pretestato, Crypt of S. Gennaro. *Air Shaft with Paintings.* 3rd century. *In situ.* Wall painting. (Photo Pontificia Commissione di archeologia sacra)

78. *Antique Christian Art.* Rome, SS. Pietro e Marcellino, vault, detail. *Jonah thrown into the Sea.* Late 3rd century. *In situ.* Wall painting, 15 3/4 by 22 3/4 in. (Photo Held)

79. *Antique Christian Art.* Rome, Catacomb of Priscilla, Cappella Greca, entrance, detail. *Head in a Medallion.* First half of 3rd century. *In situ.* Wall painting, diameter 20 3/4 in. (Photo Held)

80. *Antique Christian Art.* Rome, Catacomb of Domitilla. *Cubiculum of the Good Shepherd: Overall View of the Decorations.* Late 2nd-early 3rd century. *In situ.* Wall painting. (Photo Pontificia Commissione di archeologia sacra)

81. *Roman Art.* Rome, Pagan Mausoleum under S. Sebastiano on the Via Appia, detail. *Birds and Vine-Shoots.* 2nd century. *In situ.* (Photo Pontificia Commissione di archeologia sacra)

82. *Antique Christian Art.* Rome, Catacomb of S. Callisto, Crypt of Lucina, detail. *Fish and Eucharistic Bread.* Early 3rd century. *In situ.* Wall painting, 12 1/2 by 11 3/4 in. (Photo Held)

83. *Antique Christian Art.* Rome, Catacomb of Domitilla, detail. *Orpheus and Animals.* 3rd century. *In situ.* Wall painting. (Photo Pontificia Commissione di archeologia sacra)

84. *Antique Christian Art.* Rome, Catacomb of Domitilla, detail. *Orpheus-Christ with Animals, detail.* 3rd century. *In situ.* Wall painting, 19 1/2 by 35 1/2 in. (Photo Held)

85. *Roman Art.* Rome, Villa of Livia, detail. *Gardens and Birds: Orchard closed off by a Balustrade.* First century. Rome, Museo delle Terme. Wall painting, size of the room as reconstructed, 38 1/2 by 19 1/2 ft. (Photo Scala)

86. *Roman Art.* Rome. *Sarcophagus, detail: Bath of a New-born Babe.* 2nd century. Rome, Museo delle Terme. Relief. (Photo De Antonis)

87. *Antique Christian Art.* Rome, Catacomb of the Via Latina, Room N, niche. *Hercules and the Hydra.* Mid-4th century. *In situ.* Wall painting, 33 1/2 by 33 1/2 in. (Photo Held)

88. *Roman Art.* Rome, Underground Basilica of Porta Maggiore, detail. *Mythological Scene.* First century. *In situ.* Stucco. (Photo De Antonis).

89. *Roman Art.* Rome, Roman edifice in the Farnesina Gardens, Cubiculum D, 3rd ceiling, fragment. *Scene of a Rustic Sacrifice: Drunken Silenus, Woman with Torches (?) and Double-flute Player.* From the time of Julius Caesar (?) or Augustus. Rome, Museo delle Terme. Stucco. (Photo Alinari)

90. *Antique Christian Art.* Rome, Catacomb of Pretestato, Crypt of S. Gennaro, left wall of the vault, detail. *Winter.* First half of the 3rd century. *In situ.* Wall painting, length at the bottom 11 ft. (Photo Held)

91. *Antique Christian Art.* Rome, Catacomb of Domitilla, room in the Flavian Hall, detail. *Eros.* 3rd century. *In situ.* Wall painting, 13 by 16 1/2 in. (Photo Held)

92. *Antique Christian Art.* Rome, Catacomb of Pretestato, Crypt of S. Gennaro, wall above the entrance. *The Harvest, detail.* First half of 3rd century. *In situ.* Wall painting, 22 by 19 1/2 in. (Photo Held)

93. *Antique Christian Art.* Rome, Catacomb of Pretestato, Crypt of S. Gennaro, left wall of the vault, detail. *Winter, detail: Bird feeding its Young.* First half of 3rd century. *In situ.* Wall painting, width 21 1/2 in. (Photo Held)

94. *Antique Christian Art.* Rome, Catacomb of Priscilla, detail. *The Good Shepherd; Balaam pointing to the Star or Isaiah with the Virgin and Child.* First half of 3rd century. *In situ.* Wall painting and stucco, 10 1/2 by 51 in. (Photo Held)

95. *Antique Christian Art.* Rome, Catacomb of Priscilla, detail. *Balaam pointing to the Star or Isaiah with the Virgin and Child.* First half of 3rd century. *In situ.* Wall painting, 15 3/4 by 10 1/2 in. (Photo Held)

96. *Antique Christian Art.* Rome, Catacomb of Priscilla, Cubiculum of the 'Velatio,' back wall, detail. *Orant called the 'Donna velata.'* Mid-3rd century. *In situ.* Wall painting, overall size (with the two other groups), 31 1/2 by 79 in. (Photo Scala)

97. *Antique Christian Art.* Rome. *Sarcophagus, detail: Orant.* 3rd century. Rome, Palazzo Sanseverino, Cortile. Marble. (Photo Pontificia Commissione di archeologia sacra)

98. *Antique Christian Art.* Italy. *Sarcophagus of Flavius Julius Catervius, detail: A Philosopher.* 3rd or 4th century. Tolentino, Cathedral. Marble. Overall size 110 by 47 in. (Photo Alinari)

99. *Antique Christian Art.* Rome. *Sarcophagus of the Nereids, detail: Fisherman.* 3rd or 4th century. Rome, Museo di Pretestato. (Photo Pontificia Commissione di archeologia sacra)

100. *Antique Christian Art.* Rome, Catacomb of S. Callisto, Chapel of the Sacraments, left-hand wall, detail. *Jonah thrown into the Sea.* First half of 3rd century. *In situ.* Wall painting, 23 1/2 by 17 in. (Photo Held)

101. *Antique Christian Art.* Greece. *Relief: Orpheus.* 4th century. Athens, Byzantine Museum. Marble. (Photo Hassia)

102. *Antique Christian Art.* Rome, Catacomb of Priscilla, Cubiculum of the 'Velatio,' detail. *The Three Children in the Fiery Furnace.* Mid-3rd century. *In situ.* Wall painting, 19 1/2 by 34 in. (Photo Held)

103. *Antique Christian Art.* Rome, SS. Pietro e Marcellino, vault of a room, right side of the arch. *The Baptism of Christ.* Late 3rd century. *In situ.* Wall painting, 30 by 15 3/4 in. (Photo Held)

104. *Antique Christian Art.* Rome, Catacomb called Coemeterium Majus, arcosolium. *Orant between Two Shepherds.* Late 3rd century. *In situ.* Wall painting, 26 3/4 by 79 in. (Photo Held)

105. *Antique Christian Art.* Rome, Catacomb of S. Callisto, Chapel of the Sacraments, back wall. *Eucharistic Meal.* First half of 3rd century. *In situ.* Wall painting, 25 1/2 by 45 in. (Photo Held)

106. *Antique Christian Art.* Rome, Tomb of the Aurelii, Viale Manzoni. *The Heavenly Jerusalem (?).* 3rd century. *In situ.* Wall painting. (Photo Pontificia Commissione di archeologia sacra)

107. *Antique Christian Art.* Rome, Tomb of the Aurelii, Chamber III, on the left. *The Sermon on the Mount: The Shepherd Christ above his Flock.* Mid-3rd century. *In situ.* Wall painting, 36 1/2 by 27 1/2 in. (Photo Held)

108. *Antique Jewish Art.* Rome, Jewish Catacomb, Villa Torlonia, lunette of an arcosolium. *The City of Jerusalem and the Temple Candlesticks.* 3rd century. *In situ.* Wall painting, 47 by 71 in. (Photo Held)

109. *Antique Christian Art.* Rome, Tomb of the Aurelii, Chamber III, left-hand wall. *An Apostle (?).* Mid-3rd century. *In situ.* Wall painting, 6 1/4 by 4 1/4 in. (Photo Held)

110. *Antique Christian Art.* Rome, Catacomb of Priscilla, Cappella Greca, detail. *Eucharistic Meal: 'Fractio panis.'* First half of 3rd century. *In situ.* Wall painting, height in the centre 14 1/2 in., length 90 1/2 in., length of the table 30 1/4 in. (Photo Held)

111. *Antique Christian Art.* Rome, Catacomb of SS. Pietro e Marcellino, Hall of the Tricliniarch, lunette of an arcosolium. *Celestial Banquet.* Late 3rd century. *In situ.* Wall painting, 30 1/2 by 71 in. (Photo Held)

112. *Antique Christian Art.* Rome, Catacomb of Priscilla, Cubiculum of the 'Velatio,' back wall, detail. *The Magister.* Mid-3rd century. *In situ.* Wall painting, overall size (with the two other groups) 31 1/2 by 79 in. (Photo Pontificia Commissione di archeologia sacra)

113. *Antique Christian Art.* Rome, Catacomb of Priscilla, Cappella Greca, antechamber, detail. *Story of Susanna (before the restoration of 1952).* 3rd century. *In situ.* Wall painting. (Photo Pontificia Commissione di archeologia sacra)

114. *Antique Christian Art.* Rome, Catacomb of Priscilla, Cappella Greca, detail. *Susanna and the Elders (before the restoration of 1952).* 3rd century. *In situ.* Wall painting. (Photo Pontificia Commissione di archeologia sacra).

115. *Antique Christian Art.* Rome, Catacomb of Priscilla, Cubiculum of the 'Velatio,' back wall. *Orant called the 'Donna velata' between the Magister and the Mother and Child.* Mid-3rd century. *In situ.* Wall painting, overall size 31 1/2 by 79 in. (Photo Held).

116. *Antique Christian Art.* Rome, Catacomb of Priscilla, Cubiculum of the 'Velatio,' back wall, detail. *Orant called the 'Donna velata,' detail.* Mid-3rd century. *In situ.* Wall painting, overall size 31 1/2 by 79 in. (Photo Scala)

117. *Antique Christian Art.* Rome, Catacomb of Priscilla, Cubiculum of the 'Velatio,' back wall, detail. *Mother and Child.* Mid-3rd century. *In situ.* Wall painting. (Photo Held)

118. *Antique Christian Art.* Rome, Trasona Catacomb, Tomb of the Two Orants, detail. *Portrait of a Young Woman, detail.* Mid-4th century. *In situ.* Wall painting, overall size 38 1/2 by 19 1/2 in. (Hirmer Fotoarchiv, Munich)

119. *Antique Christian Art.* Rome, Catacomb of S. Callisto, Cubiculum of the 'Cinque Santi' (Five Saints), side wall of the arcosolium, detail. *Orant, detail.* Late 3rd century. *In situ.* Wall painting 20 3/4 by 26 3/4 in. (Photo Held)

120. *Antique Christian Art.* Rome, Catacomb called Coemeterium Majus, arcosolium. *Orant between Two Shepherds, detail.* Late 3rd century. *In situ.* Wall painting, overall size 26 3/4 by 79 in. (Photo Held)

121. *Antique Christian Art.* Rome, **Via Salaria.** *Sarcophagus, detail of the*

centre: The Good Shepherd. 2nd-3rd century. Rome, Museo Laterano. Marble. (Photo Hirmer)

122. *Antique Christian Art.* Rome, Vatican Cemetery. *Sarcophagus of Livia Primitiva, detail of the centre: The Good Shepherd.* 3rd century. Paris, Louvre. Marble. (Photo U.D.F.-La Photothèque)

123. *Antique Christian Art.* Rome, Via Tiburtina. *Sarcophagus of Baebia Hertofila, front: Busts of Husband and Wife (in the rough) on a strigilated ground.* Second half of 3rd century. Rome, Museo delle Terme. Marble: coffin 84 1/2 by 35 1/2 in., lid 84 1/2 by 14 in. (Photo De Antonis)

124. *Antique Christian Art.* Rome. *Sarcophagus, detail: Shepherd tending his Flock.* 3rd-4th century. Rome, Museo delle Terme. (Photo De Antonis)

125. *Roman Art.* Auletta, South Italy. *Pagan Sarcophagus: Ariadne and Vintaging Putti.* 3rd century. Naples, Museo Nazionale. Carrara marble, 82 1/2 by 35 3/4 in. (Laboratorio fotografico della Soprintendenza alle antichità della Campania, Naples)

126. *Antique Christian Art.* Rome, Via Prenestina. *Sarcophagus, detail: Orant and Bucolic Scene.* 3rd or 4th century. Rome, Museo Laterano. (Photo Alinari)

127. *Antique Christian Art.* Rome, Via Prenestina. *Sarcophagus, detail: The Good Shepherd and Bucolic Scene.* 3rd or 4th century. Rome, Museo Laterano. (Photo Alinari)

128. *Antique Christian Art.* Rome. *Sarcophagus, detail of the centre: Young Woman listening to a Philosopher.* 3rd century. Rome, Palazzo Sanseverino, Cortile. Marble. (Photo Pontificia Commissione di archeologia sacra)

129. *Antique Christian Art.* Italy. *Sarcophagus of Flavius Julius Catervius: The Good Shepherd and Two Philosophers separated by bands of strigils.* 3rd or 4th century. Tolentino, Cathedral. Marble, overall size 110 by 47 in. (Photo Alinari)

130. *Antique Christian Art.* Rome. *Sarcophagus, detail: Jonah.* 3rd century. Rome, S. Maria Antiqua. (Photo Alinari)

131. *Antique Christian Art.* Rome. *Sarcophagus, detail of the centre: Orant listening to a Philosopher.* 3rd century. Rome, S. Maria Antiqua. (Photo Alinari)

132-133. *Antique Christian Art. Sarcophagus, details: Story of Jonah.* 3rd century. Copenhagen, Ny Carlsberg Glyptothek. (Museum Photo)

134. *Antique Christian Art.* Rome. *Sarcophagus, detail: Shepherd carrying a Sheep and flanked by Two Other Sheep.* 3rd century. Rome, Museo dei Conservatori. Marble. (Photo De Antonis)

135. *Antique Christian Art.* Rome, S. Paolo fuori le Mura. *Sarcophagus with Old and New Testament Scenes, detail from the centre of the lower register: Daniel in the Lions' Den.* 3rd-4th century. Rome, Museo Laterano. Marble. (Photo Boudot-Lamotte)

136. *Antique Christian Art.* Rome, S. Paolo fuori le Mura. *Sarcophagus with Old and New Testament Scenes, detail from the upper register: Adam and Eve.* 3rd-4th century. Rome, Museo Laterano. Marble. (Photo Boudot-Lamotte)

137. *Antique Christian Art.* Rome. *Sarcophagus of Baebia Hertofila, detail of the lid: Eucharistic Meal.* Second half of 3rd century. Rome, Museo delle Terme. Marble. (Photo De Antonis)

138. *Antique Christian Art. Fragment of a Sarcophagus: Story of Jonah.* 3rd century. Rome, S. Maria in Trastevere, atrium. (Photo De Antonis)

139. *Antique Christian Art. Sarcophagus, detail: Baptism of Christ.* 3rd century. Rome, Museo delle Terme. Marble. (Photo De Antonis)

140. *Antique Christian Art.* Italy. *Sarcophagus with Large Figures and Small-scale Scenes, detail: Daniel in the Lions' Den; Jonah and an Orant.* Late 3rd century. Velletri, Museum. Marble. (Photo Pontificia Commissione di archeologia sacra)

141. *Antique Christian Art.* Italy. *Sarcophagus of Flavius Julius Catervius, detail: Adoration of the Magi.* 3rd or 4th century. Tolentino, Cathedral. Marble, overall size 110 by 47 in. (Photo Gabinetto fotografico nazionale, Rome)

142. *Antique Christian Art.* Provence. *Sarcophagus combining Pagan and Christian Motifs, detail: Fisherman and Orant.* 3rd century. Brignoles (Var), Church of Saint-Sauveur. Marble. (Photo U.D.F.-La Photothèque)

143. *Antique Christian Art.* Provence. *Sarcophagus combining Pagan and Christian Motifs.* 3rd century. Brignoles (Var), Church of Saint-Sauveur. (Photo U.D.F.-La Photothèque)

144. *Antique Christian Art.* Rome, Via Salaria. *Sarcophagus, detail: Seated Philosopher.* 2nd-3rd century. Rome, Museo Laterano. Marble. (Hirmer Fotoarchiv, Munich)

145. *Antique Christian Art.* Rome, Via Salaria. *Sarcophagus, detail: Orant and Group of Women.* 2nd-3rd century. Rome, Museo Laterano. Marble. (Hirmer Fotoarchiv, Munich)

146. *Antique Christian Art.* Rome, Lungotevere. *Sarcophagus, detail: Orant among Birds and Trees under an Arch; at the extremities, separated by strigils, a Good Shepherd and a Fisherman.* 3rd century. Rome, Museo delle Terme. (Photo De Antonis)

147-148. *Antique Christian Art.* Rome, Vatican Cemetery. *Sarcophagus, details: Cycle of Jonah.* 3rd century. Rome, Museo Laterano. Marble. (Photo Alinari)

149. *Antique Christian Art.* Egypt. *Sarcophagus of Constantina, Daughter of Constantine the Great, detail: Vintaging Cupids within the Loops of a Continuous Vine-Shoot.* About 350. Vatican, Museo Pio Clementino. Pink porphyry from Syene, Egypt. (Photo De Antonis)

150. *Roman Art.* Rome. *Arch of Constantine: Overall View.* 315. *In situ.* Marble bas-reliefs. (Photo De Antonis)

151. *Roman Art.* Rome. *Arch of Constantine, detail: Distribution of Subsidies.* 315. *In situ.* (Photo Gabinetto fotografico nazionale, Rome)

152. *Roman Imperial Art.* Salonica. *Arch of Galerius, detail: Scene of Sacrifice.* Between 297 and 305. *In situ.* Marble bas-reliefs. (Photo Hassia)

153. *Roman Imperial Art.* Salonica. *Arch of Galerius, detail: Scenes of War and Triumph.* Between 297 and 305. *In situ.* (Photo Hassia)

154. *Antique Christian Art.* Rome, Forum. *Basilica of Maxentius (also called Basilica of Constantine).* Early 4th century. *In situ.* (Photo Anderson)

155. *Roman Art.* Spalato (Split), Dalmatia. *Palace of Diocletian: Main Entrance preceded by an Arcaded Portico.* About 300. *In situ.* (Photo Urbanisticki Biro, Split. S. J. Marasovic)

156. *Roman Art.* Spalato (Split), Dalmatia. *Palace of Diocletian: Plan (reconstructed by E. Hébrard).* About 300. (After Heinz Kähler, *Rome et son empire*, Paris, 1963, fig. 45, p. 183)

157. *Roman Art.* Rome. *Wedding Diptych of the Nicomachi and the Symmachi: Pagan Priestess Sacrificing; Pagan Priestess at an Altar.* About 400. Paris, Musée de Cluny, and London, Victoria and Albert Museum. Ivory, 11 3/4 by 4 3/4 in. (Photo U.D.F.-La Photothèque)

158. *Roman Art.* Piazza Armerina (Sicily), Roman Villa. *Hunting Corridor: Personification of Arabia or Egypt.* 4th century. *In situ.* Mosaic pavement. (Photo Angelo Maltese)

159. *Roman Art.* Piazza Armerina (Sicily), Roman Villa. *Hunting Corridor: Capture of Wild Animals.* 4th century. *In situ.* Mosaic pavement. (Photo Angelo Maltese)

160-161. *Pagan Roman Art.* Piazza Armerina (Sicily), Roman Villa. *Girls doing Physical Exercises.* 4th century. *In situ.* Mosaic pavement. (Photo Angelo Maltese)

162. *Roman Art.* Rome. *Bridal Casket of Projecta and Secundus, detail.* 5th century. London, British Museum. Silver. (Museum Photo)

163. *Roman Art.* Daphne (Antioch). *Mosaic of the Seasons, detail: Personification of Spring.* Early 4th century. Paris, Louvre. Mosaic pavement, overall size 41 by 27 ft. (Photo U.D.F.-La Photothèque)

164. *Roman Art.* Silistra, Bulgaria. *Underground Mausoleum, detail: Deceased Couple.* 4th century. *In situ.* Wall painting. Size of the tomb 10 ft 8 in. by 8 ft 6 in. Size of the painted panel 21 1/4 by 37 1/2 in. (After Antonio Frova, *Peinture romaine en Bulgarie,* in *Cahiers d'Art,* October 1954, No. 1, Paris, 1954, fig. p. 31)

165. *Roman Art.* *Medal of Constantine I.* Early 4th century. Paris, Bibliothèque Nationale, Cabinet des Médailles. Gold. (Photo Bibliothèque Nationale)

166. *Roman Art.* *Bust of the Emperor Constantine I (?).* Early 4th century. Paris, Bibliothèque Nationale, Cabinet des Médailles. Chalcedony, height 7 7/8 in. (Photo Bibliothèque Nationale)

167. *Roman Art.* *Medal of the Empress St Helena.* Early 4th century. Paris, Bibliothèque Nationale, Cabinet des Médailles. Gold. (Photo Bibliothèque Nationale)

168. *Roman Art.* *Medal of the Emperor Constantius II wearing a Helmet inscribed with a Cross.* Mid-4th century. Paris, Bibliothèque Nationale, Cabinet des Médailles. Gold. (Photo Bibliothèque Nationale)

169. *Roman Art.* *Medal of the Emperor Constantius II holding the Labarum inscribed with the Monogram of Christ.* Mid-4th century. Paris, Bibliothèque Nationale, Cabinet des Médailles. Gold. (Photo Bibliothèque Nationale)

170. *Antique Christian Art.* Jerusalem. *The Round Church of the Holy Sepulchre and the Basilica of the Resurrection at Golgotha: Plan (reconstruction of their original state under Constantine).* 4th century. (After H. Vincent and F.M. Abel, *Jérusalem nouvelle,* Vol. II, fasc. 1 & 2, Paris, 1914, pl. XXXIII)

171. *Antique Christian Art.* Rome. *S. Costanza: View of the Interior (after a print by Piranesi).* The building dates to the first half of the 4th century; the print to the late 18th century. (Photo Bibliothèque Nationale, Paris)

172. *Antique Christian Art.* Rome. *S. Costanza: View of the Interior.* 4th century. *In situ.* (Photo Gabinetto fotografico nazionale, Rome)

173. *Roman Art.* Egypt. *Sarcophagus of St Helena: Horsemen.* Early 4th century. Vatican, Museo Pio Clementino. Pink porphyry from Syene, Egypt. (Photo De Antonis)

174. *Antique Christian Art.* Rome. *Ruins of the Mausoleum of St Helena (Tor Pignattara).* Early 4th century. *In situ.* (Photo De Antonis)

175. *Antique Christian Art.* Egypt. *Sarcophagus of Constantina, Daughter of Constantine the Great: One End with Vintaging Putti.* About 350. Vatican, Museo Pio Clementino. (Photo De Antonis)

176. *Antique Christian Art.* Bethlehem. *Church of the Nativity: Plan.* 4th century. (After André Grabar, *Martyrium, Recherches sur le culte des reliques et l'art chrétien antique,* Vol. I, Paris, 1946, fig. 27, p. 592)

177. *Antique Jewish Art.* Tell Hum, Palestine. *Synagogue: Plan.* 3rd century. (After H. Kohl and C. Watzinger, *Antike Synagogen in Galiläa,* Leipzig, 1916, pl. II)

178. *Antique Jewish Art.* Tell Hum, Palestine. *Synagogue (reconstruction).* 3rd century. (After Erwin R. Goodenough, *Jewish Symbols in the Greco-Roman Period,* Vol. III, Bollingen Series XXXVII, New York, 1953, No. 452)

179. *Antique Christian Art.* Rome, S. Martino ai Monti. *View of the Interior of the Basilica of San Giovanni in Laterano (before Borromini's alterations).* 17th-century wall painting attributed to Gaspard Poussin (Dughet). (Photo De Antonis)

180. *Antique Christian Art.* Vatican. *Old St Peter's: Plan (after Tiberio Alfarano).* Church built about 330; plan drawn in the 16th century. (After G. Dehio and G. von Bezold, *Die kirchliche Baukunst des Abendlandes,* atlas, Stuttgart, 1887, pl. 18)

181. *Antique Christian Art.* Vatican. *Interior of Old St Peter's (after a drawing by Tiberio Alfarano).* Church built about 330; painting made in the 16th century. *In situ.* Wall painting. (Photo Alinari)

182. *Antique Christian Art.* Rome, Via Appia. *Basilica of S. Sebastiano (SS. Apostoli): Plan.* 4th century. (After O. Marucchi, *Le recenti scoperte presso la basilica di S. Sebastiano,* in *Nuovo Bollettino di archeologia cristiana,* XXII, 1916, pl. 1)

183. *Antique Christian Art.* Rome (beside the rotunda of S. Costanza). *S. Agnese: Ruins of the Chevet of the Ancient Church.* 4th century. *In situ.* (Photo Archivio fotografico, Gallerie e Musei vaticani)

184. *Antique Christian Art.* Kharab Shems, Syria. *Basilica: South Arcade of the Nave.* 5th century. *In situ.* (Photo French Institute of Archaeology, Beirut)

185. *Antique Christian Art.* Ruweiha, Syria. *South Church: South Arcade of the Nave.* 4th century. *In situ.* (Photo French Institute of Archaeology, Beirut)

186. *Antique Christian Art.* Kharab Shems, Syria. *Basilica: Detail of the Arches.* 5th century. *In situ.* (Photo French Institute of Archaeology, Beirut)

187. *Antique Syrian Art.* Shaqqa, Syria. *Secular 'Basilica': Plan.* 3rd century. (After H.C. Butler, *Early Churches in Syria...,* Princeton, 1929, fig. 9, p. 16)

188. *Antique Syrian Art.* Shaqqa, Syria. *Secular 'Basilica': Cross-Section.* 3rd century. (After H.C. Butler, *Early Churches in Syria...,* Princeton, 1929, fig. 10, p. 17)

189. *Antique Christian Art.* Ephesus, Asia Minor. *Church of the Virgin (ancient gymnasium converted into a basilical church): Plan.* 4th century. (After *Forschungen in Ephesos,* Vol. IV, 1, Vienna 1932, fig. 2, p. 16-17)

190. *Antique Christian Art.* Epidaurus, Greece. *Church and Baptistery: Plan.* 4th century. (After G. Sotiriou, *Early Christian Basilicas with Timber Roofs,* Vol. I, Athens, 1952, fig. 26, p. 51)

191. *Antique Christian Art.* Salona, Dalmatia. *District of the Bishop's Palace: General Plan.* (After Ejnar Dyggve, *History of Salonitan Christianity,* Oslo-London-Leipzig-Paris-Cambridge [Mass.], 1951, fig. II, 13)

192. *Antique Christian Art.* Salona, Dalmatia. *District of the Bishop's Palace: Plan of the Baptistery.* 6th century. (After Ejnar Dyggve, *History of Salonitan Christianity,* Oslo-London-Leipzig-Paris-Cambridge [Mass.], 1951, fig. II, 25)

193. *Antique Christian Art.* Antioch-Kaoussieh. *Cruciform Martyrium of St Babylas: Plan.* Late 4th century. (After Jean Lassus, *Sanctuaires chrétiens de Syrie,* Paris, 1947, fig. 51, p. 124)

194. *Antique Christian Art.* Orléansville, Algeria. *Five-aisled Church of St Reparatus: Plan.* 4th century (the second apse dates to the 5th century). (After Stéphane Gsell, *Les Monuments antiques de l'Algérie,* Vol. II, Paris, 1901, fig. 132, p. 238)

195. *Antique Christian Art.* Salona-Manastirine, Dalmatia. *Cultic and Funerary Buildings of Unusual Plan around a Martyr's Tomb (first and second state).* 4th century. (After André Grabar, *Martyrium, Recherches sur le culte des reliques et l'art chrétien antique,* Vol. I, Paris, 1946, fig. 33, p. 594)

196. *Antique Christian Art.* Salona-Manastirine, Dalmatia. *Building of Unusual Plan converted into a Regular Basilica (third state).* 5th century. (After André Grabar, *Martyrium, Recherches sur le culte des reliques et l'art chrétien antique,* Vol. I, Paris, 1946, fig. 34, p. 595)

197. *Antique Christian Art.* Tebessa, Algeria. *Christian Basilica: Atrium. In the centre, a Fountain.* 4th century. *In situ.* (Photo Marcel Bovis)

198. *Antique Christian Art.* Tebessa, Algeria. *Christian Basilica: Nave.* 4th-5th century. *In situ.* (Photo Marcel Bovis)

199. *Antique Christian Art.* Tebessa, Algeria. *Christian Basilica, detail: Arcades in the Nave.* 4th-5th century. *In situ.* (Photo Marcel Bovis)

200. *Antique Christian Art.* Centcelles, Spain. *Mausoleum, Dome Mosaic: Face of a Child.* About 340. *In situ.* (Photo Enciro Gras)

201. *Roman Art.* Trier, Imperial Palace. *Face of a Child.* Early 4th century. Trier, Bischöfliches Museum. Ceiling painting. (Museum Photo)

202. *Antique Christian Art.* Rome, S. Costanza, Annular Vault, detail. *Birds among Branches, Flowers, Fruit and Various Objects.* 4th century. *In situ.* Mosaic. (Photo Scala)

203. *Antique Christian Art.* Rome, S. Costanza. *Annular Vault, detail.* 4th century. *In situ.* (Photo Gabinetto fotografico nazionale, Rome)

204. *Antique Christian Art.* Rome, S. Costanza, Annular Vault, detail. *Bust of Constantina, Daughter of Constantine the Great, surrounded by Vine-Shoots.* 4th century. *In situ.* Mosaic. (Photo De Antonis)

205. *Antique Christian Art.* Rome, S. Costanza, Annular Vault, detail. *Medallions with Cupids and Figures alternating with Birds and Animals.* 4th century. *In situ.* Mosaic. (Photo Scala)

206. *Antique Christian Art.* Rome, S. Costanza, Annular Vault, detail. *Birds among Branches and Various Objects.* 4th century. *In situ.* Mosaic. (Photo Scala)

207. *Antique Christian Art.* Rome, S. Costanza, Niche in the Circular Wall. *The Lord delivering the Law to Moses.* Mid-4th century. *In situ.* Mosaic. (Photo Scala)

208. *Roman Art. Medal of Constans I, reverse: The Emperor Constantine I with his Sons.* Mid-4th century. Paris, Bibliothèque Nationale, Cabinet des Médailles. Gold. (Photo Bibliothèque Nationale)

209. *Roman Art.* Aphrodisias, Asia Minor. *Statue of the Emperor Valentinian II (375-392).* Late 4th century. Istanbul, Archaeological Museum. Marble, height 70 1/2 in. (Photo Antonello Perissinotto, Padua)

210. *Roman Art. Head of Constantine I.* First half of 4th century. Belgrade, National Museum. Bronze. (Hirmer Fotoarchiv, Munich)

211. *The Emperor Valentinian I (?) in Military Costume, detail.* 4th century. Barletta, South Italy. Bronze. See also Fig. 15. (Hirmer Fotoarchiv, Munich)

212. *Roman Art. Medal of Constans I, obverse: Bust of the Emperor.* Mid-4th century. Paris, Bibliothèque Nationale, Cabinet des Médailles. Gold. (Photo Bibliothèque Nationale)

213. *Roman Art. Medal: Roman Emperor enthroned between Two Bodyguards.* Mid-4th century. The Hague, Koninklijk Kabinet. Gold. (Photo Van Munten Museum, Penningen en Gesneden)

214. *Roman Art. Coin: Apotheosis of Constantine and Hand of God.* 337. Paris, Bibliothèque Nationale, Cabinet des Médailles. (Photo Bibliothèque Nationale)

215-216. *Roman Art. Head of the Emperor Maximinus Daia (308-313).* Early 4th century. Berlin, Staatliche Museen. Limestone, height 10 1/4 in. (Museum Photo)

217. *Roman Art. Medal: Constantine I crowned by the Hand of God, and his Two Sons crowned by Victories.* Mid-4th century. Vienna, Kunsthistorisches Museum. Gold. (Photo Erwin Meyer)

218-219. *Medal, obverse: Bust of Constantius Chlorus; reverse, his Triumphal Entry into London.* Late 3rd century. Arras, Musée Municipal. (Photo Leroy)

220. *Roman Art. Medal: Conquering Emperor.* 4th century. Paris, Bibliothèque Nationale, Cabinet des Médailles. Gold. (Photo Bibliothèque Nationale)

221. *Roman Art. Medal: The Emperor Valens.* Vienna, Kunsthistorisches Museum. (Museum Photo)

222. *Roman Art.* Gaul. *Medal: The Emperor Magnentius holding the Labarum.* 351-353. Paris, Bibliothèque Nationale, Cabinet des Médailles. Gold. (Photo Bibliothèque Nationale)

223. *Roman Art.* Rome, Forum. *Arch of Constantine, detail: Constantine addressing the People.* Before 315. *In situ.* (Photo Gabinetto fotografico nazionale, Rome)

224. *Roman Art. Medal, reverse: Two Co-regnant Emperors seated on the same Throne.* 4th century. Vienna, Kunsthistorisches Museum. Gold. (Museum Photo)

225. *Roman Art.* Rome, Forum. *Arch of Constantine, detail: The Battle of the Milvian Bridge.* Before 315. *In situ.* (Photo Gabinetto fotografico nazionale, Rome)

226. *Roman Art.* Salonica. *Arch of Galerius, detail: The Emperor's Solemn*

Entry into a City, and a Battle Scene. About 300. *In situ.* (Photo Hassia)

227-228. *Roman Art.* Salonica. *Arch of Galerius, details: Scenes of War and Triumph.* About 300. *In situ.* (Photo Hassia)

229. *Antique Christian Art.* Rome, Catacomb of the Via Latina, Room N. *Partial View. In the niche at the back, Alcestis with Hercules and Cerberus.* 4th century. *In situ.* (Photo Pontificia Commissione di archeologia sacra)

230. *Antique Christian Art.* Rome, Tomb of the Aurelii, vault of an arcosolium, detail. *Christ and the Apostles.* 3rd century. *In situ.* Wall painting, 32 1/2 by 51 in. (Photo Held)

231. *Antique Christian Art.* Rome, Catacomb of Domitilla, Tomb of Veneranda, detail. *Veneranda led into Heaven by St Petronilla.* Mid-4th century. *In situ.* Wall painting, 40 1/2 by 31 1/2 in. (Photo Held)

232. *Antique Christian Art.* Rome, Catacomb called Coemeterium Majus, Chamber V, lunette of an arcosolium. *Orant Virgin and Half-length Child, or Mother and Son.* First half of 4th century. *In situ.* Wall painting, 20 3/4 by 63 in. (Photo Held)

233. *Antique Christian Art.* Rome, Catacomb of SS. Pietro e Marcellino, Crypt of the Saints. *Christ between St Peter and St Paul, detail: Bust of Christ.* Late 4th century. *In situ.* (Photo Held)

234. *Antique Christian Art.* Rome, Catacomb of SS. Pietro e Marcellino, Crypt of the Saints. *Above, Christ between St Peter and St Paul; below, the Divine Lamb on a Mound from which flow the Four Rivers of Paradise, between Sts Gorgonius, Peter, Marcellinus and Tiburtius.* Late 4th century. *In situ.* Wall painting, 86 by 94 in. (Photo Held)

235. *Antique Christian Art.* Rome, Catacomb of Panfilo. *Partial View of a Painted Tomb Chamber.* 4th century. *In situ.* Wall painting. (Pontificia Commissione di archeologia sacra)

236. *Antique Christian Art.* Rome, Catacomb of SS. Pietro e Marcellino, Crypt of the Saints. *The Divine Lamb on a Mound between Sts Gorgonius, Peter, Marcellinus and Tiburtius, detail: Two Saints.* Late 4th century. *In situ.* (Photo Held)

237. *Antique Christian Art.* Rome, Catacomb of Commodilla, ceiling, detail. *Bust of Christ.* Mid-4th century. *In situ.* Wall painting, 23 1/2 by 28 1/2 in. (Photo Held)

238. *Antique Christian Art.* Rome, Catacomb of Domitilla, lunette of an arcosolium near the crypt of Ampliatus. *Christ teaching among the Apostles, detail.* Early 4th century. *In situ.* Wall painting, 15 by 51 in. (Photo Held)

239. *Antique Christian Art.* Rome, Catacomb of the Giordani, arcosolium, detail. *Daniel in the Lions' Den.* 4th century. *In situ.* Wall painting, 30 by 25 in. (Photo Held)

240-241. *Antique Christian Art.* Rome, confessio under the Basilica of SS. Giovanni e Paolo, details. *Standing Figures and Stag Drinking; Beheading of Three Saints.* Mid-4th century. *In situ.* Wall painting. (Photo De Antonis)

242. *Antique Christian Art.* Rome, confessio under the Basilica of SS. Giovanni e Paolo. *Saint as an Orant, detail.* Mid-4th century. *In situ.* (Photo De Antonis)

243. *Antique Christian Art.* Rome, confessio under the Basilica of SS. Giovanni e Paolo. *Saint as an Orant with Two Prostrate Figures at his Feet.* Mid-4th century. *In situ.* Wall painting. (Photo De Antonis)

244. *Roman Art.* Rome, Pagan Tomb of Trebius Justus, arcosolium, detail. *The Dead Man with his Parents.* 4th century. *In situ.* Wall painting. (Pontificia Commissione di archeologia sacra)

245. *Roman Art.* Rome, Pagan Tomb of Vibia, gallery next to the Catacomb of Pretestato. *The Dead Vibia led into Paradise and invited to a Banquet.* 4th century. *In situ.* Wall painting, 44 by 39 in. (Photo De Antonis)

246. *Roman Art.* Rome, Pagan Tomb of Trebius Justus. *Masons working on a Building under the Orders of the Deceased.* 4th century. *In situ.* Wall painting. (Pontificia Commissione di archeologia sacra)

247. *Roman Art.* Rome, Pagan Tomb of Trebius Justus. *Servant leading a Horse.* 4th century. *In situ.* Wall painting. (Photo Pontificia Commissione di archeologia sacra)

248. *Antique Christian Art.* Rome, Catacomb of the Via Latina, Cubiculum B, lunette of the right-hand arcosolium. *Ascension of the Prophet Elijah; The Good Shepherd.* 4th century. *In situ.* Wall painting, 35 1/2 by 59 in. (Photo Held)

249. *Antique Christian Art.* Rome, Catacomb of the Via Latina, Room I, right-hand arch. *Aristotle (?) with his Disciples.* 4th century. *In situ.* Wall painting, 66 by 79 in. (Photo Held)

250. *Antique Christian Art.* Rome, Catacomb of the Via Latina, Cubiculum O. *End of a Gallery with Closure Slabs.* 4th century. *In situ.* Wall painting. (Photo Held)

251. *Antique Christian Art.* Rome, Catacomb of the Via Latina, Room N, right-hand niche. *Alcestis beside Hercules and Cerberus.* 4th century. *In situ.* Wall painting, 36 by 63 in. (Photo Held)

252. *Antique Christian Art.* Rome, Catacomb of the Via Latina, Cubiculum C, left-hand niche. *Abraham's Sacrifice.* 4th century. *In situ.* Wall painting, 35 1/2 by 18 in. (Photo Held)

253. *Antique Christian Art.* Rome, Catacomb of the Via Latina, Cubiculum B, right-hand arcosolium. *Jacob's Dream of a Ladder reaching to Heaven.* 4th century. *In situ.* Wall painting, 39 by 41 1/2 in. (Photo Held)

254. *Antique Christian Art.* Rome, Catacomb of the Via Latina, Cubiculum B. *Abraham entertaining the Three Angels under the Oak of Mamre.* 4th century. *In situ.* Wall painting, 39 by 37 in. (Photo Held)

255. *Antique Christian Art.* Rome, Catacomb of the Via Latina, Cubiculum O, left-hand niche. *The Raising of Lazarus, detail.* 4th century. *In situ.* (Photo Held)

256. *Antique Christian Art.* Rome, Catacomb of the Via Latina, Cubiculum O left-hand niche. *The Raising of Lazarus.* 4th century. *In situ.* Wall painting. (Photo Held)

257. *Antique Christian Art.* Rome, Catacomb of the Via Latina, Cubiculum O, right-hand niche. *The Crossing of the Red Sea.* 4th century. *In situ.* Wall painting, 42 by 53 in. and 26 by 16 in. (Photo Held)

258. *Antique Christian Art.* Rome, Catacomb of the Via Latina, Room N. *Partial View. In the niche at the back, Alcestis mourning for Admetus on his Deathbed.* 4th century. *In situ.* Wall painting. (Photo Pontificia Commissione di archeologia sacra)

259. *Antique Christian Art.* Rome, Catacomb of the Via Latina, Vault of Cubiculum B, detail. *The Flood.* 4th century. *In situ.* Wall painting. (Photo Pontificia Commissione di archeologia sacra)

260. *Antique Christian Art.* Rome, Catacomb of the Via Latina, Cubiculum F, lunette of the right-hand arcosolium. *Balaam and the Angel of the Lord standing in the Way.* 4th century. *In situ.* Wall painting, 35 1/2 by 53 in. (Photo Held)

261. *Antique Christian Art.* Tabarka, Tunisia. *Upper Side of a Tomb Slab.* Tunis, Bardo Museum. Mosaic. (Museum Photo)

262. *Antique Christian Art.* Kelibia, Tunisia. *Upper Side of a Tomb Slab.* Tunis, Bardo Museum. Mosaic, 77 by 28 in. (Museum Photo)

263. *Antique Christian Art.* Kelibia, Tunisia. *Upper Side of a Tomb Slab.* Tunis, Bardo Museum. Mosaic, 68 by 57 in. (Museum Photo)

264. *Antique Christian Art. Sarcophagus of Junius Bassus with Old and New Testament Scenes, detail: Entry of Christ into Jerusalem.* 4th century. Vatican, Grotte Vaticane. (Photo De Antonis)

265. *Antique Christian Art.* Rome, Catacomb of Pretestato. *Sarcophagus of Curtia Catiana, detail. Above (on the lid), Inscribed Cartouche flanked by Fighting and Banquet Scenes. Below (on the coffin), Portrait of a Child in a Medallion surrounded by Tritons and Nereids.* 4th century. Rome, Museo di Prestestato. Marble. (Photo Pontificia Commissione di archeologia sacra)

266. *Antique Christian Art.* Rome. *Sarcophagus, detail: Good Shepherd and Female Musician.* 4th century. Rome, Museo Laterano (No. 128). Marble. (Photo Anderson)

267. *Antique Christian Art.* Rome. *Sarcophagus: Portrait of the Deceased with Two Genii, Good Shepherd, Herdsman and Female Musicians.* 4th century. Rome, Museo Laterano (No. 128). Marble. (Photo Anderson)

268. *Antique Christian Art.* Rome, Catacomb of S. Lorenzi fuori le Mura. *Sarcophagus of Aurelius. Upper register, Portrait of the Deceased in front of a Curtain, and Jonah. Lower register, Adoration of the Magi, Daniel, Adam and Eve, Healing of the Blind Man.* 4th century. Vatican Museums. Marble. (Photo Pontificia Commissione di archeologia sacra)

269. *Antique Christian Art.* Rome. *Sarcophagus, detail: Orant with Various Figures.* 4th century. Rome, Museo Laterano (No. 161). Marble. (Photo Alinari)

270. *Antique Christian Art.* Rome. *Sarcophagus of the Two Brothers, front, detail: Portrait of the Dead Men.* 4th century. Rome, Museo Laterano. (Hirmer Fotoarchiv, Munich)

271-272. *Antique Christian Art.* Rome. *Sarcophagus of the Two Brothers, front: Old and New Testament Scenes, details.* 4th century. Rome, Museo Laterano. Marble. (Hirmer Fotoarchiv, Munich)

273. *Antique Christian Art. Sarcophagus of Junius Bassus, front: Old and New Testament Scenes.* 4th century. Vatican, Grotte Vaticane. (Photo De Antonis)

274. *Antique Christian Art. Sarcophagus of Junius Bassus with Old and New Testament Scenes, detail: Abraham's Sacrifice.* 4th century. Vatican, Grotte Vaticane. (Photo De Antonis)

275. *Antique Christian Art. Sarcophagus of Junius Bassus with Old and New Testament Scenes, detail: The Arrest of Christ.* 4th century. Vatican, Grotte Vaticane. (Photo De Antonis)

276. *Antique Christian Art.* Rome. *Sarcophagus, front: Christ seated above a Personification of the Cosmos, surrounded by Old and New Testament Scenes.* 4th century. Rome, Museo Laterano. Marble. (Photo Alinari)

277. *Antique Christian Art.* Rome. *Sarcophagus, front, detail.* 4th century. Rome, Museo Laterano. (Photo Pontificia Commissione di archeologia sacra)

278. *Antique Christian Art.* Rome. *Sarcophagus, front, detail: Judgment of Pilate.* 4th century. Rome, Museo Laterano. (Photo Pontificia Commissione di archeologia sacra)

279. *Antique Christian Art.* Rome. *Sarcophagus, front, detail.* 4th century. Rome, Museo Laterano. (Photo Pontificia Commissione di archeologia sacra)

280. *Antique Christian Art.* Rome. *Sarcophagus, detail of a short side: Moses striking Water from the Rock.* 4th century. Rome, Museo Laterano. Flat relief. Marble. (Photo Pontificia Commissione di archeologia sacra)

281. *Antique Christian Art.* Rome. *Sarcophagus of Probus, detail: Two Apostles.* About 395. Vatican, Grotte Vaticane. (Photo De Antonis)

282. *Antique Christian Art.* Italy. *Sarcophagus, front, detail: Daniel in the Lions' Den.* Late 4th century. Verona,

S. Giovanni in Valle. Marble. (Photo Calzolari, Mantua)

283. *Antique Christian Art.* Italy. *Sarcophagus, front: Standing Christ delivering the Law surrounded by Various Scenes: Christ and the Woman of Samaria, Christ and the Centurion of Capernaum, Christ and the Woman of Canaan, The Kiss of Judas.* Late 4th century. Verona, S. Giovanni in Valle. Marble. (Photo Calzolari, Mantua)

284. *Antique Christian Art.* Italy. *Sarcophagus, detail: Christ delivering the Law surrounded by the Apostles, with the Two Deceased at his Feet.* 5th century (?). Aix-en-Provence, Cathedral of Saint-Sauveur, chapel converted into a museum. Marble. (Photo U.D.F.-La Photothèque)

285. *Antique Christian Art.* Rome (found in the ruined mausoleum of the Anicii near St Peter's). *Sarcophagus of Probus, front, detail: Standing Christ delivering the Law surrounded by the Apostles.* About 395. Vatican, Grotte Vaticane. (Photo De Antonis)

286. *Antique Christian Art. Sarcophagus of the Good Shepherd, detail: The Good Shepherd surrounded by Vine-Shoots.* 4th century. Rome, Museo Laterano. Marble. (Hirmer Fotoarchiv, Munich)

287. *Antique Christian Art. Sarcophagus of the Good Shepherd: Vintaging Scenes with Cupids.* 4th century. Rome, Museo Laterano. (Hirmer Fotoarchiv, Munich)

288. *Antique Christian Art. Sarcophagus of the Good Shepherd, detail of a short side: Vintaging Cupids.* 4th century. Rome, Museo Laterano. (Hirmer Fotoarchiv Munich)

289. *Antique Christian Art. Sarcophagus of the Good Shepherd, detail: Vine-Shoots and Cupids.* 4th century. Rome, Museo Laterano. (Photo Boudot-Lamotte)

290. *Antique Christian Art. Sarcophagus, detail: Seated Christ delivering the Law surrounded by the Apostles.* 4th century. Milan, Basilica of S. Ambrogio, under the ambo in the nave. Marble, overall size 90 by 45 in. (Photo Scala)

291. *Antique Christian Art. Sarcophagus, short side, detail: Ascension of Elijah; Adam and Eve.* 4th century. Milan, Basilica of S. Ambrogio, under the ambo in the nave. (Photo Scala)

292. *Antique Christian Art. Sarcophagus, lid, detail: Portrait of a Couple in an*

'Imago clipeata' flanked by Two Scenes. 4th century. Milan, Basilica of S. Ambrogio, under the ambo in the nave. Marble, overall size: coffin 90 by 45 in.; lid 90 by 21 in. (Photo Scala)

293. *Antique Christian Art. Sarcophagus: Standing Christ delivering the Law in the presence of the Apostles.* 4th century. Milan, Basilica of S. Ambrogio, under the ambo in the nave. (Hirmer Fotoarchiv, Munich)

294. *Antique Christian Art. Sarcophagus, short side: Monogram and Symbols, Abraham's Sacrifice, Four Standing Figures.* 4th century. Milan, Basilica of S. Ambrogio, under the ambo in the nave. (Photo Alinari)

295. *Antique Christian Art.* Rome, Catacomb of Domitilla. *Sarcophagus, detail: Symbolic Image of the Resurrection flanked by Passion Scenes.* 4th century. Rome, Museo Laterano. Marble. (Photo Boudot-Lamotte)

296. *Antique Christian Art.* Rome. *Sarcophagus: Passion Scenes separated by Trees with Overarching Branches.* 4th century. Rome, Museo Laterano. Marble. (Photo Alinari)

297. *Antique Christian Art.* Rome, Catacomb of Domitilla. *Sarcophagus with Passion Scenes, detail: Judgment of Pilate.* 4th century. Rome, Museo Laterano. (Photo Boudot-Lamotte)

298. *Antique Christian Art. Sarcophagus, detail: St Peter led out to Execution.* Mid-4th century. Rome, S. Sebastiano. (Photo German Archaeological Institute, Rome)

299. *Antique Christian Art. Sarcophagus with Passion Scenes, detail: The Arrest of St Peter.* 4th century. Avignon, Musée Lapidaire. (Photo Bernard Martin)

300. *Antique Christian Art.* Rome. *Statuette of the Young Christ, detail.* 3rd century. Rome, Museo delle Terme. (Photo Alinari)

301. *Antique Christian Art.* Vicinity of Rome (Via Appia?). *Statuette of the Good Shepherd.* Late 3rd century. Paris, Louvre. Bone, height 5 3/4 in. (Photo Chuzeville)

302. *Antique Christian Art.* Rome. *Statuette of the Young Christ.* 3rd century. Rome, Museo delle Terme. Marble, height 27 1/2 in. (Photo Alinari)

303. *Antique Christian Art.* Greece. *The Good Shepherd.* 4th-5th century. Athens, Byzantine Museum. Marble with traces of colour, height 28 1/2 in. (Photo Hassia)

304. *Antique Christian Art.* North Italy. *Reliquary Casket ('Lipsanotheca'): Old and New Testament Scenes framed by Symbols; Medallions with Busts of the Apostles and the Beardless Christ.* Second third of the 4th century. Brescia, Museo dell'Età Cristiana. Ivory, height 8 1/2, width 9 1/2, length 13 3/4 in. (Hirmer Fotoarchiv, Munich)

305. *Antique Christian Art.* North Italy. *Reliquary Casket ('Lipsanotheca'), detail: Christ teaching the Apostles.* Second third of the 4th century. Brescia, Museo dell'Età Cristiana. (Hirmer Fotoarchiv, Munich)

306. *Antique Christian Art.* North Italy. *Reliquary Casket ('Lipsanotheca'), detail of the lid: Heads of Christ and Apostles.* Second third of the 4th century. Brescia, Museo dell'Età Cristiana. (Hirmer Fotoarchiv, Munich)

307. *Antique Christian Art.* North Italy. *Reliquary Casket ('Lipsanotheca'), detail: Story of Ananias and Sapphira (Acts of the Apostles).* Second third of the 4th century. Brescia, Museo dell'Età Cristiana. (Hirmer Fotoarchiv, Munich)

308. *Antique Christian Art.* North Italy. *Reliquary Casket ('Lipsanotheca'), detail of the lid: The Soldiers about to lay Hands on Christ in the Garden of Gethsemane (upper register) and Christ brought before Annas and Caiaphas (lower register).* Second third of the 4th century. Brescia, Museo dell'Età Cristiana. (Hirmer Fotoarchiv, Munich)

309. *Antique Christian Art.* North Africa. *Cup: The Apostles Peter and Andrew with their Nets; above, between them, a Small Edifice representing the Holy Sepulchre.* 4th century. Tunis, Bardo Museum. Engraved glass, diameter 7 3/4, thickness 5 to 6 millimetres. Cup found at Carthage in the Baths of Antoninus. (Museum Photo)

310. *Antique Christian Art.* Rome. *Two Figures.* 4th century. Vatican, Museo Sacro. Gold-painted glass. (Photo Held)

311. *Plan of Rome.*

312. *Map of the Mediterranean World.*

Map and plan drawn by Jacques Rochette.

Plan of Rome

Map of the Mediterranean World

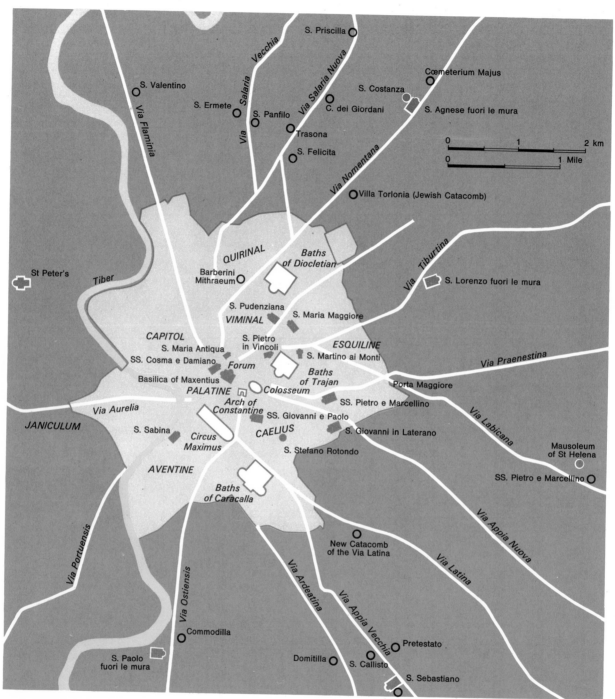

311. *Plan of Rome.*

The following labels appear on the map:

S. Priscilla

Cœmeterium Majus

S. Valentino

S. Costanza

S. Ermete

C. dei Giordani

S. Agnese fuori le mura

S. Panfilo

Via Salaria Vecchia

Via Salaria Nuova

Via Flaminia

Via Salaria

Trasona

S. Felicita

Via Nomentana

Via Tiburtina

Villa Torlonia (Jewish Catacomb)

St Peter's

Tiber

QUIRINAL

Baths
of Diocletian

S. Lorenzo fuori le mura

Barberini
Mithraeum

S. Pudenziana

S. Maria Maggiore

VIMINAL

CAPITOL

S. Maria Antiqua

S. Pietro
in Vincoli

ESQUILINE

Via Praenestina

SS. Cosma e Damiano

Forum

S. Martino ai Monti

Basilica of Maxentius

Baths
of Trajan

Porta Maggiore

PALATINE

Colosseum

Arch of
Constantine

SS. Pietro e Marcellino

Via Aurelia

SS. Giovanni e Paolo

Via Labicana

JANICULUM

S. Giovanni in Laterano

CAELIUS

S. Sabina

Circus
Maximus

S. Stefano Rotondo

Mausoleum
of St Helena

AVENTINE

SS. Pietro e Marcellino

Baths
of Caracalla

New Catacomb
of the Via Latina

Via Appia Nuova

Via Latina

Via Portuensis

Via Ostiensis

Via Ardeatina

Via Appia Vecchia

Commodilla

Pretestato

Domitilla

S. Callisto

S. Paolo
fuori le mura

S. Sebastiano

312. *The Mediterranean World.*

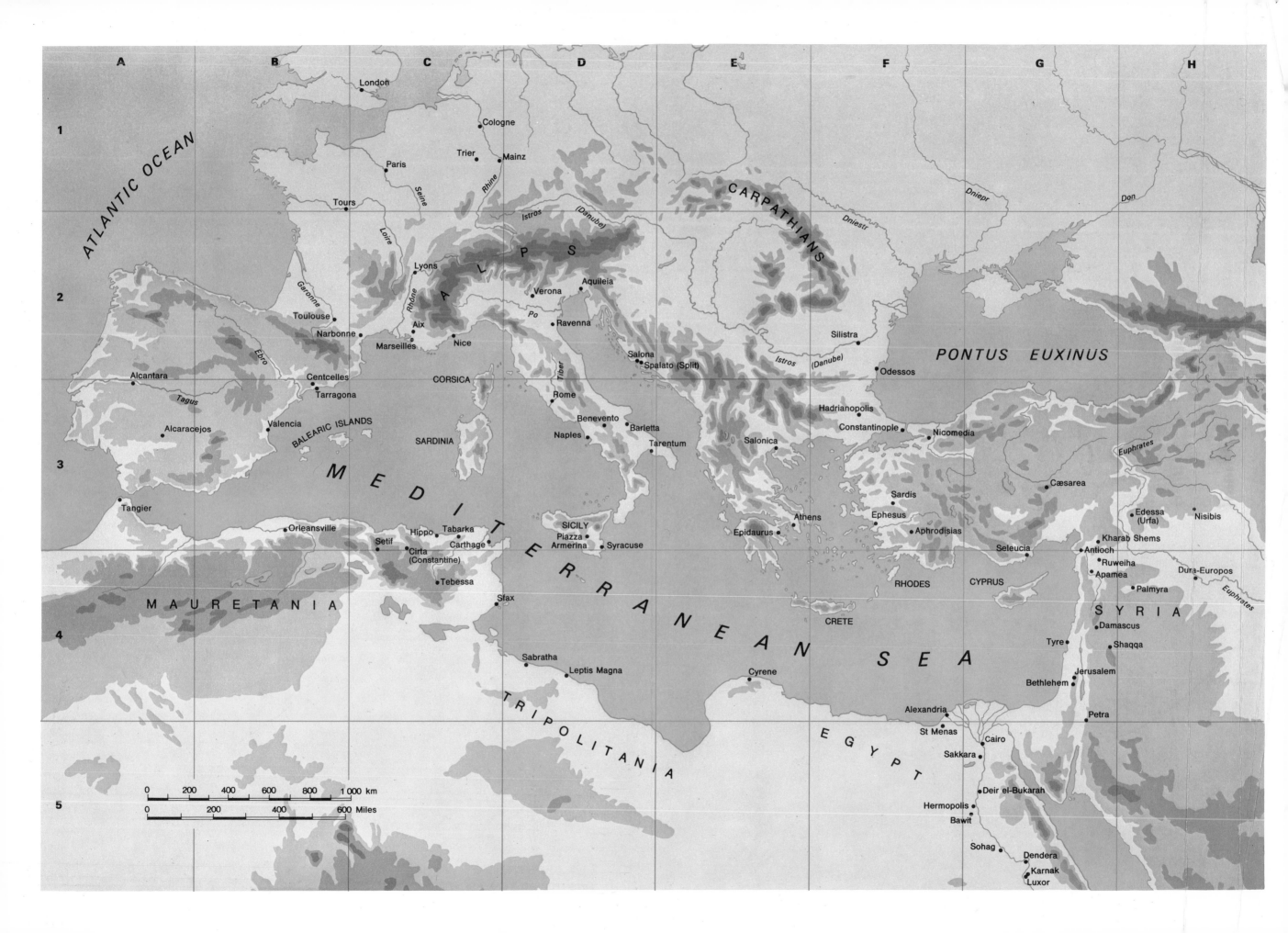

THIS, THE NINTH VOLUME OF 'THE ARTS OF MANKIND' SERIES, EDITED BY ANDRÉ MALRAUX AND GEORGES SALLES, HAS BEEN PRODUCED UNDER THE SUPERVISION OF ALBERT BEURET, EDITOR-IN-CHARGE OF THE SERIES. THE BOOK WAS DESIGNED BY MICHEL MUGUET, ASSISTED BY SERGE ROMAIN. THE TEXT, THE PLATES IN BLACK AND WHITE AND IN SEPIA WERE PRINTED BY L'IMPRIMERIE GEORGES LANG, PARIS; PLATES IN COLOUR BY L'IMPRIMERIE DRAEGER FRÈRES, MONTROUGE. THE BINDING, DESIGNED BY MASSIN, WAS EXECUTED BY BABOUOT, GENTILLY.